Abstracts of the
TESTAMENTARY PROCEEDINGS
of the
PREROGATIVE COURT OF MARYLAND

Volume I: 1658–1674

Libers: 1A, 1B, 1C, 1D, 1E, 1F, 2, 3, 4A, 4B, 4C

by
V. L. Skinner, Jr.

CLEARFIELD

Copyright © 2004
by Vernon L. Skinner, Jr.
All Rights Reserved.

Printed for
Clearfield Company, Inc. by
Genealogical Publishing Co., Inc.
Baltimore, Maryland
2004

International Standard Book Number: 0-8063-5260-4

Made in the United States of America

INTRODUCTION

Purpose of the Prerogative Court.

The Prerogative Court was the central point for probate for Provincial Maryland. It was mirrored after the Prerogative Court of Canterbury. There was a judge as well as clerk(s) of the court. Initially, all probate was brought directly to the Prerogative Court, located in the Provincial Capital. As the Province became more populous, all documents were still to be filed with the Prerogative Court; however, administration of probate was delegated to the various county courts. Even so, there are documents only in the Prerogative Court and not in the appropriate county, and vice versa.

Documents filed in the Prerogative Court.

The following documents were filed in the Prerogative Court: administration bond, will, inventory, administration accounts, and final balances. The testamentary proceedings contain the administration bond and the docket for the court. If the administrator is lax in filing documents, then a summons is also recorded.

Equity Court

The Prerogative Court was also the court for equity cases--resolution of disputes over the settlement and distribution of an estate. The case was brought before the judge and could take several years to resolve. Often depositions were taken and recorded in the minutes.

Notes on the Abstraction.

1. The left hand column contains the liber/folio number. The folio numbers are presented just as they appear in the actual document, e.g., 32a, 78½.

2. The right-hand column contains the abstraction text.

3. Various libers specify a particular session for the Prerogative Court, e.g., 1678; or, September Court 1742. This information is presented as "Court Session:" followed by the

appropriate session. Should no session have been specified, then the phrase "no date" is used.

4. An ellipsis (...) is used to indicate a continuation of the previous information, but no relevant genealogical information is present.

5. The following symbols are used in the abstraction:
```
?     difficult to read.
#     pounds of tobacco.
!     [sic].
```

Abbreviations.

The following abbreviations have been used throughout this abstraction:

```
AA   - Anne Arundel Co.        MO  - Montgomery Co.
BA   - Baltimore Co.           NE  - New England
CE   - Cecil Co.               NY  - New York
CH   - Charles Co.             NYC - New York City
CR   - Caroline Co.            p   - planter
CV   - Calvert Co.             PA  - Pennsylvania
DE   - Delaware                PG  - Prince George's
DO   - Dorchester Co.                Co.
ENG  - England                 PoA - power of
FR   - Frederick Co.                 attorney
g    - gentleman               QA  - Queen Anne's Co.
HA   - Harford Co.             SM  - St. Mary's Co.
IRE  - Ireland                 SMC - St. Mary's City
KE   - Kent Co. MD             SO  - Somerset Co.
KEDE - Kent Co. DE             TA  - Talbot Co.
LoA  - letters of              VA  - Virginia
       administration          WA  - Washington Co.
MA   - Massachusetts           WO  - Worcester Co.
MD   - Maryland
```

Court Session: 1657

Court Session: 1657

1A:1 1657. John Hammond appoints Anne Hammond his attorney with Walter Peake. Date: 16 April 1655. Witnesses: M. Fantleroy, Christ. Brownrigge.

Anne Hammond wife of John Hammond revoked the joint PoA to Walter Peake. Date: 15 November 1656. Witnesses: John Lawson, Walter Pake.

1A:2 Robert Clarke (g) assigned to Anne Hammond wife of John Hammond all his right to the plantation 1000 a. on east side of Breton's Bay. 1000 a. Date: 27 May 1656. Witnesses: John Lawson, Rob. Thimbleby.

Anne Hammond wife & attorney of John Hammond sold to Richard Hotchkeys (the Crosse) the plantation 1000 a. on east side of Breton's Bay, conveyed to her by Robert Clarke (g). Date: 18 November 1656.

1A:3 Witnesses: Walter Pake, John Lawson, Robert Thimbleby.

1A:4 John Mailam (merchant, IRE) assigned chattel to Richard Hotchkeys (merchant) & Henry Parnell (merchant). Date: 5 December 1655. Witnesses: Edward Packer, Thomas Mathewes, Pat. Graunte.

1A:5 20 July. William Boreman assigned chattel to Luke Barber. Date: 31 May 1657. Signed: William Boareman. Witness: Robert Parke.

Luke Barber registered a cattle mark. Luke Barber, Jr. registered a cattle mark.

Tho. Burdett registered a cattle mark.

3 April 1657. Ralphe Crouch executor of Mr. Lawrence Starkey vs. estate of John Pritcher (the tinker). Caveat.

5 April 1657. Thomas Mathewes attorney for William Allen (merchant, London) vs. estate of Henry Fox (Newtowne). Caveat.

Court Session: 1657

1A:6   7 April 1657. John Jarbo vs. the estate of Henry Fox. Caveat.

Philip Land vs. estate of Henry Fox. Caveat.

Patricke Forrest executor of Margarett Hatton relict of Thomas Hatton (late Secretary) vs. estate of Henry Foxe. Caveat.

Jane relict of Cuthbert Fenwicke vs. estate of said Fox. Caveat.

William Mills attorney for William Seitclere vs. estate of Henry Fox. Caveat.

17 April. Thomas Cornwaleys vs. estate of Henry Fox (Newtown). Caveat.

Philip Land vs. estate of said Foxe. Caveat.

11 May. Jane Eltonhead vs. estate of Richard Harris (Patuxent). Caveat.

17 May. Job Chandler (g) was granted administration on the estate of Simon Antonio.

1 June. Lt. James Lindsey was granted administration on the estate of Simon Antonio, as the greatest creditor.

Lt. James Lindsey was granted administration on the estate of Benjamin Gill.

Mary Harris widow of Richard Harris was granted administration on his estate.

11 March 1656. Samuell Tilghman vs. Rob. Cager. Caveat.

Thomas Cornwaleys vs. John Dandy. Caveat.

John Medley vs. John Dandy. Caveat.

1A:7   Will of Henry Fox (Newtowne). To: wife (unnamed), Mr. John Greenhill, Mr.

Court Session: 1657

John Lewger, child (unnamed), youngest daughter (unnamed) of Mary Stiles. Overseers: friend Mr. John Jarbo, Mr. Walter Hall. Witnesses: John Pille, Edm. Berkley, L.·Barber, Sen.

1A:8 Will of Lawrence Starkey, Esq. To: Raph Crouch (executor). Witnesses: Henry Parnell, George Thompson, William Boareman.

30 May 1657. William Boareman vs. Capt. William Stone. Re: land at Nangeny. Arbitrators: Job Chandler, James Lindsey. Signed: Josias Fendall.

Survey by Robert Clarke for 600 a. on Nangeny Creek, on warrant from Thomas Hatton (Secretary), being land surveyed for Capt. William Stone, adjacent to land of said Boareman.

1 June 1657. Richard Willan, age 35, deposed that in 1648, he & James Lindsey spoke to Thomas Conley about land at Mattapony called "Machell's Necke" where Mr. Collett lives.

1A:9 James Lindsey, age 37, deposed that he & Richard Willan went to Mr. Conley to get land for Thomas Mathewes.

William Eltonhead (g) assigned land to John Anderton (g): "The Island", "The Rich Necke", "Hogge Necke". Witnesses: John Anketill, John Petro, Francis Anketill.

1A:10 27 June 1657. Francis Anketill deposed to the authenticity of said deed.

In June last, John Anderton (g) delivered to the Secretary, a list of Mr. William Eltonhead. "He desired...me [John Anderton] to acquaint my mother that he left all his lands...for the good of her & her children & she to permit Robert Fenwicke & Richard Fenwicke some part of the land."

Inventory of Simon Antonio, dated 31 December 1656, before John Tomkinson,

Court Session: 1657

Mr. Thomas Carpenter, Archibald Whaakop, Richard Troope.

1A:11 John Luger (g, Newtowne) sold to Philip Land (SM) ½ his plantation on Breton's Bay, late in the joint possession of said Luger & Mary widow of Henry Fox. Date: 12 June 1657. Witnesses: John Jarbo, Forrest Patricke. Philip Land sold his right to said land to Luke Barber.
1A:12 Date: 18 December 1657. Witnesses: John Jarbo, Tho. Mathews.

Walter Hall vs. estate of William Nugent. Caveat. Date: 14 January.

James Lindsie vs. estate of William Nugent. Caveat. Date: 16 March.

Court Session: <no date>

1B:1 29 November 1659. Will of Nicholas White (p, St. Inegoes Hundred), exhibited by Markes Pheypo. Made: 22 May 1659. Heirs: wife Mary, child Ellynor. Executrix: wife. Overseers: Nicholas Keetting, Markes Pleypo (p, St. Inegoes Hundred).
1B:2 Bequests to: Mr. William Barthowse, Robert Smyth, John Mattrick. Witnesses: Peter Bathe, Richard Russell. Said Nicholas Keitting & Marke Pheypo were granted administration.
1B:3 Marke Pheypo took oath as administrator. Date: 26 November 1659. Appraisers: Thomas Mathewes, Thomas Innis. Date: 29 December 1659.

19 November. Mr. William Boreman exhibited nuncupative will of Mary White relict & late wife of Nicholas White. Said Boreman was granted administration on her estate.

Mary Clocker, alias Mary Lane, age 45, deposed that Mary White is relict of Nicholas White (dec'd) & that Mr. William Boreman is executor & to have charge of Ellynor her eldest child & Nicholas Keitting is to have charge of Mary her youngest child.

Page 4

Court Session: <no date>

1B:4 Bequests to: Emanuell Duarte, Alexander Henderson. Date: 15 November 1659.

Emanuell Duarte (p), age 31, deposed regarding the will of Mary White. Mrs. Boreman was to have charge of her daughter Ellynor & Audery wife of Nicholas Keitting to have charge of the daughter Mary. Bequest to: Marke Pheypo. Date: 15 November 1659.

1B:5 Thomas Mathewes, (g), age 37, deposed regarding the will of Mary White. Mr. William Boreman is executor. Mrs. Boreman is to care for her daughter Ellynor & Audery Keitting is to care for her daughter Mary. Date: 15 November 1659.

Johanna Howell, age 30, deposed regarding the will of Mary White. Mr. William Boreman is to be executor & to care for her daughter Ellynor. Audery wife of Nicholas Keitting is to care for her daughter Mary. Bequests to: Nicholas Keitting, Marke Pheypo. Date: 16 November 1659. Witness: Peter Bathe.

Richard William exhibited oath to William Boareman executor of Mary White relict of Nicholas White.

1B:6 ...
1B:7 Appraisers: Edward Becker (g, of St. Inego's), Walter Waterlyn (St. Inego's) with Mr. Thomas Innis.

1B:8 26 November 1659. Nicholas Guyther (sheriff, SM) was granted administration on estate of Edward Clackson, as the greatest creditor.

1B:9 ...
1B:10 Appraisers: John Metcalfe, William Heynes. Lt. Marke Pheypo to administer oath.

Nicholas Keitting vs. estate of Philip Land. Caveat.

19 December 1659. John Shertcliffe (Newtowne) was granted administration on the estate of Thomas Carpenter. Appraisers: William Browne, Henry

Court Session: <no date>
Pinkedacy. Luke Barber, Esq. to administer oath.

Ellen Phillips widow of Thomas Phillips was granted administration on estate of her husband. Appraisers: William Browne, John Shertcliffe. Luke Barber, Esq. (also Dr. Barber) to administer oath.

1B:11 William Browne & John Shertcliffe (Newtowne) exhibited will of John Thimbellby Bequests to: Pastor of the Roman Catholic Church, Mary Browne (goddaughter) all my land, John Browne, William Browne, Ann Shertcliffe & her husband, young John Shertcliffe & his brother William Shertcliffe. Executors: William Browne, John Shertcliffe. Bequests to: Margaret Browne wife of William Browne,

1B:12 Mary Browne, Robert Call (godson), William Browne, children of John Bryan. Date: 2 December 1659. Witnesses: Dennis Frissell, Jean Gwanh. Dennis Frissell, age 25, affirmed. Before: William Evans. John Gerd, age 19, affirmed. Signed: John Gwanh. Before: William Evans. Appraisers: William Browne, John Shirtcliffe. Date: 21 December 1659.

29 December 1659. William Asseter & Charles Maynard executors of estate of Thomas Diniardde were granted administration on his estate.

1B:13 1 January 1659. Will of Thomas Diniard. Executors: William Asseter, Charles Maynard. Bequests: Robert Thomas, church & Mrs. FitzHarbert due from Batt. Phillips, Charles Delahay & chattel of John Hocker & my wife, John Hamon (son of Beniamen Hamon), Arthur Delahaye to receive chattel at Mr. Gardner, Henry Thomas (son of Robert Thomas), Thomas Salmon (son of Stephen Salmon), Mary Skippe wife of Abraham Skippye, Charles Maynard & Robert Thomas,

1B:14 2 children of Thomas Thomas, Vincent Mansell. Witnesses: Barth. Phillips, Robert Thomas, Robert Joyner, David

Court Session: <no date>

	Boing, John Barrows. Robert Joyner affirmed. Date: 23 November 1659. Before: Philip Calvert. David Boing, age 24, affirmed. Date: 27 November 1659. Before: William Evans. William Asseter & Charles Maynard posted bond. Date: 28 December 1659.
1B:15	...
1B:16	Appraisers: Bartholomew Philips, Robert Thomas.
1B:17	Stannop Roberts exhibited will of John Harwood. Will made: 19 June 1659. Bequests: wife Allice Harwood, Stannop Roberts to assist my wife, Robert Cadger. Witnesses: John Lawson, Stannop Roberts, Joseph Woodward. John Lawson affirmed. Date: 19 January 1659. Said Asseter & Said Maynard were granted administration. Capt. Richard Banks to administer oath to said Alice.
1B:18	24 January 1659. William Bowles exhibited will of Edward Bowles (father of said William). Bequests: son William Bowles is executor. Signed: Edward Bowlls. Witnesses: Edward Waton, Thomas Jarues, John Douglas. John Douglas & Thomas Jarues affirmed to will of Edward Boules (Pekeawakson). Date: 14 November 1659. Witness: George Thompson. William Boules (son of Edward Boules) posted bond. Date: 24 January 1659.
1B:19	Mr. Thomas Stone exhibited will of Capt. Thomas Stone. [also cited as Capt. William Stone.]
1B:20	Bequests: son Thomas Stone as executor & if he dies, then his brother Robert Stone to be assisted by his brother John, eldest daughter Elisabeth Stone (unmarried) 900 a. at "Bustard's Island",
1B:21	wife Virlinda Stone, son Richard 500 a. in "Mannor of Nangemy", children: John, Mathew, Mary, Catheryn.
1B:22	Overseers:
1B:23	Josias Fendall, Gov. Francis Doughty (brother-in-law), Mathew Stone (natural brother). Date: 3 December 1659. Witnesses: Francis Doughty, Stephen

Court Session: <no date>

Mountague, Stephen Clifton. Peter Bathe affirmed. Date: 21 December 1660.

Mr. Thomas Mathewes (g) exhibited will of Mr. Thomas Eures.

- On 16 February 1659, John Raper, age 27, deposed that he was aboard the Elisabeth & Mary with Capt. Richard Hobs when Thomas Eures made a nuncupative will. Servants are to be consigned to Mr. Thomas Mathews & Mr. Ralph Crouch. Before: Philip Calvert.

1B:24 Mr. Mathews was granted administration.

1B:25 George Peake (Plines Point, CV) was granted administration on estate of James Hatfield (CV).

On 4 January 1659, Mr. Thomas Allanson for Ann Thomas & Daby Prichard produced will of Daby Peary. Bequests: Ann Thomas & Daby Prichard. Date: 10 December 1659. Witnesses: Thomas Alanson, Thomas Wentworth. Thomas Allanson affirmed. Thomas Wentworth affirmed.

On 25 February 1659, Frances Tucker exhibited will of Thomas Tucker (merchant).

1B:26 Bequests: John Sison, Dr. John Price (Willand) chattel from ship Constant Friendship to VA, seamen of said ship, Nathaniel Styles (merchant), Frances Tucker (mother, executrix). Date: 4 November 1659. Witnesses: Thomas Munni (now dec'd), Robert Kettell (now dec'd).

1B:27 Frances Tucker was granted administration with Nathaniel Styles.

1B:28 Will of Mrs. Jane Eltonhead. Bequests: Thomas Taylor (eldest son) land of Cedar Point, son Thomas & daughter Sarah, Roger Anderton (grandchild), 3 servants to be divided after the debts of Mr. Edward Eltonhead are paid. Witnesses: William Coursey, Katheren Coursey.

Court Session: <no date>

1B:29	Will of Philip Land. Date: 1 April 1657. Bequests: son Philip Land chattel of Mr. Chanler in part of payment for plantation that Mr. Overzee lives on & the other portion by Henry Fox, son Philip Land to receive chattel of Mr. Mathewes, son Thomas Land, son William Land, children are under age 19, wife Ann Land (as executrix), church. Overseer: Mr. Philip Calvert, Esq. Witnesses: Mr. Philip Calvert, Roger Isham. On 8 March 1659, Roger Isham affirmed.
1B:30	Will of Jobe Chandler (Portoback). Date: 24 August 1659. Bequests: wife An Chandler to receive Negro Moccaton, daughter An Chandler to receive Negro Francisco given to her by her grandmother Sarah Yardley, son William Chandler to receive Negro Alckaman, son Richard Chandler to receive Negro Ann, granddaughter Anne & son William & son Richard,
1B:31	son William to receive 1000 a. bought of Capt. Lewes & 550 a., son Richard to receive 500 a. where John Cane lives & land of Capt. Whittington & land of brother Overseyes & land of Capt. Yardly, children are under age 21, Thomas Maris, brothers in England.
1B:32	Overseers: Capt. William Stone, brother-in-law Symon Oversee, friend & brother Mr. Robert Slye. Signed: Job Chandler. Witnesses: Clement Theobald, William Eale.
1B:33	Text of Oath of an Administration.
1B:34	18 August 1658. William Stiles was granted administration on estate of Henry Bishop (d. 16 August 1658) as greatest creditor. William Stiles (Newtown) posted bond.
1B:35	...
1B:36	Appraisers: Mr. William Hall, Walter Pakes. Oath administered by Capt. Evans.

Inventory of Francis Poesey, by appraisers James Walker & Christopher Cootnall. Witness: David Prichard.

Court Session: <no date>

Payments to: Phillip Land, Henry Fox, John Luger. David Prichard. Amount: #1095.

Inventory of Henry Bishop, by appraisers Walter Hall & Walter Pakes. Amount: #975.

27 October. Elisabeth Stephenson (St. George's Hundred, SM) widow of William Stephenson was granted administration on estate of her husband.

1B:37 Thomas Cornwaleis, Esq. (the Crosse, SM) was granted administration on estate of Thomas Gregory (St. Michaell's Hundred, SM, slain at engagement at Anarundel), as greatest creditor.

30 October 1658. Thomas Cornwaleys, Esq. (the Crosse, SM) was granted administration on estate of William Nugent (g, slain at Annarundel), as greatest creditor, formerly granted to Francis Brooks.

1B:38 2 November. Peter Mills was granted administration on estate of his brother John Mills (Newtowne).

3 November. Frances the relict of Cornelius Abrahamson exhibited his will. Date: 2 May 1657. Bequests: wife, Math. Holland & my brother Frances. Witness: Robert Blinckhorne.

1B:39 Robert Blinckhorne affirmed. The widow is pregnant; commission is therefore granted to Mr. Robert Taylor.

1B:40 George Reynolds (g) was granted administration on estate of James Orris. Margarett Lloyd widow of John Lloyd (St. George's Hundred) vs. estate of James Orris. Caveat.

18 November 1658. Court. Attendees: Edward Lloyd, Esq., Thomas Todde, John Brewer, Thomas Booson, Samuell Withers, Robert Burle, Thomas Taylor.

William Henderson (AA) was granted administration on estate of Mr. John

Court Session: <no date>

1B:41   Norwood, as greatest creditor. William Galloway was granted administration on said estate. Date: 7 November 1658.

1B:42   Inventory of John Mills. Appraisers: John Shirtcliffe, Thomas Hayward, James Martin. Amount: #1901. Accounts of John Mills. Original appraisal by: John Shirtcliffe, John Jarbo. Payments to: Peter Mills (administrator), Henry Vincent (Cone), John Meadly.

1B:43   29 November. James Lyndsey was granted administration on estate of Simon Antonio, as greatest creditor. Bond: James Lyndsey (St. Thomas' Freehold, CH). Appraisers: Edmond Lyndsey, Robert Troop.

1B:44   9 December. Inventory of Cornelius Abrahams. Appraisers: John Tucker, Henry Alexander. Amount: #15045. List of debts: Edward Good, Thomas Sherridine, Susan Williams, Stephen Gary, Cornelius Johnson, James Addams, Robert Blinckhorne, John Tennis, Susan Kannaday, Gabriell Gouldin. Amount: #8836.

30 December. Owen James & Walter Pakes were granted administration on estate of Paull Simpson.

1B:45   Mr. Simon Overzee vs. estate of Francis Brookes. Caveat. Capt. Nicholas Guither vs. estate of Francis Brookes. Caveat.

31 December. Patrick Forrest was granted administration on estate of Francis Brooks, as executor of Mr. Thomas Hatton who was creditor to said Brookes.

20 January 1658/9. Appraisers to estate of Paull Simpson are: William Palmer, Francis Hill. Col. John Price to administer oath.

Court Session: <no date>

Mary Brooke (widow & relict of Francis Brooke (White Birch Freehould, St. Michaell's Hundred) was granted administration of estate of her husband.

Henry Coursey attorney for John Harris (merchant, London) was granted administration of estate of Thomas Thomas, as greatest creditor.

1B:46 24 January. George Goodrick (Portaback, CH) was granted administration on estate of Lt. William Lewes.

1B:47 Inventory of William Henderson. Date: 29 February 1658. Appraisers: Thomas Yates, John Freeman. Before: Thomas Todd. List of debts: Thomas Parsons, James Haddaway. Amount: #5355.

Accounts of William Henderson. Payments to: John Norwood, Thomas Meares, Thomas Hammond, Mr. Withers. Amount: #4603.

24 February. Inventory of Mr. Paull Simpson. Appraisers: Mr. Francis Hill, William (N).
1B:48 List of debts: Richard Nevell, Mr. James, Vincent Attchison, William Lisle. Amount: #4708.

22 February. Sampson Waring (South Cliff Hundred, CV) & James Veich (Great Eltonhead Hundred, CV) was granted administration on estate of Andrew Wilcox (Great Eltonhead Hundred, CV).

1B:49 Petition of Walter Pakes on estate of James Orris. Requests John Meadly to render chattel in his possession. Accounts exhibited. Payments to: administrator, John Shirtcliffe. Amount: #405.

Inventory of Simon Antonio. Appraisers: Robert Troop, Edmund Lyndsey. Amount: #306.

Walter Pakes vs. estate of Mr. Paul Simpson. Caveat & to satisfy Mr. Simon Overzee.
1B:50 Inventory for said Simpson. List of

Court Session: <no date>

debts: Mr. Simon Overzee. Amount: #1333.

Owen James vs. estate of Mr. Paul Simpson. Caveat.

1B:51 9 March. Zachariah Wade exhibited will of John Wade (chirurgeon, Poplar Hill, Newtown Hundred). Bequests: son Edward Wade, wife Mary Wade by Edward Attkins in the hands of Mr. George Wade (Chalversloton St.), daughter Mary (under age) due of Nicholas Houkins & his wife Elisabeth Houkins & Mr. Thomas Cheseldine & Mr. Wooddall (Chilversloton) then to son John Wade son of Ann Smith then to son Edward (under age) then to Ann Smith then to children of brother William Wade (Cocill, Warwickshire), Ann Smith & her son John Smith & my son Edward Wade & my daughter Mary Wade, Mary Foxe (servant), William Wright & Zacharias Wade & John Harwood & James Johnson. Mentions: Mr. Collett (St. Katherine's Dock), Mr. James Nuttall (St. Katherine's Lane). My attorney Zachariah Wade to pay Mr. Mr. Meese & Mr. Benbo. Date: 9 September 1658.

1B:52 Witnesses: Edmond Brent (now dec'd), William Backhouse (now dec'd). Zachariah Wade was granted administration, with sureties: Richard Banks, Patrick Forrest.

1B:53 Appraisers: John Lawson (Poplar Hill), John Harwood (Newtowne). Capt. Banks to administer oath.

15 March. George Reynolds (Little Britton, Newtown Hundred) was granted administration on estate of James Orris (Meadley), as greatest creditor. Appraisers: John Shirtcliffe, Walt. Hall.

Robert Coale (St. Clement's Hundred) was granted administration on estate of Beniamin Gill on 27 May 1658. James Neale administrator of William Bretton (Little Brittaine, Newtown Hundred) was given administration.

1B:54 William Britton (g, Little Brittaine) &

Page 13

Court Session: <no date>

John Thimbleby (g, Newtown Hundred) attorneys for James Neale (g) who married Ann (daughter & heir of Benjamin Gill (dec'd)).

Mary Brooks administratrix of her husband Francis Brooks (dec'd) was recalled, & Nicholas Guither (St. Michael's Hundred) & Patrick Forrest (St. George's Hundred) were granted administration on estate of Francis Brooks (White Burnt Freehould), as greatest creditors.

1B:55   21 March. George Reynolds administrator of James Orris to pay Walter Pakes.

23 March 1658. Will of Peter Sudborough (p, Patuxent) was exhibited. Bequests: servant, 5 children & wife (who is pregnant). Witnesses: Thomas Middleton, John Sutton.

1B:56   21 April 1659. Court. Attendees: Edward Lloyd, Esq., Mr. Thomas Todd, John Brewer, Thomas Howell, Mr. Samuel Withers, Mr. Robert Burle, Thomas Taylor.

Hester Caplin relict of Henry Caplin (AA) was granted administration on his estate. Appraisers: Mr. George Puddington, George Nettlefeild, Edmond Townell. Before: Francis Stockett.

22 March 1658. Anne Arundel Co. Court. Attendees: Col. Nath. Utie, Edward, Robert Burle, Capt. Thom Howell, Mr. Thomas Todde, Samuel Withers, Thomas Besson.

Mrs. Rose Scotcher administratrix of her husband John Scotcher. Mentions: 2 servants
1B:57   in the hands of William Cole.

28 March. Capt. Richard Hobbs (commander of the Elisabeth & Mary, London) was granted administration on the estate of George Baldwin (who died aboard said ship).
1B:58   Witnesses: Godfry Bayly, Peter Bath.

Page 14

Court Session: <no date>

1B:59	Arther Dickeson (p, King's Creek, York River VA) & Thomas Perry (p, Carter's Creek, York River VA) were granted administration on the estate of John Burlin (King's Creek, York River VA). Date: 20 May 1659.
1B:60	Witnesses: Richard Willan, Patrick Forrest, Peter Bath.
	28 June. Patrick Forrest administrator of estate of Mrs. Margaret Hatton. Appraisers: Randall Hanson, Jeremy Dickenson, Henry Ellery.
1B:61	2 August. Will of Thomas Gates was exhibited, affirmed by Daniel Walker, Edward Bates. Bequests: Michaell Bellott & John Hollowdays plantation, children of Edward Dorsey. Witnesses: Daniell Walker, Edward Bates.
	Capt. Nicholas Guither administrator of Francis Brooks (dec'd). Appraisers: Mr. William Boreman, Mr. Edward Packer. Mr. Thomas Mathews to administer oath.
1B:62	Michaell Bellott & John Hollowdays were granted administration on the estate of Thomas Gates (AA).
1B:63	17 August. Will of Jeremiah Haseling. Bequests: countryman James Sudward, 2 children Marie (under age) & Phebia Haseling (under age). Witness: Anthonie Demondidier. Date: 17 April 1659. Anthony Demondidier affirmed. Date: 1 August 1659. Witness: William Bretton. Thomas Emerson deposed. James Sudward was granted administration on said estate.
1B:64	Inventory of John Scotcher. Date: 20 June 1659. Appraisers: Col. George Utie, Ensign William Pither.
1B:65	Amount: #20290.
1B:66	18 August. Inventory of Mr. John Wade (chirurgeon, of Poplar Hill). Mentions: boy servant, maid servant, ...
1B:67	Mr. Luke Barber, Mr. John Goodrick.

Page 15

Court Session: <no date>

1B:68 List of debts: John Cornelius, William Marshall, George Reade, Richard Nevett, Harves Bell, John Masses, Thomas Ringe, Thomas Jackson, William Hughes, John Williams, Capt. William Evans, William Hatton, William Woodriffe, John Hawkins, Emperour Smith, the Scot at Perry Point, Mr. Dodman, John Cammell, Richard the Irishman, Mr. John Coursey, Mr. Miles, Richard Bennett, Mr. Robert Brooks, Christo. Gooddeker, William Cannaday, Robert Joanes, Thomas Philips, John Stearman, Thomas Howard, Mr. Thomas Hatton, Richard Nevitt, John Hudson, Mr. Richard Cole, John Coates, Capt. Guither, Mr. Francis Brooks, Walter Gees, Capt. Stone, William Watson, William Meles, John Boague, Robert Cadger, William Wright, Zachariah Wade. Appraisers: John Lawson, John Harwood.

1B:69 2 September. Mr. Samuell Withers & Mrs. Alice Durand exhibited nuncupative will of William Pell (AA).
- Grace Deavor, age 40, deposed that William Pell on 20 March 1654 made his will. Bequests: his maid servant Alice Ward, Mrs. Durand & her daughter.
- Alice Ward, age 30, deposed that her master William Pell asked for wife of Thomas Tallie & the wife of Richard Devour to attest to his will. Bequests: deponent, Mrs. Alice Durand & her daughter Elisabeth.

Samuel Withers & Alice Durand were granted administration on said estate.

1B:70 3 September. Anne Arundel Co. Court. Attendees: Col. Nath. Utie, Edward Lloyd, Esq., Mr. Samuell Withers, Robert Burle, Thomas Howell.

Ann Seares relict of Joseph Seares petitioned for administration on his estate. Appraisers: Col. Nathaniell Utie, Mr. Samuell Withers, Richard Blunt. Azadiah Hill who married the relict was granted administration.

Court Session: <no date>

1B:71
6 September. Capt. Nicholas Guither was granted revocation of Mr. William Boreman & Marks Pheypo as appraisers of Francis Brooks. New appraisers: Mr. Richard Hoskeys & Daniell Clocker. Mr. Thomas Mathews to administer oath.

1B:72
10 September. Mr. Peter Bathe exhibited of Mr. Thomas Rapier. Bequests: 2 boy servants George & Jacob Mills, Mr. Thomas Eures. Date: 4 December 1658. Witnesses: Mathew Long, John Burlein. Peter Bath was granted administration on estate of Thomas Raper (g, London).

1B:73

1B:74
29 September 1659. Col. John Price was granted administration on estate of Owen James. William Wilkinson affirmed. Richard Loyd affirmed. Will of Owen James. Bequests: William Palmer, Mr. John Lawson & Mr. Robert Cager, my goddaughter Dorothy Cager daughter of Robert Cager, my goddaughter Ellen Ring daughter of Thomas Ring, John Lawson son of John Lawson, Rebecca Frissell daughter of Alexander Frissell, Sarah Frissell & Rebecca Frissell wife & daughter of Alexander Frissell, Humphry Beech (servant), Harbert Homan (servant) & Harrie (servant), estate of John Wheatlie, kinsman Col. John Price, Mr. Wilkinson (minister). Date: 18 September 1659. Witnesses: Alexander Frissell, Sarah Frissell, William Wilkinson, Richard Lloyd. Col. John Price was granted administration. Appraisers: Mr. Richard Willan, Mr. Nicholas Young, Daniell Clocker. Mr. Thomas Mathews to administer oath.

1B:75
Col. John Price exhibited will of John Wheatlie. Bequests: my children, friends Mr. Richard Willan & Mr. Barnabie Jackson & Mr. Thomas Mathews as executors. Children to be brought up as Roman Catholics. Date: 23 January 1657. Witnesses: John Price, William Edwin.

Court Session: <no date>
Inventory of John Wheatlie.

1B:76 14 October. Inventory of Andrew Wilcox.
Date: 12 July 1659. Appraisers: Robert
Blinkhorne, Patrick Mullikin.

20 October. Inventory of Mrs. Hatton.
Appraisers: Randall Hanson, Jeremie
Dickenson.
1B:77 Amount: #910.

22 October 1659. Mrs. Ann Tilney
exhibited nuncupative will of Richard
Hotchkeyes.
• Thomas Mathews (g, SM) deposed that
on 15 October past, Richard
Hotchkeyes (g, the Crosse Mannor)
appointed Mrs. Ann Tilney (the
Crosse) as executrix.
• John Abingdon (g, SM), age 24,
deposed that on 15 October past,
Richard Hotchkeyes (g, the Crosse
Mannor) appointed Ann Tilney (the
Crosse Mannor) as executrix.

1B:78 10 November. Inventory of Mr. Richard
Hotchkeyes.
1B:79 Amount: #17606. Date: 3 November 1659.
Appraisers: John Bateman, Nich. Young.

1C:1 2 December 1660. Cuth. Fenwick, William
Mills, & John Bogue exhibited will of
Jane Fenwick (Patuxent, CV). John
Bateman exhibited oath to appraisers
George Reade & John Reade.
1C:2 Will of Jane Fenwick (widow). Bequests:
3 sons Robert (eldest, under 18) &
Richard & John Fenwick to have property
divided by Cuth. Fenwick & William Mills
& John Bogue, Cuthbert Fenwick (under
21), Cuthbert & Ignatius Fenwick (under
age), Teresa Fenwick (under 16),
1C:3 Negro Dorothy, Henrietta (maid servant),
1C:4 John Turner, old Indianman Thomas,
William Payne (Negro boy servant), Roman
Catholic Church,
1C:5 John Bogue, William Mill, John Wright,
Edmund Scott. Date: 24 November 1660.
Witnesses: John Wright, John Turner,
Edmund Scott.

Court Session: <no date>

1C:6   William Mill & William Innis guardian of the orphan of Robert Batterson was granted administration on his estate. Date: 3 January 1660.

1C:7   Appraisers: George Reade, Allexander Watt.

8 December 1660. Mrs. Elisabeth Overzee relict of Symon Overzee was granted administration on his estate.

Inventory of Joseph Hatfield. Appraisers: John Cobrath, Walt. Car. Date: 13 June 1660. Amount: #12415.

1C:8   18 January 1660. James Lindsey was granted administration on estate of John Webb (carpenter). Appraisers: Capt. Christopher Russell, John Ashbrooke, Henry Adams.

13 January 1660. George Reade (Patuxent River, CV) was granted administration on estate of John Morris (p, Patuxent). Appraisers: William Mill, Andrew Robison. Mr. John Bateman to administer oath.

George Reade was granted administration on estate of David Stephens, as greatest creditor. Appraisers: William Mill, Andrew Robison. Mr. John Bateman to administer oath.

Thomas Stone (g, Nangemy, CH) was granted administration on estate of his father Capt. William Stone.

1C:9   Appraisers: Joseph Harrison, John Chaireman. John Lawson to administer oath.

Isaack Abrahams was granted administration on estate of Thomas Reade. Date: 11 December 1660.

Francis Carpenter attorney for Capt. Leonard Chamberlaine was granted administration on estate of Richard Hix (Patuxent). Date: 8 January 1660. Will of Richard Hix. Bequests: daughter Mary Hix (executrix), my landlord John Sinklear, Capt. Leonard Chamberlaine

Court Session: <no date>

1C:10 (Kent Co., Yorke River) as overseer, John Sinklear & his wife Jane Sinklear, William Sampell, Mr. Gilles Sadleir as attorney. Date: 5 April 1660. Witnesses: Francis Carpenter, William Sampell. Will proved 21 January 1660. Capt. Leonard Chamberlayne (Kent Co., Yorke River VA) gave PoA to Francis Carpenter. Date: 5 December 1660. Witnesses: Samuell Mane, James Eirne (?).

1C:11 Charges at burial of Mr. Richard Hix. Date: 16 April 1660. Amount: #1248. Witness: Peter Knight. At Poropothankeun, Yorke River. Date: 10 June 1660.

1C:12 Inventory of Mr. Richard Hix. Date: 7 April 1660. List of debts: Samuell Graves, Andrew Dickeson, Robert Kingsborough, Richard Bently & Thomas Serchwell, Mr. Jules Sadler, Alexander Magruder, Tho. Parry, William Graves, Thomas Barbary, Thomas Sheridan, Cornelius Canady, William Turner, Tho. Cobham, William Howes, Mr. Robert Taylor, Patrick Dew, William Samphell, James Jolley, Andrew Dickeson, Samuel Graves, Thomas Pary, Francis Lacy. John Sinklear acknowledged the bills. Date: 13 April 1660. Witness: Fran. Carpenter.

1C:13 19 January 1660. Morgan Williams & William Hemsley executors of Thomas Dikes (KE) were granted administration on his estate. Will of Thomas Dikes. Date: 2 December 1660. Bequests: Mecom Mekeny, Fran. Brook & Thomas Brooke, Morgan Williams & Mr. William Hemsley as executors. Mentions: Mr. William Leeds. Witness: Mecom Mekeny.

20 January 1660. Morgan Williams executor of Robert Houlton was granted administration on his estate. Will of Robert Houlton. Date: 20 November 1660. Bequests: Mathew Erickson (son of John Erickson), Sarah Williams, William Hemsley, Mr. Morgan Williams as executor. Witnesses: Thomas Dikes,

Court Session: <no date>

William Hemsley. William Hemsley affirmed.

1C:14 Mrs. Juliana Russell (widow) executrix of Capt. John Russell (g, KI) was granted administration on his estate. Will of John Russell. Bequests: wife Juliana (executrix) plantation (KI) & 100 a. called "Great Thicketts" (KI) & 250 a. on Eastern Shore called "Russendall",

1C:15 3 servants John Lawleme & Disborough Bennett & Thomas Mathewes, my goddaughter Mary Winchester. Date: 7 January 1660. Codicil: bequest: cousin Edmund Carpenter, John Morgan, Sr. Witnesses: William Hemsley, Morgan Williams. Will proved 18 January 1660. Security: Morgan Williams.

1C:16 30 January 1660. Mr. Thomas Ringould for Ann Hill widow of Assidia Hill (KE) was granted administration on his estate.

23 February. Richard Foster & his wife An were granted administration on estate of her brother Thomas Jackson, as next of kin. Appraisers: Luke Gardner, Robert Cole.

2 March. Mr. William Bretton father-in-law of Mary late wife of William Thompson was granted administration on his estate. Lt. Col. John Jarbo attested that William Thompson desired his wife should administer his estate & his father-in-law Mr. William Bretton as overseer of his children.

1C:17 Walter Pakes attested to the same. Francis wife of Walter Pakes attested to the same. Date: 26 February 1660. Col. William Evans to administer oath.

3 April 1661. Richard Crackborne was granted administration on estate of Thomas Elstone (SM), as greatest creditor.

John Williams (CH) deposed that Ursly Lynton desired: the youngest son of John

Court Session: <no date>

Delahaye have chattel, John Delahaye to have her husband's clothes, wife of John Delahaye to have clothes, Mrs. Jane Tompkinson, Francis Pope. Executor: said Pope. Date: 17 April 1661

1C:18 **19 April 1661.** John Bouge was granted administration on estate of Edmund Scott. Mr. Bateman to administer oath.

Capt. Fendall was granted administration on estate of William Warren.

18 June. Mr. Robert Slye was granted administration on estate of William Empson (CH).

10 June. Mr. Richard Willan & Hugh Lee to appraise estate of Peter Bathe. Mr. Thomas Mathews to administer oath.

20 June. James Walker & Francis Pope to appraise estate of William Empson. Mr. Henry Addams to administer oath.

26 June. Elisabeth Gunnion was granted administration on estate of James Gunnion.

1C:19 Mary Bulline was granted administration on estate of Henry Bulline.

John Cobret attorney for Mrs. Billingsley was granted administration on estate of Maj. John Billingsley.

John Ashcombe & William Steevens were granted administration on estate of Richard Reynolds.

John Cobrith, James Allen, & William Mackdoc were granted administration on estate of James Dick.

John Cobreth was granted administration on estate of William Long.

John Vanhack was granted administration on estate of John Mackenny.

Dorothy Day was granted administration on estate of John Day.

Court Session: <no date>

1C:20   27 June. William Turner was granted administration on estate of William Bromall.

1C:21   Will of Mr. Peter Bathe. Bequests: brother Christopher Bathe all estate of my father in Ireland (testator is sole executor of his father), son Richard Bathe, overseer Marke Pheypo, Emanuell Edwards to get chattel at Mr. Mathews & Humphry Howell, Mr. Edward Arthur (merchant), Mr. Abbington. Overseers: Mr. Patricke Higgins, Mareke Pheypo, William Brook (g). Date: 12 April 1661. Witnesses: John Mas, Anna Land.

1C:22   Inventory of Mr. Peter Bathe. Appraisers: Mr. Hugh Lee, Mr. Richard Willan. ...

1C:23   Inventory of Capt. William Stone. Date: 3 December 1661.

1C:24   Servants: Jeremiah Dickerson, Thomas Alcox, William Greengoe, Tho. Livinstone, Walter Browne, William Pollett, Robert Maston, Hercules Hayes, John Poole, Tho. Banister, George Lyngham, Negro Philip, Negro Margarett, Elisabeth Thomas, Lettis Seamore.

1C:25   List of debts: Thomas Sampson, Mathias Brian, Tho. Kelley, James, Tho. Wentworth, Frankham, Mr. Lindsey, Mr. Lindsey creditor for John Webb, John Webb, Edmund Lindsey, Mr. Chandler, Mr. Goodridge, Mr. Turner, Serjeant Nevett, WIlliam Whittle, Tho. Ennis, John Mansfield, Brother Sprigge, John Bisco, Symonds, Robert Marland, Samuell Harris, Walter Pakes, Tho. Frizell, John Harwood, Robert Troope, Armpow Forster, John Metcalfe, William Boreman, John Coats, Humphry Howell, Martin Kirke, Capt. Jenkins, Samuell Harris, Capt. Whittington, Andrew the Scot, James Lee, Tho. Robbinson,

1C:26   Samuel Harris, Mr. Mountigue, Joseph Harris, Mr. Clifton his servant.

4 July. Hugh Lee was granted administration on estate of Sampson

Court Session: <no date>
Cooper. Appraisers: Daniell Clocker, Tho. Innes. Mr. Mathews to administer oath.

Will of William Martine. Bequests: wife, daughter-in-law Mathew Nedham then to my youngest daughter Dorothy Needham then to eldest daughter-in-law Margarett Needham then to overseers John Vanhack & Cesar Prince. Witnesses: John Vanhack, John Macckenny.

1C:27   Will of Richard Reynolds. Bequests: brother John Reynolds & cousin Mary Hassard due from Mr. Bateman, Mr. John Ashcombe & Mr. William Steevens, cousin William Hassard, John Odber. Overseers: Mr. John Ashcombe, Mr. William Steevens. Date: 1 August 1660. Witnesses: John Odber, William Steevens. Capt. John Odber affirmed. Date: 9 February 1660.

1C:28   Will of Robert Taylor. Bequests: sons Robert Taylor & Henry Taylor land, eldest son Samuell Taylor 800 a., Mary Butmore, sons Robert Taylor & Samuell Taylor, son Henry Taylor & daughter Mary Taylor, sister Alce Reade,
1C:29   brother Mr. George Reade & son Samuell Taylor as executors. Date: 25 February 1660. Witnesses: Robert Kingsbury, Richard Garrett.

        Will of William Johnson (g, St. Wynefride). Bequests: nephew Mr. William Langworth son of my brother James Langworth (g, St. Wynefride) 500 a. called "St. Wynefride's" & to pay annually to Francis Fitzherbert, Esq., wife Emma Johnson,
1C:30   brother James Langworth, sister Mrs. Agatha Langworth chattel in the custody of my brother Langworth, sister Mrs. Elisabeth Morris, niece Mrs. Mary Langworth, Mr. James Langworth (executor) to pay Lawrence Sarkey, Esq. & Catholic priest & John Gardner (son of Luke Gardner),
1C:31   mother Elisabeth Morris, sister Mrs. Elisabeth Price, Emma Shankes (daughter of John Shankes (p, St. Clement's

Court Session: <no date>

Hundred)), daughter Elisabeth Johnson. Date: 7 June 1656. Signed: William Johnson, Emma Johnson. Witnesses: Luke Gardner, Robert Cole, William Thompson.

1C:32 Will of Augustine Herman. Bequests: sons Ephraim Georgius Herman (minor) & Casparus Herman (minor) land in "Mannor of Bohemia" on Bohemia River in East Baltimore Co. Date: 24 May 1661. Witnesses: John Collett, Francis Riggs.

1C:33 Will of Thomas Millner (p, Elvon River, CH). Date: 23 February 1659. Bequests: Thomas Robinson, Joseph Harrison, John Thompson 200 a. in Westmoreland Co. VA bought of Mr. Garr. Fookes & bounding Sarah Thompson called "Redd Clift", John Thompson to pay James Lees. Witnesses: Thomas Robinson, Samuell Palmer. Samuell Palmer affirmed. Date: 12 December 1662.

Will of James Langworth (g, St. John's, CH)
1C:34 Bequests: Francis Fitzherbert, Esq. & Catholic priest, son William Langworth 800 a., 2nd son John Langworth 300 a. on St. Clement's Bay,
1C:35 wife Agatha Langworth, eldest daughter Mary land, daughter Elisabeth,
1C:36 wife & 5 children,
1C:37 goddaughter & niece Jane Constable (under 18), daughter of my brother Mr. Marmaduke Constable), Mr. Fitzherbert,
1C:38 Margarett Parsons (maid servant hired of Mr. Starkey), godson John Gardner (son of Mr. Luke Gardner (St. Clement's Bay)), goddaughter & niece Elisabeth Johnson,
1C:39 goddaughter & niece Mary Turner (daughter of my brother Mr. Thomas Turner (St. Clement's Bay)), brothers & sisters Mr. & his wife Elisabeth and Mr. Thomas Turner & his wife Emma, my kinsman Mr. Robert Greene,
1C:40 my brother John Sens.
1C:41 Executrix: wife Agatha Langworth. Sons at age 21; daughters at age 16; children to be brought up Roman Catholic.
1C:42 Mentions: Thomas Haling (servant).

Court Session: <no date>

Date: 18 August 1660. Witnesses: Zachary Wade, Henry Adams, Tho. Brooke, Tho. Simpson.

1C:43 Will of Col. John Price (St. George's Hundred, SM). Bequests: servants Herbert Howman & William Styles, Mr. William Wilkinson, son-in-law Joseph Bullett (under 20), servants,
1C:44 daughter Ann Price (under 18), William Hatton & Daniell Clocker & George Macckall & Thomas Dent. Date: 10 February 1660. Witnesses: William Wilkinson, Tho. Dent, William Hatton.
1C:45 William Wilkinson, Thomas Dent, & William Hatton affirmed. Date: 11 March 1660.

29 June. Francis Pope was granted administration on estate of Joseph Lenthall.

9 July 1662. Will of Thomas Peteate. Bequests: wife Anne Peteate assisted by Walter Cotterill & John Guy. Date: 19 January 1650. Witnesses: Ralph Beane, Tho. Jackson.

1C:46 Anne Guy was granted administration on estate of Henry Lilly. Francis Pope to administer oath.

Will of William Brumale. Bequests: 3 sons Luke Brumale & Richard Brumale & Charles Brumale. Overseers: William Parrett, William Turner. Mentions: Joseph Dowkins (servant).
1C:47 Date: 4 December 1660. Witnesses: Humphry Warren, James Veich, John Willen, Tymothy Goodridge.

Will of James Dicke. Bequests: William Mackdodalt, John Cobreth 200 a., James Allen, Henry Allexander. Date: 5 February 1660. Witnesses: Nicholas Horner, Michell Gillinge.

1C:48 Inventory of Mr. Robert Taylor. Appraisers: John Boage, William Mills. Date: 13 April 1661. Mentions: 3 servants: Thomas Sweetsad, Stephen Britting, Mary Jackson.

Court Session: <no date>

1C:49 Amount: #17716. Date: 16 April 1661. List of debts per Mr. Sadleir: Thomas Cherendine, John Davis, Richard Wills, Robert Warrine, Mr. Gyles Sadleir, Robert Kingsbury, Walter Peake,
1C:50 Mr. Belcher, Mr. John Bateman executor of Belcher, William Bromall, Richard Cloufeild, Philip Comes, Tho. Fresell, Geo. Bussy, Richard Prestoe. Debts due: Edmund Hinshman, William Mallett, Richard Garrett, wife of John Sutton, John Anderson, John Read.

2 August. George Peake was granted administration on estate of Thomas Davies.

Guenbtheon Blaye was granted administration on estate of William Blaye.

7 August. Inventory of Phillip Conner (KI).
1C:51 ...

1C:52 Will of Henry Potter (age 40). Date: 22 December 1659. Bequests: daughter Audry. Witnesses: Marcks Pheypo, Brian Dal. Brine Daly affirmed. Date: 25 June 1662.

14 August. Inventory of Thomas Jackson. Date: 5 August 1661.
1C:53 Amount: #4002. Appraisers: Luke Gardner, Robert Cole.

Inventory of John Day. Date: 6 August 1660.
1C:54 ...

1C:55 20 August. George Read was granted administration on estate of Robert Taylor.

27 August. Henry Spinke & John Shertcliff to appraise estate of Thomas Elstonhead. Col. Evans to administer oath.

Tho. Dent, William Hatton, Dan. Clocker, & Geo. Macckall were granted administration on estate of Col. Price.

Page 27

Court Session: <no date>

Thomas Turner was granted administration on estate of William Johnson.

1C:56 Will of John Salter (p, KI). Bequests: daughter-in-law Rebecca Lumbard, wife Jane. Overseers: Mr. William Coursey, Mr. Henry Morgan. Date: 20 March 1660. Witnesses: Moses Stagwell, Tobye Wells. Moses Stagwell & Toby Wells affirmed. Date: 1 March 1661.

1C:57 16 October. Inventory of John Salter. Date: 2 August 1661. List of debts: Gregory Murrell, Henry Clay,
1C:58 Anthony Griffen, Moses Stagwell, Richard Blunt, John Ellis.

Will of John Medley. Bequests: eldest son John Medley (under age) 600 a., son George Medley (under age) 350 a., son Thomas Medley (under age) 300 a., son William Medley (under age) 550 a. on Bretton's Bay,
1C:59 Mr. Fitzherbert, Col. William Evans, Mr. Richard Willan. Mentions: Mr. Thomas Gerrat. Witnesses: Robert Shell, Edw. Elliott.

1C:60 Will of John Coursey. Bequests: brother Henry Coursey chattel bought of Capt. Thomas Bradnox, John Barke (servant), father Mr. Henry Coursey "Courseyton" at the Chester River, brother William Coursey chattel at Robert Smithe, sister Mrs. Katherine Coursey, Nicholas Bradway, Mrs. Juliana Russell chattel at Morgan Williams, Sarah Williams (daughter of Morgan Williams),
1C:61 sister Mrs. Katherine Coursey chattel at Henry Carline, brother James Coursey chattel at Henry Morgan, brother William (executor) chattel at John Salter, brother William chattel at John Smith, Rodger Baxter & his children, Thomas Mathews & Desboro Bennett & Anne Rodgers, brother James Coursey 400 a. near mouth of Chester River. Witnesses: William Coursey, Thomas Mathews, Disborough Bennett. Codicil: bequests: niece Mary Coursey, sister Mrs. Jane Southcote.

Court Session: <no date>

1C:62 Will of Nicholas Keiting. Date: 20 April 1657. Bequests: wife, son Thomas & daughter Ellenor, wife, chattel in VA for ammunition for Governor Calvert, estate in Ireland to son Thomas. Overseers: wife, Mr. Fitzherbert, Mr. John Metcalfe, Marks Pheypo, Nicholas White. Witnesses: John Metcalfe, Marks Pheypo. Will proved 10 October 1661.

Jane Salter was granted administration on estate of John Salter.

1C:63 Will of Samuell Parker at house of Mr. Robert Slye with him & Mr. Edmund Nanfann. Bequests: wife, William Hurde, John Dougles. Date: 10 October 1661.

Inventory of Col. John Price. Date: 13-14 May.
1C:64 ...
1C:65 Servants: Francis Ward, William Cartland, Henry Scutt. List of debts: William Palmer, Mr. Nicholas Guyther, Alice Harwood, Francis Walton, Auth. Griffith, William Bowles.
1C:66 Servants at Herring Creek: William Keate, Thomas Steele, Herbert Howman, Elisabeth Bodwell. Appraisers: Richard Banckes, Randall Hanson.

1C:67 20 October. Patience Martine widow of William Martine was granted administration on his estate.

5 November. Inventory of Henry Bulling. Appraisers: Mr. John Halfehead, Thomas Martine.

1C:68 27 November. Jane Fenwick relict of Cuthbert Fenwick was granted discharge.

William Heard was granted administration on estate of Joane Parker.

Henry Adams & Francis Pope to prove will of Samuell Lambert. Date: 5 November 1661. Will of Samuell Lambert. Bequests: John Williams, brother John Lambert. Date: 14 October 1661. Witnesses: Tho. Wentworth, Robert

Court Session: <no date>

1C:69 Ostrine. John Lambert was granted administration on said estate.

1C:70 Francis Pope & Henry Adams to prove will of John Guy. Will of John Guy. Bequests: wife Anne Guy. Date: 26 February 1658. Witnesses: Gyles Tompkins, John Douglace.

1C:71 Inventory of Widd Linton. Appraisers: Mr. Thomas Bates, John Nevell. Amount: #10500.

19 December 1661. William Biss was bound to Richard Ward (merchant, Bristoll). Samson Waring became bound to said Ward. Said Biss drowned. Said Waring was granted administration on estate of said Biss.

1C:72 Hannah Lee was granted administration on estate of Hugh Lee. Sureties: Nich. Guyther, Vincent Atcheson.

29 December. Inventory of Mr. Edmund Scott. Appraisers: John Reed, John Wright. Amount: #510.

29 January. Mr. Robert Slye was granted continuance on estate of William Empson.

1C:73 10 February 1661. Mary Bradnox was granted administration on estate of Capt. Thomas Bradnox. Bond: Mr. Collett.

11 February. Walter Senserfe & Henry Sewall were granted administration on estate of James Scapes.

15 February 1661. Susan Atcheson was granted administration on estate of James Atcheson. Bond: Patrick Camell.

Hen. Hooper vs. estate of Richard Goate (Herring Creek). Caveat.

Capt. James Neale was granted administration on estate of David Abercromby.

Court Session: <no date>

2 April 1662. Inventory of Thomas Ellstone. Appraisers: John Chercliffe, Henry Spinke.

1C:74 Inventory of William Warren by Capt. Fendall. Appraisers: William Smootes, John Moris.

1C:75 Inventory of Robert Houlton. List of debts: Capt. Thomas Bradnox, William Richard, William Davis, William Hemsley, chattel given to Mathew Erickson (son of John Erickson), chattel given to Sarah Williams (daughter of Morgan Williams). Appraisers: William Hemsley, Will. Grainger. Date: 18 November 1662.

Inventory of John Mackinnie. Appraisers: William Leucas, George Willson. Date: 29 June 1661. List of debts: John Mackine for Col. Evens.

1C:76 Inventory of John Hall. Date: 19 June 1660.
1C:77 ...
1C:78 List of debts: William Parker, George Whittell, Thomas Manning, Henry Michell, William Irland, Henry Kent, Armigell Greenewood, John Wilson, Robert Peeke, William Kent. Appraisers: Thomas Taylor, Thomas Hooke, Will. Hunt. John Cumber.

1C:79 Inventory of William John Sonn by Thomas Turner. Date: 24 February 1661.
1C:80 Appraisers: William Barton, Robert Cole.

28 March 1662. Joseph Harrison was granted administration on estate of Thomas Milner. Bond: Thomas Robinson.

21 April 1662. Inventory of Thomas Dickes. List of debts: Mr. William Leeds, William Piper, legacies to Frances Brooke & Thomas Brooke, Andrew Skiner.

Inventory of William Martine. Date: 20 December 1662.

1C:81 Inventory of William Long. Amount: #2760. Date: 20 July 1662. Appraisers:

Court Session: <no date>

James Allen, Mark Cleares.

1C:82
1C:83
Inventory of Thomas Davis. Date: 27 December 1662.
...
Appraisers: Mark Clare, Walter Car. Before: Ben. Brassears.

1C:84
23 April 1662. Will of Forker Frissell. Bequests: William Harper (seaman) & his wife, Mary daughter of James Halles, Rebecka Frisell (daughter of Allexander Frisell), Joane Mackahill (daughter of George Mackahill), the Church, John Makey, Mr. Willkinson, William Harper my plantation for 7 years then to Denish Frisell. Executors: George Mackahill, Francis Hill.
Date: 13 December 1661. Signed: Forker Frizell. Witnesses: William Baker, William Harper, Mary Bruckfeld, Elisabeth Harper, William Stanfort. William Stanford, Mary Bruckfeld, George Mackahill, & Francis Hill affirmed. George Mackahill & Francis Hill were granted administration. Bond: Peter Carwaren.

1C:85
Will of William Wright. Date: 3 June 1660. Bequests: wife Mary, 3 children, son William, eldest daughter, Randall Hendson & John Lawson (Poplar Hill). Witnesses: Richard Bankes, Richard Bennet, John Cammell. Richard Bankes & John Cammell affirmed. Peter Carwaren was granted administration. Bond: Francis Hill.

26 April 1662. Richard Russell was granted administration on estate of John Coleman. Bond: Marks Phepo.

26 May 1662. Barbary Sutton (Patuxent River) was granted administration on estate of John Sutton. Bond: Enock Cambes.

1C:86
3 June 1662. Additional inventory of Col. John Price. Amount: #1784. Appraisers: Richard Bankes, Randell Hanson.

Court Session: <no date>

Mr. Robert Slye was granted administration on estate of Samuell Smith. Date: 11 April 1662. Bond: Mr. Thomas Gerrard.

4 June 1662. Mr. John Abington attorney for Mrs. Ann Tillny was granted administration on estate of Roger Isham.

11 June 1662. William Evans vs. estate of Gyles Sadler. Caveat.

1D:1   25 March 1662. Inventory of James Scapes by Mr. Robert Smith.
1D:2   List of debts: William Mills, Thomas Sprigge, Robert Pery, George Reade, Robert Cheaswick, Francis Huntchens, James Mullikin, Robert Blinkhorne, Allexander Watts, Thomas Leacthworth, Francis Armestrong, Thomas Perry, Andrew Roberson, Edward Keene, John Bagby,
1D:3   John Anderton, John Potts, Thomas Morkin, James Forbes, Hatton Bond, James Jolley, James Wilson, John Boage, James Godsgrace, John Bateman, Thomas Booth. Amount: #19588. More debts: Sanders Magruder, Thomas Harper, Thomas Sheiredin, William Pritchett, Thomas Trueman, the Governor, Ignatius Fenwick, Gilles Sadleir, John Little, John Askom. Amount: #8575. More debts in the hands of Henry Sewall: James Jolley, William Huntington, Samson Warren, William Mills,
1D:4   Phillip Coomes, Robert Parrey, John Edmondson, Thomas Markin, John Titmash, Michaell Craordley & Thomas Paggett, John Brigger, Edward Wood, John Satton, Enock Coomes, Jonathon Prether, Mathew Smith, Thomas Taylor (down the River), James Thomson & Richard Games, John Greeer & Andrew Dickeson, Stephen Clifton, George Alderson. Amount: #12558. More debts: Francis Carpenter, John Bulner, Abraham Watson at James Jolley, James Elton at Mr. Manning, John Senott at Lyons Creeke on plantation of William Parrett, Francis Armestrong, Stephen Benson, John Berrymore, James Cortney at Mr. Manning, Capt. Manning, Robert Clarck, John Hilliard, Richard

Court Session: <no date>

1D:5 Bentley by Cooper, William Chease, William Dutton, John Rallings, John Boge on estate of Mr. Fenwick (dec'd), Thomas Burdett, Stephen Garey. Amount: #3211. More debts: Richard Upgate, Henry Osborne. More debts: Daniell Browne, Henry Robinson, Peter Sharp, John Marke, John Felton, William Graves, Henry Corsey, William Howes, Tobias Mills, Thomas Brookes, John Pott, William Simson, John Mirth, Michaell Brookes, Peter Joy, John Paynter, Christofer Frame, Thomas Robinson, William Pritchett, John Platts,

1D:6 Cornelius Johnson, John Littell, Andrew Henderson, Thomas Stone. Amount: #2637.25 Additional inventory by Walter Senserf & Henry Sewall administrators.

17 June 1662. Will of Capt. Thomas Brodnox (KI).
1D:7 Bequests: wife Mary Brodnox (executrix). Date: 20 October 1661. Witnesses: Tobey Wells, Edward Sparks. Toby Wells affirmed. Date: 25 December 1661. Edward Sparks affirmed. Date: 7 February 1661.

1D:8 Will of Christofer Carnell. Bequests: John Pyper (executor) for my daughter Elisabeth Carnell. Overseers: John Gouldsmith, said Pyper. Date: 25 November 1661. Witnesses: Samuell Harris, John Norman, Samuell Dobson.

Inventory of William Empson (CH). Appraisers: Francis Pope, Mr. James Walker.
1D:9 Amount: #1137.5. Additional inventory. Appraisers: Francis Pope, Mr. Thomas Hussey. Amount: #1050. List of debts: William Hurd,
1D:10 Francis Fearnley, Richard Rowes. Amount: #5351.5. Accounts. Payments to: Robert Slye, John Courts, Thomas Baker, my father Gerrard, James Johnson. Date: 10 April 1662. Amount: #4810.5.

Will of Andrew Wardner. Bequests: wife Mary Wardner & children,
1D:11 daughter Izabel guardian is William

Court Session: <no date>

Lucas, George guardian is John Vanhack. Mentions: land of William Lucas, William Coles, John Vanhack. Signed: Andrew Warner. Date: 5 October 1660. Witnesses: William Kelley, George Mee. Will proved 27 March 1662.

1D:12
18 June 1662. Inventory of James Acheson.
Amount: #3640.

Inventory of Thomas Millner. Appraisers: John Warde, William Alline. Date: 26 May 1662. Amount: #4148.

1D:13
Zachary Wade, age 34, deposed that he was present at the house of Thomas Bushell in March 1653 when he made his will. Bequests: wife & children, brother William Bushell.

John Wahob, age 30, deposed that he was present when Thomas Bushell made his will. Bequests: wife, children, brother William Bushell. Sworn: 12 February 1661.

16 June 1662. Marks Pheypo was granted administration on the estate of Henry Potter. Security: George Marchall.

25 June 1662. Richard Cragbone was granted discharge Thomas Elston.

1D:14
Inventory of William Thompson (Bretton's Bay). Appraisers: Walter Peake, William Assiter. Date: 11 March 1660.
1D:15
Amount: #9571. List of debts: John Sewwll, George Reynolds.

1D:16
27 June 1662. Inventory of John Gwy. Amount: #7946. Appraisers: Francis Pope, Robert Henly.

John Gouldsmith was granted administration on the estate of Christofer Carnell. Bond: John Norman.

1D:17
Inventory of John Parker. Amount: #12077. Appraisers: John Douglass, Henry Pier. Walter Ben to administer oath.

Court Session: <no date>

29 June 1662. John Lambert was granted administration on estate of Samuell Lambert.

1D:18 Thomas Williams (Lancaster Co., Rappahannock River, VA), brother to John Williams (dec'd), gave PoA to Mr. Joseph Harrisson (Nansemick, CH). Date: 23 April 1662. Witnesses: Tho. Robinson, Luke Greene.

1D:19 4 August 1662. David Holt vs. Christian Bromefield (alias Christian Hoult) administrator/administratrix of Robert Hoult.

John Vanhack was granted administration on estate of Hugh Beaven. Bond: William Cole. Will of Hugh Beaven. Bequests: John Vanhack & William Lucas. Date: 16 October 1661. Witnesses: Josias Smith, Phillip Mackeaneday. Josias Smith affirmed. Date: 24 November.

Joseph Harrison administrator of Thomas Williams. Date: 1 August 1662. Bond: Frances Bacheler.

5 August 1662. Inventory of James Dick. Mentions: John Cobreath 100 a.
1D:20 By John Cobreth. Amount: #3924.

Inventory of Major Billinstia. Appraisers: James Allen, Mark Clare. List of debts: Thomas Mortine, Edward Moring, John Morris.

1D:21 Will of Henry Potter. Date: 22 December 1659. Bequests: daughter Adory, Church. Mentions: Robert Hooper. Witness: Marks Pheybo. [See f. 110.] Attested. Date: 23 June 1662.

21 August 1662. Will of George Meese. Bequests: John Cronheeck per will of George Mee land on Deep Branch, wife. Mentions: Tho. Mathews.
1D:22 Witnesses: George Wilson, Thomas Ward. Will proved 21 August 1662.

25 August 1662. Inventory of William Biss. Appraisers: Walter Car, Markes

Court Session: <no date>

1D:23 Clare. Date: 30 December 1661.
Servants mentioned: John Smith, William
Rallings. Amount: #6244. List of debts
by Judith now wife of Mr. John Norwood.
List of debts: John Marakin, Thomas
Rockhould,
George Stronge, William Greere. Amount:
#6450. Before: Mr. George Pake. Date:
30 December 1661.

1D:24 Inventory of Robert Holt. Date: 14
August 1662.
...
1D:25 List of debts: Vincent Accheson, James
Johnson, Mr. Mansfeild, Francis Hill,
William Pawmer, Ellick Frizell, Robert
Holte. Amount: #10242. Appraiser: Tho.
Mathewes. Witness: William Penrin.

1D:26 Nathaniell Utye, Esq. (Spetulia, BA) was
bound to John Benbow, John Harris, &
Henry Meese (merchants, London). Date:
14 September 1660. Recorded: 3 April
1662. Witnesses: Phillip Calvert, John
Bateman, Peter Bathe.

1D:27 Henry Corbyn (g) discharges Mr. Henry
Meese of all debts. Date: 22 May 1661.
Witnesses: Tho. Cornwaleys, Andrew
Cooke, Samuell Crissey.

1D:28 James Lee was granted administration on
estate of John Delahay (CH).
Appraisers: Humphry Hacket, Zachary
Wade. Warrant to: Joseph Harris.

Inventory of David Crombe. Appraisers:
Thomas Bennett, John Machie. Date: 17
February 1661.

12 September 1662. Inventory of David
Crombe in the hands of John Lawson (g).
Appraisers: said Lawson & Capt. Richard
Banckes. Date: 24 April 1662.

15 September 1662. William Smoote
(carpenter), age 65, deposed the value
of the ship St. George (sunk in
Wiccacomoco River). Date: 10 May 1662.

1D:29 20 September 1662. Gift of Robert Holt.
Date: 2 March 1661. To: his wife

Court Session: <no date>

Christian Holt, 2 daughters Elisabeth Holt & Dorothy Holt 50 a. Witnesses: Richard Browne, John Lafel, John Benson.

1D:30 Will of Samuell Lambert. Bequests: John Williams chattel from my brother John Lambert, John Lambert. Date: 14 October 1661. Witnesses: Thomas Trent, Robert Oston. Thomas Trent affirmed. Date: 21 November 1661. Witnesses: Henry Adams, Francis Pope, Sam. Lambert. Robert Oston affirmed. Date: 28 February 1661. Witnesses: Henry Adams, Francis Pope.

Will of John Guy. Bequests: Ann Guy. Date: 26 February 1658. Witnesses: Gyles Tomkins. 2 witnesses affirmed before Henry Adams & Francis Pope. Date: 28 January 1661. [Paragraph in Latin. Mentions: Georgius Thompsonus.]

1D:31 Inventory of Mrs. Jeane Fenwicke (widow, Patuxent, CV). Appraisers: George Read, John Read. Date: 14 November 1660.

1D:32 ...

1D:33 Signed: George Reade, John Reade.

1D:34 Will of Christopher Russell. Bequests: burial per Church of England, 2nd son Walter Russell to have servant Robert Landon, daughter Elisabeth Russell to have servant William Smith, Katherine Budd for looking after my 3 children, son William Russell (executor), friends Capt. Josias Fendall & Mr. Robert Handley. Date: last March 1662. Witnesses: Tho. Lomax, George Shourtie, George Tayler.

1D:35

1D:36 Thomas Lomax & George Tayler affirmed. Date: 30 July 1662.

9 October 1662. Capt. Josias Fendall & Robert Handley were granted administration on estate of Christopher Russell.

18 October 1662. David Holte was granted administration on estate of David Holt. Bond: Francis Jackson (g).

Court Session: <no date>

1D:37	Inventory of Capt. Thomas Brodnox (KI). Date: 1 August 1662. Mentions: 1000 a. on Chester River, 500 a. on Chester River, 400 a. his plantation. ...
1D:38	List of debts: Mr. Loyd, Robert Holton, John Morgan. Administratrix: Mary Bradnox. Additional Inventory.
1D:39	List of debts: Thomas Stagwell, William Tayler, Thomas Phillips, the Governor, Richard Steevens, Capt. John Tully, Mr. John Hatton, Mr. John Browne, Edward Clarkston, Mr. Nathaniell Styles, Mr. Edward Keerke,
1D:40	Thomas Hill, Mr. Henry Morgan, Tobye Wells. Amount: #5700.
	30 October 1662. William Calvert deposed on 27 October 1662 that on 18 August 1662, Mr. Thomas Coughing while at Mr. Mathews made his will. Bequests: Mathew Stone & Thomas Sprigg & Thomas Trueman to look after my father's business. Appraisers: John Reed, George Reed. William Turner to administer oath.
1D:41	Inventory of John Setton. Date: 28 June 1662. Amount: #3597. Appraisers: Francis Lane, Robert Kingsboro.
1D:42	George Macall & Francis Hill administrators of Forker Frizell were granted continuance.
	Peter Carwardin administrator of William Right was granted continuance.
	Inventory of Hugh Beven. Date: 13 September 1662. Amount: #310. Appraisers: George Willson, Thomas Ward. Administrator: John Vanhack.
1D:43	6 November 1662. Margery Battin administrator of her husband William Battin was granted administration on his estate. Appraisers: James Walker, John Bowles. Will of William Battin. Bequests: Charity Adams & William Love, wife Margery Battin (executrix), daughter Edia Newman & her 3 children George & William & Margerite Newman, my

Court Session: <no date>

sister Jone Smute & her son William Smute, my son George Newman. Overseers: Capt. Josias Fendall, Mr. Rob. Henly, my brother-in-law Thomas Smute. Date: 29 May 1662. Witnesses: Samuell Clarke, Mary Oonell, Tho. More, Edmund Pinsonn.

1D:44 7 November 1662. Capt. James Neale vs. estate of Hugh Lee possessed by Hannah Lee relict of said Hugh. Caveat.

Will of Tho. Wallton. Bequests: wife Ellinor Walton. Date: 8 October 1662. Witnesses: Richard Collett, John Wisman. Will proved 21 November 1662.

28 November 1662. John Anderson was granted administration on estate of Thomas Wallton. Bond: John Elzey.

Margery Battin was granted administration on estate of her husband William Battin. Date: 6 October 1662.

1D:45 2 December. Will of John Cornelos. Bequests: Ann Dorrington & her children. Overseer: William Dorrington over John Winale. Witnesses: Richard Bond, John Allenson. Will proved 30 November 1662.

1D:46 William Dorrington was granted administration on said estate. Bond: John Bateman.

1 December. Inventory of Capt. Christopher Russell. Date: 11 November 1662. Appraisers: John Bowles, John Price.

1D:47 Will of William Palmer. Date: 6 November 1662. Bequests: my mother then Alexander Frizall, James Atwick 25 a., Herbert Homan, Alexander Frizall, my mother & brother, Henry Banyster, Daniell Smyth, John Atwick. Mentions: Capt. Cooke. Witnesses: Roger Atkeson, Richard Downes.

1D:48 4 December 1662. John Nutwell vs. Henry Sewall, Esq. & Walter Sensarfe administrators of estate of James Scape.

Court Session: <no date>

3 December 1662. Alexander Fryzall was granted administration on estate of William Palmer. Bond: Walter Peake.

9 December 1662. Inventory of Robert Holt (d. 29 December 1662).

1D:49   10 December. George Bradshaw was granted administration on estate of Thomas Killy. Bond: William Boareman.

Henery Ellery was granted administration on estate of William Stephenson.

1D:50   24 December 1662. Inventory of Christopher Kernall. Date: 11 May 1662.
1D:51   Appraisers: John Gie, Edward Turner. Amount: #7572.

1D:52   Inventory of Gyles Sadler.
1D:53   Amount: #24688.

Inventory of Mr. Hugh Standley. Date: 11 August 1662. Servants mentioned: Henery Vizard, John Owen.
1D:54   Amount: #12103. Appraisers: Francis Carpenter, Henry Alexander.

2 January 1662. Will of Richard Smith. Bequests: Mathew Smith my wife & child,
1D:55   William Williams (under age) 50 a. Overseers: Francis Pope, Mr. Turner, Mr. Bates.
1D:56   Date: 25 November 1662. Signed: Richard Smoth. Witnesses: Robert Robines, James Johnson. Will proved 2 January 1662. John Hatch, Arthur Turner, & Frances Pope were granted administration on estate of Richard Smith. Bond: Patrick Forrest.

1D:57   23 January 1662. Will of Thomas Turner (St. Winefreds, SM). Bequests: Mr. Francis Fitzherbert for baptism in Roman Catholic Church,
1D:58   wife Emma & 3 children (of age at 16) Thomas & Mary Turner & Elisabeth Johnson estate in several parishes in Audlen (Essex, ENG) as by my father's will. Overseers: Mr. William Bretton, Mr. Luke Gardner.
1D:59   Date: 2 October 1662. Witnesses:

Court Session: <no date>

William Rosewell, Chas. Alexander. Will proved 21 January 1662.

Anne Beach (widow) gave chattel to her children from estate of her husband Elias Beach (dec'd): her eldest daughter Mary Beach (b. 30 January 1653), her youngest daughter Rebecca Beach (age 3), her youngest son Thomas Beach (age 1). Date: 22 January 1662.

1D:60 Witnesses: Tho. Innes, John Boulton.

1D:61 20 February. Will of Richard Gott (Herring Creek, AA). Bequests: Richard Gott (under age 17) plantation, wife Susan. Date: 20 November 1660. Witnesses: John Stanesby, Edward Parish, Jeffery Lambert. Henry Hooper was granted administration on estate of Richard Gott (said Henry married the relict). Bond: Thomas Manning.

1D:62 Roger Grosse to prove said will.

22 February. Additional inventory of William Empson by Robert Slye (g). List of debts: Humphry Attwicks.

27 February. Mr. John Lawson exhibited oath of Mr. Richard Banks & John Camell, appraisers of estate of William Wright. Inventory of William Wright (Poplar Hill, SM). Date: 24 February 1662.

1D:63 ...

1D:64 Will of William Bouls (p, Pukiawaxen, CH) Bequests: wife Sarah (executrix) 200 a. & 200 a. in possession of Humphrey Attwicks & Thomas Gibson, Robert Robins, uncle John Boules & my kinsman James Tyre. Date: 15 February 1662. Signed: William Boules. Witnesses: William Ayliffe, William Lewis.

1D:65 Will proved 27 February 1662. Sarah Boules was granted administration. Bond: Robert Robins. Appraisers: William Heard, Thomas Smoote. Mr. Francis Pope to administer oath.

2 March. Mr. John Lawson exhibited will of William Palmer dated 3 December 1662, with probate. Appraisers: George

Court Session: <no date>

1D:66 Maccall, William Edwin. John Lawson to administer oath. Date: 26 February 1662. Inventory of William Palmer. Appraisers: George Maccall, William Edwin. Date: 26 February 1662. Amount: #6003. Alexander Frizell administrator of William Palmer was granted continuance.

1D:67 Mr. John Lawson exhibited will of Forker Frizell, with probate. Appraisers: Peter Waters, David. Duncun. Inventory of Forker Frizell. Date: 9 March 1662. Amount: #4675. Appraisers: Peter Waters, David Duncun.

1D:68 Mr. Joseph Harrison exhibited will of John Delahay, with probate. Appraisers: Zachary Wade, Humphrey Haggatt. Oath on 4 March 1662. Inventory of John Delahay. Administrator: James Lee. Date: 9 March 1662. Mentions: 300 a. Amount: #1904. Appraisers: Humph. Haggott, Zachary Wade.

Mr. John Nutthell exhibited will of George Mee, with probate. Appraisers: William Cole, George Willson. Oath on 28 February 1662. Inventory of George Mee. Mentions: 400 a. Amount: #15300.

1D:69 Inventory of Samuell Lambert. List of debts: Rich. Dod, Daniel Browne, Andrew Watson, Robert Dauner, Clem. Theobald. Appraisers: William Jeffers, Henry Franckcum.

1D:70 26 March 1663. Will of John Shirtcliffe (SM). Bequests: wife Anne Shirtcliffe plantation of 300 a. on Bretton's Bay then eldest son John Shirtcliffe, eldest son John Shirtcliffe 200 a. out of patent for 600 a. due on assignment from John Mansell (dec'd) on Bretton's Bay, youngest son William Shirtcliffe 100 a. at head of St. Clement's Bay called "Shirtcliffe Runne", youngest son William Shirtcliffe 200 a. due from Thomas Spalding & servants belonging to Mr. John Lewger the younger,

Court Session: <no date>

1D:71 eldest daughter Mary Shirtcliffe 100 a. out of 200 a. due from Joseph Dorazell & Elisabeth Morgan & John Bayly & Elisabeth Abrahams, youngest daughter Ann Shirtcliffe 50 a. out of 200 a., cousin Thomas Spalding 50 a. out of 200 a.,

1D:72 Mr. Francis Fitzherbert for Catholic Church of Newtowne, brother-in-law Henry Spinke & friend Peter Mills to aid wife. Date: 2 December 1661.

1D:73 Witnesses: Edward Clarke, Edmond Smith, Leonard Greene. Edward Clarke & Leonard Greene affirmed. Date: 26 March 1663. Anne Shirtcliffe was granted administration. Bond: Edward Clarke. Appraisers: William Assiter, William Tetershall. Col. William Evans to administer oath.

Anne Hammond widow & administratrix of John Hammond was granted administration on his estate. Bond: Mr. Richard Willan. Appraisers: John Jarbo, William Tetershall. Col. William Evans to administer oath.

1D:74 Bridget Sheale widow of Robert Sheale was granted administration on his estate. Bond: William Wood. Appraisers: Mr. John Jarbo, Henry Spinke. Col. William Evans to administer oath.

William Hollis was granted administration on estate of Thomas Sampson (BA). Bond: Capt. John Collier. Appraisers: William Hollins, Capt. John Collier. Capt. Thomas Howell to administer oath.

1D:75 Mr. Henry Adams exhibited will of John Williams (CH), with probate. Appraisers: William Allen, Thomas Burdett. Date: 17 December 1662. Inventory of John Williams. Date: 29 January 1662.

1D:76 Amount: #3271. Appraisers: Thomas Burdett, William Allen, Sr.

9 April. Henry Ellery deposed that he travelled to New England in the catch

Court Session: <no date>

1D:77 (called the Methew) of Mr. Legg, with Richard Grimes. Before they arrived at Manahawtans, said Grimes died. Mentions: John Hawkins. Will of said Grimes. Bequests: deponent to return chattel to Mr. Robert Kedger. Administrator: Robert Kedger. Bond: Henry Ellery. Appraisers: Mr. Henry Hyde, William Edwin. Mr. Thomas Dent to administer oath.

Inventory of John Coleman. Appraisers: John Nicholls, George Wright. Date: 18 April 1662. Amount: #3720.

1D:78 William Turner vs. estate of William Bromall (p, CV) in trust of John Hilliard (overseer). Caveat. [Petitioner taking a voyage to VA.] Appraisers: James Veitch, Samuel Groves. Capt. Thomas Manning to administer oath.

1D:79 30 April. Will of Alice Harwood. Date: 16 November 1660. Bequests: Stanop Roberts plantation, John Wallcops son & his daughter Elisabeth, Dorcas Lawson, Frances Philips (daughter of Thomas Philips), John Lawson, Richard Ringe (son of Thomas), Walter Frizell. Witnesses: John Lawson, Suncomb Phrizell, John Wilkinson. Will proved 30 April 1663. Administrator: Stanop Roberts.

Estates left in public hands: Edward Cotton to Thomas Mathewes & Raph Crouch.

1D:80 19 June. Inventory of William Bromall (p, St. Leonard's Creek, CV). Servants mentioned: John Dowkins, Robert Hobbs, John Love.
1D:81 Amount: #20471. [Deceased died on 8 December 1660.] Appraisers: James Veitch, John Helyard. Date: 6 April 1663.
1D:82 Appraisers: James Veitch, Samuell Graves.

Inventory of Thomas Sampson. Appraisers: Thomas Overton, John Hill. Date: 21 May 1663.

Court Session: <no date>

1D:83 ...
1D:84 Amount: #9830.

25 June. Inventory of Capt. William Battin (CH). Appraisers: Mr. James Walker, John Bowles. Date: 12 February 1662.
1D:85-94 ...
1D:95 Amount: #88416.

Inventory of Robert Sheale. Appraisers: Col. John Jarbo, Henry Spinke. Date: 7 April 1663.
1D:96 Amount: #2430.

1D:97 Inventory of John Hammond. Date: 7 April 1663. Appraisers: Col. John Jarbo, William Tetershall. List of debts: Christian Bromfield, John Luombroz, William Hemstead, Mr. Standley.
1D:98 Amount: #6640.

Inventory of Richard Grimes (mariner) by his administrator Henry Ellery (SM). Appraisers: Mr. Henry Hyde, William Edwin. Date: 13 April 1663.
1D:99 Amount: #3405.5.

1D:100 Inventory of John Shirtcliffe. Appraisers: William Assiter, William Tetershall. Date: 7 April 1663.
1D:101-103 ...
1D:104 Amount: #10517.

1D:105 Francis Pope (g) one of administrators of Richard Smith (CH) was granted continuance.

1D:106 Inventory of Alice Harwood relict of John Harwood. Date: 12 June 1663. Mentions: 100 a. on Blacke Creek.
1D:107 Administrator: Stanop Roberts.

22 July. John Brewer (g, AA) was granted administration on estate of John Hatton (merchant). Bond: Francis Holland.

Mr. John Nutthall to administer oath to John Reynolds & Edward West appraisers
1D:108 of Hugh Lee.

Court Session: <no date>

1D:109	30 July. Will of Humphrey Haggett. Bequests: wife Anne Haggett (executrix). Servants: James Williams, Henry Price, Daniel Russell, Rachel White. Mentions: Mr. Joseph Harrison. Date: 30 December 1660. Witnesses: Francis Bacheler, Thomas Lomax, Thomas Wentworth, Thomas Steade. Thomas Wentworth affirmed. Thomas Stead affirmed.
1D:110	Anne Haggett was granted administration. Appraisers: Thomas Robinson, John Wheeler. Mr. Zachary Wade to administer oath.
	31 July 1663. Marks Pheypo affirmed the will of Henry Potter.
1D:111	Will of Anthony Goddard (Swingdon, Wilts, England & Rapahanock VA). Executor: Mr. William Burges (AA). Date: 28 July 1663. Witnesses: John Gray, Nath. Heathcoate. Mr. John Brewer to administer oath.
1D:112 1D:113	Will of Richard Talbott. Bequests: my eldest son Richard "Poplar Knowle", my other sons Edward & John "Talbott's Ridge", my son of age at 21 & daughter Elisabeth of age at 16, my eldest sons Richard & Edward chattel from their grandfather. Executrix: wife. Date: 21 April 1663. Witnesses: Rich. Galloway, Jacob Duhatto, Tho. Tailer.
1D:114 1D:115	Robert Paca administrator of John Hall petitioned for discharge. ... Discharge granted to Robert Paca for:

- Mary Connor administratrix of Philip Connor.
- Henry Alexander administrator of James Gunnell. Date: 18 February 1662.
- Peter Carwardin administrator of William Wrighte. Date: 8 September 1663.
- Stanop Roberts administrator of Alce Harwood. Date: 8 September 1663.
- Joseph Harrison administrator of Thomas Milner. Date: 8 September

Court Session: <no date> 1663.

- Joseph Harrison administrator of John William. Date: 8 September 1663.
- Sampson Waring administrator of William Bisse Date: 8 September 1663.
- John Vanhack administrator of Hugh Bevin. Date: 8 September 1663.
- John Vanhack administrator of John Mackenny. Date: 8 September 1663.

1D:116   Will of William Styles. Date: 21 April 1663. Bequests: wife Mary Stiles, my children. Witnesses: William Wood, Mordecai Hammond. William Woods, age 25, affirmed. Date: 31 October 1663. Mary Styles was granted administration. Appraisers: William Tettershall, Walter Pakes.

Mr. Samuell Withers exhibited oath of Mr. Roger Grosse & Capt. William Burges, appraisers of estate of John Hatton. Date: 14 July 1663.

1D:117   Will of Woodman Stockley. Bequests: wife America, 4 children (of age at 18) James & Elisabeth & Ann & Oliver. Overseers: friends Michaell Brooke, James Berry, William Berry, William Allomby. Date: 22 February 1659. Witnesses: William Allomby, John Whiston, John Winall, William Burke, Geo. Aldeson.

1D:118   <u>30 October.</u> William Burke affirmed said will.

Will of Robert Cole (yeoman, of St. Clement's Bay). Date: 2 March 1662. Bequests: Mr. Francis Fitzherbert that the testator die a Roman Catholic, son-in-law Francis Knott, my own children,
1D:119   my son Rob. Cole, my daughters Mary Cole & Elisabeth Cole, my son Robert Cole plantation then his brother William then his brother Edward,
1D:120   Francis Knott 50 a., my 3 sons 600 a. (have warrant for 450 a. & rights for transporting John Elton, Sibel Johnson,

Court Session: <no date>

1D:121 & Isabella Joanes), estate in England to children after my mother Mrs. Jone Cole (Heston, County Middlesex). Mentions: Ann Harinton, John Wheeler. Executors: Col. William Evans, Capt. Luke Gardner (both of St. Clement's Bay), my cousin Mr. Henry Hanckes (Holborne, London). Children of age at 21, & to be raised Roman Catholic. Witnesses: Thomas Brooke, James Thompson, Edward Clark.

1D:122 Codicil: son Robert Cole b. 15 October 1652, daughter Mary Cole b. 26 January 1653, son William Cole b. 23 June 1655, son Edward Cole b. 9 November 1657, daughter Elisabeth Cole b. 2 March 1659. Francis Knott is 3 years older than my son Robert. Date: 25 April 1662. James Thompson affirmed. [Said Cole was bound for England.] Date: 8 September 1663. Thomas Brooke (g) affirmed. Date: 16 September 1663.

1D:123 8 December. Accounts of William Palmer. Payments to: Dr. Barber, Capt. Cooke, Mr. Dent, William Hewes. Amount: #4619.

Samuell Cooper (son of Sampson Cooper (Rippon, Yorke River, alderman)) chose as his guardian Barnaby Jackson (SM).

1D:124 Will of Mary Brasseur (widow, the Clifts). Bequests: my children: Robert 200 a., Benjamin 200 a., John 200 a., son Robert, Benjamin, son John land adjoining land sold to my brother-in-law Robert Brassieur, daughter Mary (under age 16),

1D:125 daughter Ann (under age 16), daughter Susanna (under age 16), daughter Martha (under age 16), daughter Elisabeth (under age 16).

1D:126 Overseers: Thomas Starling, brother-in-law Robert Brassieur. Date: 25 May 1663. Witnesses: Theophilus Lewis, James Pugsley. Thomas Starlinge & Mary Brassieur posted a marriage bond. Said Mary is the late wife of Benjamin Brassieur.

1D:127 Date: 25 July 1663. Signed: Thomas Starling. Witnesses: Robert Heighe, James Hume.

Court Session: <no date>

4 January 1663/4. Thomas Billingsley (the Clifts, CV) exhibited will of James Billingsley.

1D:128 John Lawson deposed that about 8 December last, at the house of William Tenahill, David Duncan declared that said Will. was to receive all. Date: 28 January 1663.

28 January 1663/4. William Tenahill was granted administration. Appraisers: John Lawson, John Cammell. Mr. Thomas Dent to administer oath.

Sampson Waring was granted administration on estate of Antony Roy. Date: 1 December.

1D:129 Will of William Wilkinson. Bequests: Elisabeth Buddens (daughter of Margarett Buddens (my last wife)), my 2 grandchildren William Dent eldest son of Tho. & Rebecka Dent & William Hatton eldest son of William &
1D:130 Elisabeth Hatton, my son-in-law Thomas Dent & his wife Rebecca, my son-in-law William Hatton & his wife Elisabeth. Executors: my 2 sons-in-law. Date: 29 May 1663. Witnesses: Randall Handson, San. Smith.
1D:131 Codicil: Bequests: my son-in-law William Hatton land bought of Capt. William Stone called "Hulls Neck". Date: 8 July 1663.

Francis Pope exhibited oath of William Heard & Thomas Smoote, appraisers of estate of William Bowles. Date: 27 February 1662.
1D:132 Inventory of William Bowles. Appraisers: William Heard, Thomas Smote.
1D:133 Amount: #17850.

Henry Adams exhibited oath of John Bowles & Thomas, appraisers of Rich. Smith, sworn on 10 January 1662. Inventory of Richard Smith. Date: 1 February 1662. Appraisers: John Bowles, Mr. Thomas Smootes.
1D:134-135 ...
1D:136 Mentions: 3 servants: John Cather,

Court Session: <no date>

1D:137 Nathaniel Button, William Barnes.
Witness: John Worland.
Amount: #23308.

13 February 1663. Discharge was granted to Hugh Standley administrator of Giles Sadler (late sheriff of CV).

Discharge was granted to George Thompson administrator of Daniel Jordan.

1D:138 Will of John Bateman.
Bequests: wife Mary Bateman received of her mother Margarett Perrey, said Margaret Perry "Resurrection Mannor" & "Thorpe Freehould" 400 a., daughter Mary Bateman,
1D:139 Overseer: Phillip Calvert, Esq. Date: 20 November 1662. Witnesses: Thomas Truman, John Gittings. Codicil: Date: 3 December 1662. Witnesses: John Gittings, Stephen Clifton, Thomas Truman.
1D:140 Inventory of John Bateman, Esq. (Resurrection Mannor, CV). Appraisers: Arthur Ludford, William Mills. Date: 5 January 1663.
1D:141-144 ...
1D:145 Amount: #35388.

1D:146 Will of Richard Willan.
Bequests: daughter Elisabeth Willan, son Phillip Willan, daughter Grace Willan, eldest daughter Mary Mills,
1D:147 wife Sarah Holland (executrix), sons of age at 18, daughters of age at 16. Overseers: Capt. Luke Gardner, Mr. John Shercliff. Date: 25 October 1662. Witnesses: Patrick Forrest, Thomas Hatton. Will proved 5 September 1663
1D:148 by Pattrick Forrest. Idem: Thomas Hatton.

Will of Suzan Cannaday. Bequests: son James Cannady, Mr. Norton & Mr. Leagwort, daughter Suzan, son William, son John. Date: 11 July 1663. Witnesses: John Tany, William Graves. Will proved on 26 February 1663.

1D:149 26 February 1662. Thomas Leitchworde & Tobias Norton granted administration on

Court Session: <no date>

estate of Suzan Kennaday (also Suzan Cannaday). Appraisers: Arthur Ludford, Hugh Standly.

Inventory of Mr. William Turner. Appraisers: Richard Smith, Henry Alexander. Mentions: servants: Simon Hubbar (boy), Richard Phare, James Denrell, John Barber, Suzanna Griffin.

1D:150 ...
1D:151 Date: 22 April 1664. Before: Hugh Standley.

1D:152 Inventory of Anthony Goddard. Appraisers: Thomas Beeson, Richard Orson. Date: 25 August 1663. Amount: #3289. Before: John Brewer. Date: 25 August 1663. Appraisers: said Capt. Thomas Beeson & Mr. Richard Ewens.

1D:153 Inventory of John Cornelius. Appraisers: Arthur Ludford, John Bigger.
1D:154 List of debts: William Graves, James Compton.

1D:155 Will of Mordecay Nicolas. Bequests: Andrew Woodberry. Alexander Cole & Mrs. Mary Cusale affirmed. Date: 11 January 1663/4. Witnesses: Sanders Coale, Mary Oonelle. Henry Addams & Thomas Mathews affirmed.

1D:156 Inventory of John Hatton. Date: 30 July 1663.
1D:157 ...
1D:158 Amount: #16910.

1D:159 Accounts of John Brewer. Administrator: John Hatton. Date: 1 March 1661. Payments: Thomas Gates, Tho. Billingsley, John Wolcott, John Edwards, Abraham Coffin, Samuell Skipwith, Will. Leeds, Will. Elliott, John Jenkins, Thomas Taylor, Richard Gott, Robert Martin, Will. Bissie, George Utye, Tho. Tolley, Patrick Dunkin, Mathew Clarke, Will. Davis, Will. Neale, Rich. Ewen, John Jones, Samuell Chew, Godfrid Herman, Alexander Towerson, Will. Davis, John Cumber, Anne Coudle, Elinor Boud, Will. Bamsday, Edmond Townhill, Henry

Court Session: <no date>

1D:160 Tootle, Will. Richards, John Bruer, John Eason, Robert Burley, Rich. Acton, James Bigby, Capt. Robert Vaughan, Samuell Withers, Richard Deaver, John Stansby, Abr. Bishop, Will. Coursey, Mr. Philip Calvert, Richard Cheyney, John Scarlett, Anthony Griffin, Will. Coursey & his brother John, Oliver Sprye, Rober Parker, Thomas Bevett, Thomas Snow, Macam Mecammey, Andrew Eclinor (?), John Winchester, Josias Lambert, Grehan Crumell, Nicholas Prichard,

1D:161 Joseph Weeks, Mary Bradnox, Morgan Williams, Henry Clay, Will. Taylor, Rich. Woolman, James Maxall, Franc. & Thomas Stockett, Fra. Hillan, Will. Hunt, James Sowthward, Seth Foster, Godfry Bayly, Franc. Trippe, Nathaniell Styles, Thomas Odovell, John Collier, Will. Hemsley, Will. Champe, John Morgan, Sr., John Spurdance, Robert Tyler, Rich. Blunt, Will. Stanly, James Warner. Amount: #65419.

1D:162 Mentions: patents for: 600 a. bought of Mr. Sprye "Spry's Hill", 350 a. bought of Godfrid Herman "Herman's Mount", 400 a. bought of James Bigby "Scimmon Point", 300 a. bought of William Hemsley "White Clift" on Chester River, 100 a. bought of Thomas Bennett on St. Michael's River. Date: 39 (!) July 1663. Appraisers: Rog. Grosse, William Burges.

Stephen Brooks Clifton petitioned for Charles Brooks to swear Richard Smyth & Henry Alexander to appraise the estate of William Turner. Date: 15 April 1664.

Francis Armstrong administrator of Cornelius Abrahamson was granted discharge. Date: 13 May 1664.

John Pyper administrator of Christopher Camall was granted discharge. Date: 13 May 1664.

1D:163 Inventory of William Edwin. Date: 11 January 1663. Appraisers: Robert Cager, Henry Ellery. List of debts: Thomas Crakson, Humphry Fuller, Andrew Wastson,

Court Session: <no date>

William Palmer & Nicholas Brookes, Mr. Robert Henley, Robert Mosely & Robert Austure, John Walton, David Pritchard, Daniell Johnson, John Ward, William Hinsey, William Smoote, William Heard, Richard Morris, Peter Carr, John Nevell, Henery Peare, Mr. Arthur Turner, Edmond Linsey, Symon Thomas, James Lindsey, John Waddis, John Hall, John Coddington, Robert Jones, Edward Solman, Thomas Shaw, Edward Rogers, John Gardner, Henry Roach,

1D:164 Thomas Tolley & William Courte, William Robinson, George Thompson, Bartholomew Gatherill, Joseph Harrison, William Barton, William White, John Deynly, John Duglas, Mrs. Verlinda Stone, Mr. Daniell Hill, Thomas Smoote, George Newman, James Lee, John Delahay, Mr. Francis Pope, Francis Wast, Walter Beane, William Bowles, Mr. Horton, Richard Dodd, Daniell Collins, William Love (Ocquia), William Greene, John Mathewes, William Soward, Michael Hill, Mr. Mountague, John Eure (Great Wiccocomico), James Makgreger, Edward Hawley, James Clayton, Robert Such, Anthony Linton, Daniell White,

1D:165 Martha Smith, John Morris, Francis Gray, Phillip Caryduter, Edmond Nanton, Richard Robinson, Joseph Cooy, Richard Watson, George Day, Thomas Humphreys, William Beath, Nicholas Rushell, Samuell Mutterslued, John Harbott, John Bogisse, Thomas Peryne, Richard Hitchcoke, Abraham Joyne, Percivall Hamond, John Kent, Richard Dennis, Samuell Mayhan, John Price, Alexander Sherwood, Thomas Williams, Richard Rice. Amount: #74844. List of debts: Thomas Sheares, James Makgreger, John Lane, Nicholas Purqua, Mr. Colclough,

1D:166 Mr. Wright, Thomas Hackett, Jonathon Hewes, Symon Richardson, Edward Wood, Thomas Hamper, Henry Graw, Elias Blake, Michaell Carter, Robert Clarke, John Thomkinson, Samuell Lamberd, Henry Spkinke, Peter Ackellis, Zachary Wade, William Marshall & Walter Beane, Thomas Shelton, Robert Wilson. List of debts: Alexander White, Christopher Rushell, John Lord, Richard Haybeard, John Hatch,

Court Session: <no date>

Absolom Covey, Christopher Carmell, Robert Robins, John Blakwell, Mathew Clarke, John Roper, Mr. Muttershed, Richard Rich, Richard Brawne, Robert Hickes,
1D:167 Richard Tarlin, William Empson, Richard Perie, Mr. Spencer, Nicholas Ferman, George Mettcope, Robert Hewes, William Cleamond, Dr. Mattix, Thomas Beadle, Thomas Early, William Lamman, William Ruske, Francis Clay, Thomas Bumbery, Francis Symons, Richard Flint, Richard Webley, Peter Presley, John Bennitt, Edward Henley, Mr. Vinson, Thomas Addams. Amount: #26954. Account by Capt. Will. Battin. Payments to: Edmond Lyndsey, Edward Goodman, Richard Rich, Thomas Baskett, George Markhes, Walter Pake, John Baker, William White,
1D:168 Thomas Johnson, Col. Fowke for Jacob Lumbro, Francis Gray, Robert Robyne, William Freak.

Nicholas Temple & Will. Streete deposed regarding the will of Capt. Ralph Story (ENG). Date: 25 December 1663. Executrix: wife Avis Story. Bequests: brother's children, John Price (chyrurgeon), John Doyne (my mate), Thomas Gold (my mate), Will. Streete, Thomas Atkins (boy).
1D:169 Will proved 6 January 1663.

7 January 1663. Appraisers: Robert Frankling, Richard Huggins.

13 January 1663. Samuell Withers administered oath.

Inventory of Capt. Ralph Story. Date: 13 January 1663.
1D:170 ...
1D:171 List of debts: Will. Piper, Daniell Hutt, Charles James, Nicholas Wiett, Ralph Williams, Henry Morgan, John Cumber, Thomas Howell, Edward Kedmore, Richard Huggins, William Leeds, Anthony Griffin, Joseph Chew, James Maxfeild, Robert Franklin, Mr. Thomas Gerrard, Samuell Withers,
1D:172 Mr. Mannder, Daniell Johnson, John Hutch, Col. Evans, John Goldsmith,

Court Session: <no date>

Francis Sisson, Cornelius Howard, Sarah Marsh, Robert Clarkson, William Neale, Edward Skidmoare, Thomas Hamond, James Sowthward, James Maxfeild, Henry Cattlin, Thomas Underwood, Nathaniell Utye, Richard Bennett, Henry Sewell, William Hopkins, Thomas Howell, Nicholas Wyett, Jonathon Neale. Amount: #71925. List of debts: Mr. Sly for Mr. Thomas Edwards, Mr. William Baker, Mr. Thomas Gerrard, Thomas Howell. Amount: £30.6.8.

1D:173 Appraisers: Robert Francklin, Richard Huggins. List of debts: Ralph Hayward.

1D:174 Will of John Sison (p, AA). Bequests: wife Frances Sison plantation of 420 a., eldest daughter Jeane Sison, wife & Katheryne Davis & George Loudell, wife & John Herman, Jeane Sison & Richard Hill & Richard Warfeild & John Bennitt, Elisabeth Sison 200 a. bought of Mr. Edward Lloyd, brother Benjamin Sison, brother Cornelius Howard, Richard Huggins. Witnesses: William Wilson, William Gaymes.

William Price & William Greengoe deposed on will of William Edwin. Date: 13 October 1663. Bequests: wife then eldest son Michaell Edwin, grandchild Mary Hall.

1D:175 12 February 1663/4. Inventory of William Edwin.
1D:176 Appraisers: Henry Ellery, Robert Cager.

Will of Robert Hopkins. Date: 22 March 1661. Bequests: Thomas Hopkins, father & 2 brothers. Witnesses: John Hambleton, Robert Sorell.

1D:177 Inventory of Thomas Kelly. Amount: 496. Date: 2 February 1663. Administrator: Mr. George Brad. Appraisers: Robert Trupp, John Browne.

Will of John Wright (Newtown). Date: 2 November 1663. Bequests: landlord William Asiter. Witnesses: John Daves, Gaberell Woodmorson.
1D:178 Date: 1 December 1663. William Assiter

Court Session: <no date>

was granted administration on estate of John Wright. Will proved by John Daves & Gaberell Woodmorson. Date: 27 December 1663.

1D:179 Will of Susannah Billingsley. Bequests: brother Richard Ewen, brother John Ewen, brother-in-law Edmond Billingsley, husband James Billingsley (dec'd), Walter Caree, sister Ann Ewen, brother Richard Ewen, sister Elisabeth Talbott chattel at plantation of my father-in-law Capt. Burges, sister Suffia, Edward Parrish. Mentions: John Cumber the younger, John Cray. Date: 9 February 1663/4.

1D:180 Deposition: Stephen Hammett was my mate & died in Anne Arundel Co. on 3 November. Mentions: Mr. John Dunch (master of the Golden Lyon). Signed: James Conaway. Date: 7 November 1663. Said James granted administration. Appraisers: John Howard, Cornelius Howard. Mr. John Brewer to administer oath.

1D:181 Inventory of (N). Date: 5 December 1663. Appraisers: William Tettershall, Henry Spinke. Amount: #4920. Mentions: John Bryant. Signed: James Pateson.

1D:182 Will of James Billingsley (p, CV). Bequests: brother Walter Carr, brother Thomas Billingsley, 3 cousins in Rapahanock, wife Susannah. Date: 19 November 1663. Witnesses: William Carr, Rich. Briscoe. Will proved 6 January 1663.

Will of Jacob Odenhanway. Date: 23 October 1663. Bequests: daughter Elisabeth, wife. Witnesses: James White, John Ewen.

1E:1 Will of William Turner (g, Patuxent, CV). Bequests: oldest son William Turner 350 a., son Edward Turner, Edward & Richard Turner to divide 400 a. in Choptank, daughter Jone Clifton, son William & grandchild William Clifton to

Court Session: <no date>

1E:2
divide warrant for 600 a., residue between 3 sons William, Edward, & Richard Turner & grandchild William Clifton. Executors: son-in-law Stephen Clifton, son William. Date: 11 June 1663. Witnesses: Francis Tractman, Francis Lane. Francis Tractman attested. Date: 20 August 1663. Francis Lane attested. Date: 22 December 1663. Stephen Clifton (chyrurgeon) was granted administration. Appraisers: Mr. Richard Smith, Mr. William Dorrington.

1E:3
Will of Edward Cotton. Date: 4 April 1653. Mentions: agreement with Barnaby Jackson for work for Richard Willan. Executors: Thomas Mathewes, Ralph Crouch. Bequests: David Thomas (servant), Mr. Starkey provided he give to John Warren & to his eldest son Ignatius Warren, George Prouse, James Grinoway, Thomas Mathews the younger,

1E:4
Mr. Darby Flanagan, eldest daughter of John Wheately.

1E:5
Mentions: William Ramsey, George Sprouce. Witnesses: John Pyle, Walter Pekes. John Pile &

1E:6
Walter Pekes attested. Date: 22 April 1653.

1E:7
Will of Christopher Goodeker. Date: 18 January 1663. Bequests: Dorothy, son Richard. List of debts: Mr. Walter Hall, John Sissell, Thomas King, John Baxter, Peter Carridine, Edward Fowler. Debts owed: Mr. Nottley, Mr. Robert Slye, Robert Jones, the Smith, John Lawsone. Witnesses: John Lawson, William Tenahill, Susanna Whitle. John Lawson & William Tenahill attested. Date: 28 January 1663.

13 December 1663. Capt. Robert Troope & John Browne to appraise estate of Thomas Killy (CH). Mr. Joseph Harris to administer oath.

1E:8
Rand. Hanson exhibited PoA to act on behalf of wife & children. Signed:

Court Session: <no date>

John Cummins. Date: 24 March 1662/3. Witnesses: John Wood, Andra Woodbury. Andrew Woodbury deposed to validity of PoA of John Cummings. John Verd attested. Date: 30 April 1663.

James Billingsley gave to his brother Thomas Billingsley 300 a. Mentions: James' wife Susan. Date: 12 November 1663. Witnesses: John Stansby, John Troster, Robert Teighe. John Troster attested. Date: 6 January 1663.

1E:9   24 December 1663. Cuthbert Fenwick, Arthur Ludford, James Tompson, & William Mills to appraise estate of John Bateman (CV). Oath given to Mr. Arthur Ludford & Mr. William Mills. Date: 5 January 1663.

1E:10   Inventory of William Bowls. Date: 22 January 1663. Appraisers: William Haird, Thomas Smote. Mentions: 200 a. Amount: #17850. Mr. Francis Pope made oath. Date: 27 February 1662.

1E:11   Inventory of Stephen Hamond. List of debts: Mr. Franlyn, Mr. Yates, Richard Bamby, Mr. Dyke, Joseph Wild, Ralph Salmon, John Pollard, sisters of Richard Mosse, Benjamin Rico, Henry Mitchell, Guy White, Patrick Dunoons, John Longworth, Jonathon Hopkins, William Bateman, Mrs. Norwood for self & son Ben., Joseph Gallion, William Wilson, Thomas Turner, John Sandford, George Chamon, Henry Sewell, John Howard, Rowland Johnson, William Barker, Richard Huggins, Wheatley, John Gray, Bartholomew Glevin, James Warner, Robert Parkes, Mathew Clarke, Robert Prooter, Richard Kemon. Appraisers: Cor. Howard, John Howard. Additional inventory of Stephen Hammett. Date: 8 February 1663.

1E:12   Amount: #2041.
1E:13   Additional inventory of Richard Smith. Administrator: Francis Pope. Amount: #26658.

Cornelius Howard is administrator of estate of John Sizon. Mentions: William

Court Session: <no date>

1E:14	Crymer, William Wilson. Date: 3 February 1663. Affirmation of said will of John Sisson (AA). Date: 16 March 1663. Inventory of John Sisson. Date: 13 February 1663.
1E:15-16	...
1E:17	Appraisers: William Crouch, William Hills.
1E:18	Date: 3 February 1663/4. Witness: Mr. Samuell Withers (AA). William Crouch & William Hills attested. Date: 9 February 1663.
1E:19	Mary relict of Benjamin Brasseur now wife of Thomas Sterling was granted administration on his estate. Said Mary cannot travel to the Office. Capt. Thomas Mannyng & George Peake (CV) to administer oath. Appraisers: James Humes, John Cobrath. Date: 24 February 1663.
1E:20	John Brookes vs. Frances relict of Michaell Brookes. Date: 2 February 1663.
1E:21	Will of John Bolayn. Overseers: William Marshall, Peter Carr for my children. Bequests: my children to receive 1/2, wife & her children to receive other 1/2. Date: 3 May 1663. Witnesses: John Courte, Alexander Smith, Meverell Tulley. Before: Thomas Mathews, Henry Adams. Will proved on 3 November 1663. Inventory of John Bolayn (CH). Date: 23 November 1663.
1E:22	Filed on 5 December 1663. Appraisers: Francis Pope, John Nowell. Elisabeth wife of John Bolayn was granted administration.
1E:23	...
1E:24	Date: 3 November 1663. Mr. Francis Pope & Mr. John Nevill to appraise estate of John Bolanie. Date: 3 November 1663.
	Accounts of William Bysse. Administrator: Sampson Waring. List of debts: Thomas Bisse, Richard Ware (Bristol),

Court Session: <no date>

1E:25 John Tench for Phill. Miller, Robert Blinkhorne. Amount: #4904. Date: 8 September 1663. Paul Kinsey, now administrator, allows account.

Inventory of William Bisse. Date: 3 December 1661. Appraisers: William Carr, Markes Claris. Servants: John Smith, William Rallus, John Long (age 7).
1E:26 Amount: #6244. Additional inventory in hands of Mr. John Norwood. List of debts: John Marcekin, Thomas Rockhould, George Strong, William Iperer. Paule Kinsey, who married the relict, was granted administration.

Accounts of Robert Taylor. Executor: George Mee. Payments to: William Parrett, Mrs. Jane Fenwicke, William Turner, Thomas Hactcoot, William Muffett for schooling the children, Stephen Clifton, Thomas Bysse, Robert Kinsborro, Stephen Clifton (chyrurgeon), James Furbus,
1E:27 John Six, Mr. Pollard, Henery Keene, Richard Gerrall, Henry Sewall, Robert Kinsborro, Mr. Tho. Turner for schooling the children, Henry Mees, Henry Keene, Gills Sadler, Edmond Kinsman, John Sutton, John Read. Legacies paid by George Read: Eleis Read, Mary Bulleyne, George Read. Amount: #18049. This account was in the inventory of Mr. Sadler, per: Mr. Maning, Mr. Sprigg, Maj. Brooke.
1E:28 Payments for maintaining 4 children for 3 years. Signed: George Read. Date: 8 September 1663.

Inventory of Mr. Hugh Lee. (He died 16 February 1661.) List of debts: Tho. Souchorne, Nich. Bradaway, Mr. Clifton on Anderton, Francis Carpenter, John Baman, John Reed, Francis Wine, edm. Pinson, St. Mary's from Mr. Nicholas Gwyther, (AA), Mr. Collett, German Gillett, Walter Pake, John Brackenbury, Mr. Burdett, Robert Sheeles, William Lawrence,
1E:29 Mr. Bretton, Robert Hooper, Richard Foster, Henry Elery, Nicholas Rawlings,

Page 61

Court Session: <no date>

1E:30 Mr. Hall, Thomas Hughes, Richard Russell, Mr. Metcalfe, Robert Joyner, Andrew Basha, Thomas Wheeler, Richard Grimes, Robert Maston, Thomas Courtney, Mr. Hampstead, William Palmer, Capt. Gwyther, Mr. Pheypo, Tho. Walton, Richard Games, Tho. Griffin, Robert Cageer, Thomas Howker, William Greene, John Boy, Jerman Gillett, William Lucus, William Cole, Samuell Brockett, Phillip Calvert, Esq., Mr. Lloyd, Vincent Acheson, Mr. Clarke, Mr. Collett, Bryan Daly, Patrick Forrest, Mr. Gittings, William Harper, Mr. Halfehead, Mr. Lomax, Mrs. Land, Mr. Dent, Mathias, John Mastrix, Tho. Tayler, John Vanheek, Mr. Zacharias Wade, Mr. Hamond, Mr. Thompson, Mr. Gerard, Mr. Bateman, Mr. Smith, Mr. Jackson, Mr. Kinsbury, William Price. Amount: #46839.

1E:31 Additional inventory of Mr. Hugh Lee. Date: 4 June 1664. Servants: William Price, Mary. Appraisers: John Raynoldes, Edward West. Amount: #8120.

1E:32 Payments to: Mr. Collett for Augustine, widow Bodlam, Mr. Bateman, Mr. Cowch doctor for Capt. Tilghman, Capt. Tilghman, Mr. Preston, Mr. Dent, William Edwyn, Joseph Edley, Mr. Wilkenson, Mr. Ennis, Richard Armstrong, Andrew Bashey, Mr. Horsley, Mr. Abington, William Smith, Mr. Burdett, Mr. Hoskins, Mr. Hall, Mr. Gaylard, Mrs. Land, Capt. Brent, Mr. Mathew Rhoden. Amount: #45069.

1E:32A Capt. Josias Fendall & Mr. Robert Hundley are executors of Richard Russell. Will dated 9 October 1662.

1E:33 5 April 1664. Robert Henley who married Sarah relict of Francis Batchelor was granted administration on said estate. Bond: George Newman. Appraisers: Henry Franckcum, Daniell Johnson. Zachary Wade to administer oath.

6 April. John Ewens was granted administration on estate of Zuzan relict of James Billingsley. Bond: Capt. William Burges. Appraisers: Robert

Court Session: <no date>

Heigh, John Cobreth, George Pascall, James White. Roger Grosse & George Peake to administer oath.

1E:34   4 June 1664. John Nuttall to administer oath to John Reynolds & Edward West as appraisers of estate of Hugh Lee.

30 June. Stephen Clifton was granted administration on estate of William Turner (CV). Security: George Alderson.

Stephen Clifton was granted administration on estate of Francis Lacy, as greatest creditor. Bond: Francis Tratman. Appraisers: Geo. Alderson, Francis Tratman. Hugh Standley to administer oath. [Tratman being since dec'd, Tho. Perry sworn.]

1E:35   16 July. Elisabeth Mattingly widow of Thomas Mattingly was granted administration on his estate. Appraisers: William Rosewell, Raphael Haywood. Capt. Luke Gardner to administer oath.

1E:36   Inventory of David Duncan. Date: 2 March 1663. Amount: #3001. Appraisers: John Lawson, John Camell.

1E:37   Will of Robert Clarke. Executor: eldest son John Clarke. Bequests: son John Clarke, son Robert Clarke (age 12), son Thomas Clarke (age 10), daughter Mary Clarke (under age 18). Date: 14 July 1664. Witnesses: Thomas Mathews, George Goodricke.

1E:38   Thomas Mathews attested. Date: 21 July.

21 July 1664. Henry Adams & Will. Marshall to take the oath of George Goodricke.

30 July. Thomas Perry, guardian of Will. Bind. Tratman, was granted administration on estate of Francis Tratman. Bonds: said William Perry, Stephen Clifton. Appraisers: Samuell Groves, John Stincklow. Mr. Hugh Stanley to administer oath.

Court Session: <no date>

1E:39 Will of William Bushell (St. George's Hundred, SM). Executor: William Watts, Sr. Bequests: William Watts, Jr., Robert Frizell, Fran. Stephenson, Frances Barnum.

1E:40 Witnesses: Henry Hyde, Thomas Andrewes. Will proved 1 August.

Inventory of John Wright. Appraisers: Richard Bennett, Henry Spinke. Date: 3 December 1663.
1E:41 Amount: #502. Additional inventory: list of debts: William Sanders.

3 September 1664. John Brookes (chyrurgeon) was granted administration on estate of Thomas Purnell (CV) on behalf of the orphans. Bond: Bernard Ebben. Appraisers: Samuell Graves, Thomas Perry. Charles Brooke (g) to administer oath.

1E:42 29 September 1664. Barnaby Jackson, guardian to Samuell Cooper (son of Sampson Cooper (Rippon, County York, England)), was granted administration on estate of said Sampson. Bond: Geo. Gooddricke.

Will of Sampson Cooper (alderman, of Rippon, County Yorke). Requests burial on land of Col. John Trussell. Overseers: Maj. George Collough, Col. John Trussell (both of Northumberland Co. VA). Bequests: son Samuell Cooper all chattel in VA & to be bound to Mr. Samuell Cock (silkeman).
1E:43 Mentions: wife Bridget Cooper, Mr. John Connyers (Rippon). Bequests: son Samuell land bought of Mr. Gregory Paulgrave ""Sinckbury"", son Jonathon Cooper ""Coatestoole Close"" bought of Mr. Edward Wright & his brother Nicholas & Miles Smyth, son Jonathon land near Leonard Pick & Mrs. Jefferson, son Jonathon land near Mr. Jarnings & Thom. Day bought of Francis Plumland & his son Thomas,
1E:44 Maj. George Cullough, Col. John Trussell, Capt. John Rogers & Mr. William Presley, Mr. David Lindsey (minister), William Bedlam (landlord) &

Court Session: <no date>

his wife Elisabeth, Hanna Fountlin, Thomas Haselridge. Executors: sons Samuell & Jonathon & wife Bridgett. Overseers: Mr. Nicholas Kitchin, Mr. Ant. Bramhaite (alderman). Mentions: Mr. Cock (silkman, of London), Mr. Bruntwhite.

1E:45   Date: 11 August 1659. Witnesses: William Bedlam, Thomas Haselridge, Hanna Franckling, John Trussell. Will proved in Northumberland Co. VA by William Bedlam & Tho. Haselridge. Date: 20 February 1659.

1E:46   29 September. John Sike (taylor) was granted administration on estate of John Pritt (CV). Bond: John Hunt. Appraisers: John Halfhead, John Hunt. Richard Collett to administer oath.

4 October. Margarete Read relict of John Read (CV) was granted administration on his estate. Bond: Rob. Kingbury. Appraisers: Robert Kingbury, Jonathon Prater. Tho. Brooke to administer oath.

Dr. Francis Clifton administrator of Francis Lacy was granted continuance. Date: 6 October 1664.

Mary Bateman executrix of John Bateman, Esq. was granted continuance. Date: 10 October 1664.

1E:47   7 October. Thomas Brooke (KI) was granted administration on estate of Walter Jenkin. Said Brooke married the relict. Robert Vaughan & William Richards to prive will, written by Joseph Wicks. Appraisers: Morgan Williams, Joseph Wicks. Capt. Vaughan to administer oath.

4 November. Thomas Owen, on behalf of George Puddington, was granted administration on estate of Daniel Dike (AA). Capt. Thomas Besson & Roger Grosse to administer oath to said Puddington. Security: Robert Francklin. Appraisers: Murrian Duvall, Neale Clarke. Capt. Besson to administer

Page 65

Court Session: <no date>

oath.

1E:48 29 November 1664. Guy White (CV) was granted administration on estate of John Brimston (CV). Nuncupative will of John Brimston. Date: 13 November 1664. Bequests: Guy White. Signed: William Singleton. Thomas Darling deposed the same. Security: William Singleton. Appraisers: Geo. Read, Richard Bayley. Reymond Staplefort to administer oath.

1E:49 28 November 1664. William Chaplin was granted administration on estate of John London, as greatest creditor. Security: Guy White.

Will of Abraham Houldman (BA). Date: 28 December 1663. Bequests: son Abraham Houldman (under age 18) land on Buch River 150 a. called ""Buchwood"" & 100 a. on Gunpowder River called ""Holmwood"" & 150 a. ""Hunting North"", wife Izabell 50 a. on Seaverne,
1E:50 brother-in-law Robert Burly & Stephen Burly, John Collier. Mentions: Joseph Gallyan.
1E:51 Executrix: wife. Bequests: Hendrick (servant). Witnesses: John Collier, James Phillipps, Robert Kenington.

John Brooke (chyrurgeon, CV) is administrator of Thomas Burnett & guardian to orphans of said Burnett. Date: 2 December 1664.

1E:52 Petition of Robert Morris on behalf of self & John Harris (merchant, London). Mentions: Thomas Jordan (dec'd), Capt. Morris. Capt. Robert Morris is empowered to seize accounts of John Harris (merchant) or Thomas Jordan.
1E:53 Date: 29 December 1664.

Petition of Henry Scarburgh (merchant, London). Mentions: Mary Bateman relict & administratrix of John Bateman (merchant, dec'd).
1E:54 ...
1E:55 Thomas Truman, Richard Smyth, & William Groome to appraise estate of said Bateman. Mr. Thomas Brookes or Mr.

Court Session: <no date>

Thomas Sprigge to administer oath.
Date: 28 December 1664.

1E:56
Will of Bernard Ubbin. Executrix: wife.
Bequests: Mr. Walter Senserse. Date:
20 November 1664. Signed: Baerman
Ubbin. Witnesses: Edward Armstronge,
John Brooke. Will proved 31 December
1664. Appraisers: Samuell Groves,
Thomas Perry. Mr. William Dorrington
to administer oath.
Walter Senserse was granted
administration on said estate.
Security: William Dorrington.

Will of William Beeston (carpenter).
Bequests: Mrs. Mary Bateman.
Executrix: Mrs. Mary Bateman. Date: 29
February 1663. Witnesses: Robert
Parrey, John Berredge. Will proved 3
January 1664.

1E:57
Will of Stephen Clifton (chyrurgeon,
CV). Bequests: wife Jone Clifton & son
William Clifton. Overseers: Capt.
Thomas Mannyng, William Dorrington,
brother William Turner. Date: 24
December 1664. Witnesses: Abraham
Wattson, William Smyth, Edward Savage.
Will proved by Abraham Wattson. Date:
12 January 1664. Jone Clifton was
granted administration on estate of her
husband Stephen Clifton. Bond: John
Stansby. Appraisers: Thomas Perry,
Samuell Graves. William Dorrington to
administer oath.

1E:58
Marguarite Perry vs. executrix of John
Bateman. Petition of Henry Scarburgh,
creditor to said estate. Appraisers:
Tho. Trueman, William Groome, Richard
Smyth. They are to report to Tho.
Sprigg or Maj. Thomas Brookes. Former
bondsman: John Gittings (dangerously
sick). Bondsmen: Tho. Nottley
(merchant), Thomas Manning (g).

1E:59
Date: 14 January 1664. Accounts (paid
by Michael Brooke (before his death) &
others). Payments to: Thomas Jordan
(Presbiterian), Mr. Andrew Cooke,
Thomas Gane, James Forke (for making
clothes for the children), Mr. Preston.

Court Session: <no date>

Amount: #1869. Inventory. Mentions items left out for use of Mary Smyth. Signed: James Veitch.

1E:60 Inventory of Michael Brooke. Date: 11 June 1664. Servants mentioned: Richard Owen, Elisabeth Jackman, John Turner, Anth. Taylor, David Rogers.

1E:61 Amount: #21015. Appraisers: Arthur Ludford, James Veitch. Sperate debts: Peter Sharpe, Henry Sewall, Nicholas Spencer, Henry Thickpenny, Sam. Chew,

1E:62 Rich. Balye, John Bogue, Michaell Basy, Tho. Barbery, Thomas Ennes, Andrew Robinson, Hen. Robinson, Edward Coodery, John Read, Hugh Stanley, Alexander Watts, John Sewall. Amount: #12347. Desperate debts: [torn] Kendall (Accomac Co.), [torn]penser (Accomac Co.), [torn] Wise (Accomac Co.), John Watts (Accomac Co.), Nehemiah Coventon (Accomac Co.), Mr. Hoskins (Accomac Co.), John Perkins for John West (Accomac Co.), Isack Foxcroft (Accomac Co.), John Parramore (Accomac Co.), William Thorne (Accomac Co.), Tho. Burdett, Tho. Stone, Mr. Hackett, Rich. Armstrong, Rich. Armstrong & Guy Knowles,

1E:63 Guy Knowles, Capt. Henfield, Godfrey Harmer, John Lewes (Accomac Co.), Anthony Gosson, Thomas Harper, Alphonsus Balls, Rich. Hill (Accomac Co.), Daniell Goulson, Charles Scarburgh (Accomac Co.), William Presley (Chiccacone), Stephen Gerry, Robert Macklyn, Geo. Whittle, James Atcheson, Michael Vandervorte. Amount: #15432 & 288 gilders. Sperate accounts: Lt. General, Hugh King, John Bagby, Secretary Sewall, Capt. Neale, Capt. Manning, John Jones. Amount: #4525. Mentions: Belcher's plantation. Amount: #15503.

1E:64 Additional inventory. Amount: #4950. Appraisers: Arthur Ludford, William Mills. Additional inventory. Amount: #1660. Appraisers: William Calvert, Luke Barber, John Viccaris. Desperate accounts: Roger Scott, John Elzey, John Robinson, William Grimsted, Geo. Colclouch, Capt. Gwyther, Henry Hooper, Jacob Micheelson, William Coursey, Philip Thomas, Richard Bayly, Rich.

Court Session: <no date>

1E:65 Wright, Rich. Hodgkeys, Capt. Fendall, John Read, Mr. Francis Jackson, Cornelius Comages, Arthur Ludford. Amount: #11069. Totals: 65546. Desperate accounts: Godfrey Harmer, Rich. Armstrong, Guy Knowles, Anthony Gosson, William Kendall (Accomac Co.), Mr. Rich. Wright, Capt. Henfield. Signed: Mary Bateman.

Inventory of Francis Tratman. Amount: #930. Date: 1 August 1664. Appraisers: Hugh Stanly, Samuell Graves. John Sinclare to administer oath.

1E:66 Inventory of Francis Batchelor. Appraisers: Daniell Johnson, Henry Francum.

1E:67 Inventory of Thomas Burnett. Date: 10 September 1664.
1E:68 Amount: #4589. Appraisers: Samuell Prater, Thomas Perey.

Inventory of Suzan Billingsley. Date: 18 April. Appraisers: Robert Heigh, John Cobreath.
1E:69 Signed: John Cobreath, Robert Heighe, George Veake. Additional inventory of Suzan Billingsley in Anne Arundel Co. Appraisers: George Pascall, James White. Date: 13 May 1664.
1E:70 ...
1E:71 Amount: #7988. Signed: Roger Grosse. Date: 8 June.

1E:72 Will of Robert Clarke. Executor: eldest son John Clarke. Bequests: son John Clarke, son Robert Clarke (age 12), son Thomas Clarke (age 10),
1E:73 daughter Mary Clarke (under age 18), son John Clarke lands. Date: 14 July. Witnesses: Thomas Mathewes, George Goodricke. Will proved 21 July 1664
1E:74 by Thomas Mathews. Will proved 10 August 1664 by George Goodricke.

21 July 1664. Mr. Henry Addams to swear Thomas Mathews & George Goodricke to appraise said estate.

Court Session: <no date>

1E:75 Inventory of Robert Clarke, Esq. Date: 10 August 1664.
List of debts: Isack Abrahams, Peter Sharpe, Francis Armstrong, Thomas Alonson, Tho. Baker & Richard Dod.

Will of John Mott. Bequests: daughter Elisabeth Mott, wife. Witnesses William James, Wa. Phelps. Will proved on 29 October 1664 by William James & Walter Phelps.

1E:76 Inventory of Francis Lacie. Amount: #5696. Date: 1 August 1664. Appraisers: George Alderson, Thomas Perey. Before: Hugh Stanley.

Capt. Luke Gardner to swear William Rosewell & Raphel Haywood to appraise the estate of Thomas Mattingley (SM). Date: 25 July 1664.

Thomas Dent to swear John Lawson & John Cammell to appraise the estate of David Duncan (Poplar Hill). Date: 28 January 1663.

1E:77 Will of William Howes (carpenter). Bequests: William Hatton eldest son of William & Elizabeth Hatton, William Dent eldest son of Thomas & Rebecka Dent.
1E:78 Witnesses: John Dent, John Wynn. Date: 2 December 1662. Will proved on 8 November 1664.

Robert Sench, age 33, deposed that Francis Rigges bequeathed all to John Edmondson & Rich. Collett. Signed: Robert Sech. Date: 3 October 1664. Before: John Rogers.

Mary Sench, age 33, deposed that Francis Rigges bequeathed all to John Edmondson & his children & Richard Collett.
1E:78½ Date: 3 October 1664. Before: John Rogers.

Thomas Langley, age 35, deposed that Francis Rigges bequeathed all to John Edmondson & Richard Collett at the house of Robert Sench at Chickacome River VA. Date: 12 October 1664. Before: Francis

Court Session: <no date>

Anketile.

Margaret Perry said land belonging to John Bateman are to be appraised. Date: 17 January 1664. Appraisers: Mr. Richard Smyth, Mr. William Groome. Tho. Brooke to administer oath. [cf. f. 58.]

1E:79 Inventory of John Bateman, Esq.
1E:80-82 ...
1E:83 Mentions: 400 a. of land. Amount: #139,971. Appraisers: Tho. Truman, William Groome, Richard Smyth.

20 January 1664. Putuxent. Tho. Manying attorney for Mrs. Margaret Perry received in estate of Mr. John Bateman from his executrix Mrs. Mary Bateman. Signed: Tho. Manynge. Witnesses: Tho. Truman, Tho. Sprigg, Rich. Smyth, William Groome.

1E:84 January 1664. Richard Collett was granted administration on estate of Francis Riggs. Bond: Thomas Campher. Appraisers: Mr. John Anderson, Mr. Thomas Taylor. Mr. Francis Anketill to administer oath.

Will of William Heard (p, Puttomacke River). Overseers: Henry English, John Douglas. Bequests: wife Bridgett Heard. Date: 4 January 1664. Witnesses: Walter Story, Andrew Ward.
1E:85 Will proved 26 January 1664.

25 January 1664. Bridgett Heard was granted administration on estate of her husband William Heard. Security: John Douglas.

8 February. Michaell Higgins was granted administration on estate of Robert Foott on behalf of orphan James Moore. Security: Richard Gibbs. Appraisers: Thomas Perry, Samuell Graves. William Dorrington to administer oath.
1E:86 Inventory of the goods on the barque Johannah of New England of Master Bartholomew Cadd.
1E:87 Appraisers: Zachariah Gillam, Daniel

Court Session: <no date>
Jinifer.

1E:88	Will of John Nevill (Portobacco, CH). Bequests: wife Johannah Nevill, son William Nevill plantation, daughter Ellen Lambert, son John Lambert, grandson John Lambert. Executor: son William Nevill. Mentions: William Price, Date: 15 January 1664. Witnesses: Hen. Baily, Andr. Bashachis. Will proved 4 February 1664. John Lambert & William Price appeared on behalf of William Nevill administrator of John Nevill & were granted administration on said estate. Security: Thomas Payne. Date: 4 February. Appraisers: Fran. Pope, Robert Troope. Tho. Mathews or Henry Adams to administer oath.
1E:89	Inventory of Daniell Gordion. Administrator: George Thompson (g, CH). Date: 30 April 1664). Amount: #6707. Appraisers: Jo. Lumbrozo, Tho. Baker. Accounts. Payments to: Dr. John Lumbrozo for attendance on Mary Gordion,
1E:90	Mr. Bradshaw, Richard Trew, Isaac Woodberry, Mr. Thomas Mathews, Dr. Lumbrozo, for a servant due from Henry Moore. Amount: #9266.
	11 February 1664. John Sherm (mariner, of New England) was granted administration on estate of Bartho. Pudd (who drowned in St. George's River). Security: Nicholas Young. Appraisers: Zachariah Gillum, William Hollingsworth.
1E:91	22 February. John Boyce & John Price administrators of Ralph Story were granted discharge.
	Thomas Mathews & Henry Adams for proving the will of John Bolayn, the widow is able to travel. [cf. f. 22.]
	Susannah Whittle, age 38, deposed on 16 November 1664 that Thomas Ringe made a nuncupative will. Bequests: his wife. Witness: William Lawson.

Court Session: <no date>

24 February. John Booth was granted administration on estate of Thomas Ringe, said Booth married the relict. Security: William Whittle. Appraisers: Peter Carwardin, William Tunnehill. John Lawson to administer oath.

1E:92 Inventory of Benjamin Brasseur (g, CV). Appraisers: James Humes, John Cobrath. Date: 24 February 1663/4.
1E:93 ...
1E:94 Amount: #68050.

1E:95 Inventory of Daniell Dike. Date: 13 December 1664. Bills received: James Chilcott, Jonathon Hopkinson, John Gray, George Homes, Bartholomew Gleven, Nicholas Gassaway, Dennis Macannark. Amount: #3838. List of debts: Capt. Thomas Besson, Thomas Besson, Jr., Robert Franklin, John Harwood, Robert Prestone, George Pascall, Fernando Batty. Amount: 34706. Signed: Maren Duvall executor of Neale Clarke.

1E:96 3 March 1664. John Gray (AA) was granted administration on estate of Theophilus Lewis (AA). Security: Capt. William Burges. Appraisers: Capt. William Burges, Capt. Thomas Besson. George Puddington to administer oath.

4 March 1663. Inventory of Susan Canady (widow, CV).
1E:97 Amount: #7444. Appraisers: Arthur Ludford, John Ringe. Signed: John Bugg, Arthur Ludford. Before: Hugh Stanley.

1E:98 6 March 1664. Mary Goulden relict of Gabriel Goulden (CV) was granted administration on his estate. Security: Robert Blinkhorne. Appraisers: Robert Blinkhorne, John Hawkings. Mr. William Dorrington to administer oath.

Randall Hanson was granted administration on estate of John Cummines, as greatest creditor.

1E:99 Will of Gabrill Goulding. Bequests: wife Mary Goulding (pregnant) 550 a., Annah Austin (servant), Daniell

Court Session: <no date>

Figett (son of Mary Waller & Richard Walker) & his second brother Walker. Date: 15 February 1664. Witnesses: Tho. Studd, Peter Bennett. Will proved 6 March.

1E:100 7 March 1664. Jone Watts was granted administration on estate of her husband Saunders Watts. Security: Richard Bayly. Appraisers: Richard Bayly, William Singleton. Reymond Stapleford to administer oath.

Petition on inventory of John Bateman. Date: 1 March 1664. Signed: Tho. Truman, Ri. Smith, William Groome.

1E:101 Inventory of Bartholomew Cadd. Amount: #28973. Date: 19 February 1664. Appraisers: William Hollingsworth, Zachariah Gillem.

1E:102 15 March 1664/5. John Ellye was granted administration on estate of Lathline Ahalwen. Appraisers: Joseph Horsley, John Nevill. William Dorrington to administer oath. Will of Lathline Ahalwen. Bequests: John Elie. Date: 7 January. Witnesses: William Macdowall, Peter Caton. Will proved 15 March 1664/5.

1E:103 1 April 1665. Thomas Billingsley (CV) was granted administration on estate of Paull Turlen (CV). Bond: Henry Hooper (CV). Appraisers: John Trostes, Robert Heigh. George Peake to administer oath.

11 April. John Douglas was granted administration on estate of Bridget Heard relict of William Heard. Humphrey Waring (merchant) was nominated, but relinquished.

1E:104 Bond: John Douglas. Appraisers: Francis Pope, John Cage. Date: 11 April 1665. Will of Bridget Heard. Bequests: son William Heard (under age), sister Mary Yowkins & John Douglas (son of John Douglas (Pickwaxton)). Executors: John Douglas, Sr., Humfry Warren (Wiccocomico River).

1E:105 Bequests: mother Katherine Yowkins,

Court Session: <no date>

Margaret Stephens (servant), Andrew Ward, Sr. Date: 4 March 1664. Witnesses: John Emerson, Walter Story. Will proved 11 April 1665.

1E:106 Will of Henry Sewall, Esq. (Patuxent River, about to travel to England on ship "The Maryland Merchant".)
1E:107 Bequests: wife Jane 2000 a. promised by Hon. Charles Calvert, Esq., brother Samuell Sewall 200 a., cousin Richard Dudley 100 a.,
1E:108 wife & children: Nicholas, Elisabeth, Mary, Anne Sewall. Overseers: Charles & William Calvert, Esq. Witnesses: William Bretton, Edward Savage.
1E:109 Will proved 17 April 1665.

4 April 1665. Jane widow & executrix of Henry Sewall was granted administration on his estate. Security: Hon. Charles Calvert, Esq. Appraisers: William Groome (g), William Dorrington (g). Maj. Charles Brooke to administer oath.

1E:110 Will of Henry Osbourn (Leonard's Creek, Putuxent). Bequests: wife Katherine Osbourne, children. Executrix: wife. Date: 6 August 1664. Witnesses: Hen. Tripp, Robert Day, Tho. Purnell. Will proved 22 April 1665.

28 March 1665 Patuxson. Richard Bayley & William Singleton to appraise estate of Sand. Wats. Signed: Raymund Staplefort.

1E:111 6 April 1665. George Reed & Richard Bayley to appraise estate of John Brimstone. Signed: Raymund Staplefort.

Inventory of Langhnel Hollen. Date: 18 April 1665. Appraisers: John Hortley, John Nevill.

Inventory of Margaret Read.
1E:112 Amount: #11505. Additional inventory. Amount: #7235.
1E:113 List of bills. Amount: #10293. Further list of bills. Amount: #5315. Additional inventory.

Page 75

Court Session: <no date>

1E:114 Inventory of John Brinstone. Appraisers: Mr. George Reed, Richard Bayly. Date: 6 April 1665. Amount: #4100. Signed: George Rede, Rich. Baylye.

1E:115 Inventory of Tho. Ring. [Oaths by Mr. John Lawson.] Date: 18 March 1664. Appraisers: William Tenahills, Peter Carwardine.

1E:116 Inventory of Mr. Tho. Mattingley. Date: 25 July 1664. Appraisers: William Rosewell, Raphael Haywood. List of debts: Capt. Luke Gardner. Amount: #5690. List of debts paid by Walter Packyt who married the relict: Dr. Swanson, Capt. Luke Gardner, Capt. Gardner for Mr. Sly & Mr. Nottly.

1E:117 28 April 1665. William Marlow was granted administration on estate of William Sandum, as greatest creditor. Bond: William Whittle. Appraisers: William Asiter, James Martin. William Rosewell to administer oath.

John Lawson exhibited oath of Peter Carraden & William Tunnhill, appraisers of Tho. Ringe (Poplar Hill).

1E:118 Inventory of Bridget Heard. Date: 22 April 1665.
1E:119 ...
1E:120 Will proved 4 May 1665. Appraisers: Francis Pope, John Cage.

Inventory of William Heard (SM). Date: 17 February 1665.
1E:121 ...
1E:122 Will proved 4 May 1665. Appraisers: Francis Pope, John Cage. Walter Beane administered oath.

1E:123 Sarah Bowles administratrix of her husband William Bowles.

1E:124 29 May 1665. John Harrington who married Mary relict of Francis Mugg was granted administration on said estate. Security: John Davies. Appraisers:

Court Session: <no date>

Nicholas Gwyther, John Reynolds. John Vanheeck to administer oath.

Sarah Jordan relict of John Elzey (g) & since widow of Tho. Jordan was granted administration on estate of said Elzey. Bond: Capt. William Thorne (the Eastern Shore),
1E:125 who is to administer oath to said Sarah.
1E:126 ...
1E:127 Bond: Charles Ballard.
1E:128 Date: 5 July 1665. Signed: Stephen Horsey, William Thorne. Appraisers: Roger Woollford, James Came. Date: 29 June 1665.

1E:129 Will of Francis Mugg. Date: 9 March 1663. Bequests: wife Mary Mugg, daughter Mary, Sarah Coleman (daughter of John Coleman). List of debts: Mr. John Raper, Fabby Roberts, Mr. Bagley, Mark Phepo. Debts due from: Mr. John Raper, John Bryan, Mr. Vanhacke. Witnesses: John Metcalfe, Jerome Harrington, John Fleming. Will proved on 18 May 1663 by
1E:130 John Metcalfe & Jeremy Harrington.

Inventory of William Sandum. Date: 10 May 1665. List of debts: John Warring,
1E:131 Mr. George Reynolds, Col. Evans for children of John Medley, William Marlow, Imben Monyan. Amount: #2955. Appraisers: William Asiter, James Martin.

Will of Mr. William Bozman. Date: 5 August 1664. Bequests: 1200 a. to be divided amongst John Bosman & George Bosman provided William Bosman receives some land, sons John & William & George (of age at 17). Executrix: wife Ellenor. Overseers: Capt. William Thorne, Mr. Thomas Bloyss.
1E:132 Bequests: daughter Bridget (at age at 15), daughter Katherine, daughter Anne (of age at 15), son John to go to Mr. Thomas Bloys until he is age 17, my 4 daughters Katherine & Bridget & Anne & Mary,
1E:133 Laserus Maddox,
1E:134 Date: 5 August 1664. Witnesses: Roger

Court Session: <no date>

1E:135 Woolford, Thomas Clarke, Thomas Walley. Ellinor Bosman granted administration. Stephen Horsey & James Davies to prove will. Appraisers: Roger Woollford, Thomas Walley. Stephen Horsey to administer oath. ...

1E:136 William Dorrington exhibited oath of Robert Blinchorne & John Hawlings, appraisers of estate of Gabriell Goulding. Date: 6 March 1664. Inventory of Gabriell Goulden (CV). Date: 1 May 1665. Appraisers: Robert Blinchorne, John Hollins. Amount: #10890.

1E:137 Inventory of John London by William Chaplaine. Received of: Richard Preston, Thomas Mannyng, Charles Brooke, John Brooke. Amount: #2500. Signed: William Chaplin.

1E:138 Inventory of Henry Sewall, Esq. Sworn by Richard Collett. Date: 8 May 1665. Mentions: Madam Sewall. List of debts: Roger Towell, Tho. Miles, Jonas Jordan, John Addison, John Cooke, William Kenckby, Joyce Rubel, Elisabeth Greene, George Aldridge,

1E:139 Abraham Rhodes, Jeremy Cunikin, William Hardginson, Elisabeth Woodward, William Thompson, William Turvile, William Braban, Christopher Barns, Joseph Hatch, Anne Davies, Edw. Savage, Walter Greene. Amount: #73520. Appraisers: William Dorrington, William Groome.

William Rosewell exhibited oath of William Assiter & James Martin, appraisers of William Sandum (SM).

1E:140 Will of William Phillips (CV). Bequests: wife & 2 sons, eldest son William (under 18) land, 2nd son, Cornelius Boule (servant), Mary Sewall.

1E:141 Executrix: wife Alice Philips. Date: 24 November 1664. Witnesses: Nath. Stone, Edw. Ourmstronge.

1E:142 Inventory of Stephen Clifton. Amount: #9346. Date: 6 February 1664.

Court Session: <no date>

Appraisers: Thomas Perey, Sam. Graves.

1E:143
4 July 1665. Alice relict of William Philips was granted administration on his estate. She is now wife of Charles Buttler. Security: James Thompson. Appraisers: Mathew Stone, Cuthbert Fenwick. Thomas Letchworth to administer oath.

John Vanheck exhibited oath of Nicholas Gwyther & John Reynols, appraisers of Francis Mogg, sworn 2 June 1665.

Josias Lambert was granted administration on estate of Tho. Giles (TA). Date: 17 March 1664. Security: Samuell Winslow. Appraisers: Samuell Winslow, Robert Curtis.

1E:144 Stephen Horsey & James Davies proved the will of William Bosman. Date: 3 July 1665. Inventory of William Bosman. Date: 3 July.
1E:145 ...
1E:146 Servants: Thomas Lupton, John Dawse, Robert Fenly, William Hattly, Mary Allin.
1E:146! Appraisers: Roger Wolford, Tho. Walley. Additional inventory. List of debts: John Allsta, Thomas Clarke, Nehemiah Covinton, William Smyton, John Maskhum, John Wilson, Mr. John Tilney.

Inventory of Mrs. Sarah Jordan. Date: 13 July 1665.
1E:147 ...
1E:148 [This is actually the inventory of Mr. John Elzey.] Appraisers: Roger Wolford, James Bann.

27 July 1665. Anne Pope relict of Henry Pope (CV) was granted administration on his estate. Security: John Brooke. Appraisers: John Brooke, Arthur Ludford. Hugh Standley to administer oath.

28 July 1665. Randolph Handson was granted continuance on estate of John Cummins.

Court Session: <no date>

1E:149   Will of William Robeson. Bequests: son George (under age) land, son Charles (under age), wife Susanna. Executrix: wife.

1E:150   Date: 20 January 1664. Witnesses: Daniell Johnson, Richard Randall.

1E:151   Inventory of Robert Foote. Amount: #4919. Date: 18 February 1664. Appraisers: Thomas Perey, Samuell Graves.

1 August 1665. Richard Smith was granted administration on estate of Dr. Thomas Wylde. Appraisers: John Stanson, James Veitch. William Dorrington to administer oath.

1E:152   Inventory delivered by Henry Hares from Richard Collett. Due from Francis Riggs. List of debts: Hugh Stanley, William Parker, Richard Bennett, William Ellingsworth, Francis Armstrong, Lt. General, John Edmunds, Absolam Covant. Amount: #14768. Date: 30 January 1665. Appraisers: John Anderton, Thomas Taylor.

27 August 1665. Francis Anketill to swear John Anderton & Tho. Taylor to appraise the estate of Francis Riggs.

1E:153   Inventory of Paul Tinton. Amount: #3040. Appraisers: John Trostes, Robert Heighe. Date: 19 May 1665.

1E:154   Inventory of Sander Watts (CV). Appraisers: William Singleton, Richard Bayly. List of debts: William Dorrington, John Sinkler. Amount: #17090. Date: 19 April 1665.

1E:155   Inventory of Mr. Nevill. Appraisers: Mr. Francis Pope, Capt. Robert Troope. Date: 24 March 1664/5. Amount: #24210. Date: 28 June 1665. Additional inventory.

1E:156   Total amount: #51153.

4 September 1665. Henry Goodridge was granted administration on estate of John

Court Session: <no date>

Brett.

1E:157   16 September 1665. Augustine Herman was granted administration on estate of John Brett, as greatest creditor. Security: Thomas Browning. Appraisers: Thomas Browning, Francis Overton. Thomas Howell to administer oath.

1E:158   Inventory of Francis Mugg. Appraisers: Nicholas Gwyther, John Reynolds. Amount: #7750.

1E:159   Thomas Sprigg exhibited oath of Cutbeard Fenwick & John Sewell, appraisers of William Phillips (CV), sworn 30 September 1665. Inventory of William Philips (Petuxent River). Amount: #16805.

1F:1   John Cobreth (p, CV) attorney of Elisabeth the widow of John Billingsley had been granted administration on his estate. William Burgh who married said Elisabeth is granted administration. Witnesses: Robert Burrisone, William Kydd.

          Inventory of Henry Foxes. Date: [torn] August 1665. Amount: #110.

1F:2   Alice Philips relict of William Philips (Petuxent River) was granted administration on his estate. New appraisers: John Sewall, Cutbord Fenwick. Thomas Sprigg to administer oath. Date: 27 September 1665.

          16 October 1665. Toby Wells who married Mary relict of William Richards was granted administration on his estate. Security: Henry Coursey. Appraisers: John Viccoredge, Thomas Brookes. Morgan Williams to administer oath.

1F:3   John Viccoredge (KE) who married the widow of Capt. Thomas Bradnox exhibited accounts.

          Henry Warren, Esq. petitioned regarding estate of Bartholomew Philips (St. Clement's Mannor). Said Philips gave to

Page 81

Court Session: <no date>

1F:4 Mr. Francis FitzHerbert. Margaret the relict & now wife of Robert Perry has administration & conceals the will. Date: 24 October 1665.

Will of Richard Young (Clifts). Executor & Overseer: father-in-law Capt. Samson Waring. Bequests: Basill Waring (son of said Samson) & brother William Young & sister Elisabeth. Date: 4 April 1665. Witnesses: Pallidere Pritchard, John Vaughen, James Thompson. Samson Waring was granted administration on said estate.

1F:5 Thomas Mannyng & George Peake to prove will. Date: 28 October 1665. Appraisers: James Farloe, James Thompson. George Peake to administer oath.

1F:6 William Head who married the relict of Henry Carlile was granted administration on his estate. Morgan Williams & Deliverance Loboty to prove will. Date: 28 October 1665. Appraisers: Thomas Ringgould, Edward Jones. Nicholas Pickett to administer oath.

1F:7 George Puddington exhibited oath of Capt. William Burgess & Capt. Thomas Besson, appraisers of estate of Theophilus Lewis (AA). Inventory of Theophilus Lewis. Amount: #5533.

10 November 1665. Peternelle Chivers vs. estate of Thomas Darling.

1F:8 24 November 1665. Richard Gardner & John Smyth were granted administration on estate of Thomas Gibbs. Nuncupative will was given in presence of Thomas Truman & John Chittam. Appraisers: John Beage, John Bigger. Tho. Truman to administer oath.

27 November 1665. Rebecca Strowd was granted administration on estate of James Strowd. Appraisers: William Watts, Stannup Roberts. Randall Hanson to administer oath.

Court Session: <no date>

1F:9   Will of James Strowd. Bequests: wife Rebecca Strowd 150 a. Date: 10 November 1665. Witnesses: John Carrington, John Bonner. Will proved on 23 November 1665.

Depositions by Tho. Truman & John Chittam, that on 8 September last at the plantation of Mr. William Groome on south side of Petuxent River, Thomas Gibbs made his will that Richard Gardner & John Smyth should receive all. Date: 25 October 1665.

William Groome to prove nuncupative will of Thomas Darling, declared by Frances Beckwith & John Martin, wherein he bequeathed all to Peternelle Chivers (Petuxent River).

1F:10   Will of Bulmer Mitford (SM). Bequests: wife Fortune Mitford, son Thomas Mitford. Executrix: wife.
1F:11   Overseers: Philip Calvert, Esq. (Chancellor), Mr. Francis Jackson. Cousin John Moricroft to come to MD. Date: 23 July 1665. Witnesses: William Champe, James Young, John Smith.
1F:12   Petition of Fortune Metford late wife of Bulmer Metford.

20 November 1665. Fortune Mitford relict of Bulmer Mitford was granted administration on his estate. Security: John Morecroft. Appraisers: Henry Ellery, John Niccolls.

1F:13   5 December 1665. Samuell Cressey, who married Susannah relict of William Robinson, was granted administration on his estate. Thomas Mathews & Francis Pope to swear Daniel Johnson & William Price, 2 of the witnesses of the will. Security: Walter Peake. Appraisers: Francis Pope, Thomas Baker. Tho. Mathews to administer oath.

1F:14   Margarite Bankes, age 38, deposed on 19 July 1665, concerning the will of Thomas Kempe. Mid-June last, the deponent was at the house of William Whittle where she heard Thomas Kempe make his will.

Court Session: <no date>

- Bequests: mother & sister, Saunders the Scotchman, Mr. Nicholas Young, William Whittle.

1F:15 Nicholas Young was granted administration on said estate. Date: 30 November 1665.

4 December. Thomas Mannyng & George Peake exhibited will of Richard Young dated 21 November 1665, proved by Palador Prichard & James Thompson.

Inventory of John Cummines. Administrator: Randall Hanson.

1F:16 Will of Bartholomew Philips. Date: 12 June 1662. Bequests: daughter Elisabeth Philips plantation at mouth of St. Clement's Bay, wife Margarite Philips, son-in-law John Tonge.

1F:17 Witnesses: Raphael Haywood, James Martin. Will proved 6 November 1665.

7 December 1665. Robert Perry who married Margarite the relict of Bartholomew Philips was granted administration on said estate. Security: William Rosewell.

Will of George Houldcroft. Date: 21 September 1665.

1F:18 Bequests: Susanah Houldcroft,
1F:19 brothers Michaell Houldcroft & Valentine Houldcroft, wife Susanah Houldcroft,
1F:20 brother Michaell Houldcroft estate in England. Executrix: wife Susanah Houldcroft. Witnesses: Abraham Lemactre, James Edmonds. Will proved by Abraham Lemaistre on 2 December 1665.

8 December 1665. Susannah Holdcroft was granted administration on said estate. Appraisers: John Smyth, James Edmonds. Robert Slye to administer oath.
1F:21 Security: Robert Slye.

11 December 1665. Peternelle Chivers was granted administration on estate of Thomas Darling (CV). Will was proved by John Martin & Fran. Beckwith wife of George Beckwith.
1F:22 Appraisers: Gwy White, Richard Bayley.

Court Session: <no date>

William Groome to administer oath.

Will of Thomas Darling, per John Martin. John Martin, age 18, deposed that Mrs. Becworth asked Thomas Darling about his bequests. Bequests: Peter Nell, Mrs. Becworth. Date: 7 December 1665.

1F:23 Inventory of Thomas Wylde. Appraisers: John Stansby, James Veitch.
1F:24 Date: 29 August 1665. Signed: John Stanesby, James Veitch. Additional inventory. List of debts: Samuell Lands, Philip Boages. Date: 21 October 1665.
1F:25 Additional inventory. List of debts: Richard Preston, William Berry, Edw. Keene, Richard Keene, Peter Sharpe, Mr. Henry Hooper, George Read. Amount: #9638.

Will of Robert Brasheurs the elder. Bequests: Tovey Tho., Tho. Frost & Tho. Smith, Robt. Jerves,
1F:26 Robert Jervis chattel that was my brother's, cousin Mary Brashieur, John Cobreth. Date: 4 December 1665. Witnesses: John Cobreth, Marke Clear, John Bennett.

16 December 1665. Thomas Tovey, Thomas Frost, & Thomas Smith were granted administration on said estate. [This is void & given to Sampson Waring guardian for & on behalf of Robert Brassieur, Jr. See f. 37.]

1F:27 Appraisers: John Troster, Robert Heigh. George Peake to administer oath.

Inventory of Thomas Gibbs. Date: 2 November 1665. Amount: #1820. Appraisers: John Bigger, John Beage. Thomas Truman administered oath.

1F:28 Will of Adam Staneley (p, Clifts, CV). Executor: Stephen Benson (p, Clifts, CV). Bequests: William Benson son of Stephen Benson chattel at plantation of Sampson Waring, Elisabeth Benson daughter of Stephen Benson chattel at plantation of Sampson Waring.

Court Session: <no date>

1F:29 Date: 24 March 1664. Witnesses: John Hortley, Hen. Michell, Tho. Manyng. Codicil: date: 24 October 1665. Will proved by Thomas Manyng on 4 January 1665.

1F:30 Will of Anthony Wilson. Date: 14 November 1665. Bequests: Thomas Wright, William Stokter, William Singleton. Executor: Ishmaell Wright. Witnesses: John George, Rich. Walker.

Inventory of Henry Carlile (KI). Appraisers: Thomas Ringould, Edward Jones.
1F:31 Morgan Williams & Deliverance Lovely administered oath.
1F:32 Amount: #20510. Signed: Thomas Ringold, Edward Jones.

Inventory of Richard Young. Appraisers: James Verlo, James Thompson.

1F:33 Date: 28 December 1665 List of debts: Richard Moss. Amount: #4168. Signed: James Tomson, James Varlo. George Peak administered oath.

1F:34 Inventory of Mr. William Richard (KI). Appraisers: Mr. John Vickorice, Mr. Thomas Brooke. Date: 1 January 1665.
1F:35 ...
1F:35½ List of debts: John Winchester, Arthur Jenus, Henry Gotts, Peter Fensons. Amount: #33595.

1F:36 Ismaell Right (CV) executor of Anthony Willson appointed William King as his attorney. Date: 24 January 1665. Witnesses: Phine Blackwood. William Stockden.

25 January 1665. William King was granted administration on estate of Anthony Wilton. Security: Guy White. Appraisers: Abedlow Martin, Richard Bayley. William Groome to administer oath.

1F:37 20 January 1665. Petition of Sampson Waring guardian to Robert Brasseur, Jr.

Court Session: <no date>

1F:38	(son of Robert Brasseur, Sr.) for administration on said estate, formerly granted to Thomas Tovey, Thomas Frost, & Thomas Smyth. Signed: John Cobreath. Date: 15 January 1665. Witnesses: Tho. Mannyng, George Peake.
1F:39	Marke Clare, age 30, deposed that on 1 December last, Capt. John Cobreath brought the will of Robert Brassieur for said Mark to witness. [Will of said Robert dated 4 December 1665.] Date: 15 January 1665. Witnesses: Thomas Mannyng, George Peake.
	John Bennett, age 21, deposed that Mark Clare said correctly. Date: 15 January 1665. Witnesses: Thomas Mannyng, George Peake.
1F:40	Commission to prove the will of Robert Brasseur. Date: 15 January 1665. Signed: Thomas Mannyng, George Peake. Sampson Waring was granted administration on estate of Robert Brassieurs.
1F:41	Security: Francis Hudgins. Appraisers: James Humes, Henry Kent. George Peake to administer oath.
	19 January 1665. Rebecca relict of James Strowd was granted continuance.
	Inventory of Capt. Nicholas Gwyther. Administrator: Philip Calvert, Esq. (Chancellor).
1F:42	Inventory of George Holdcroft (chyrurgeon, of St. Clement's Hundred). Appraisers: John Smith, John Edmonds. Date: 16 January 1665.
1F:43	...
1F:44	Amount: #9883.
	Will of Nicolas Hammond (CV). Bequests: wife Alice Hammond, Tobias Miles (son of Tobias Miles), Bazill Waring (son of Sampson Waring). Witnesses: William Burnett, Sampson Waring.
1F:45	16 February 1665. Sampson Waring on behalf of Alice Hammond was granted

Court Session: <no date>

administration on estate of Nicolas Hammond. Capt. Thomas Mannyng & George Peake to prove said will. Security: Sampson Waring. Appraisers: Sampson Waring, Tobias Miles. Capt. Thomas Mannyng to administer oath.

1F:46   20 February 1665. Richard FitzAllen on behalf of Mary Glevin (KE) widow of Bartholomew Glevin was granted administration on his estate. Nicolas Pickord & Morgan Williams to prove said will. Security: William Hemsley. Appraisers: Richard FitzAllen, William Head. Nicholas Pickord to administer oath.

1F:47   Sara Young, age 27, deposed that about a fortnight before James Oazey died at the house of Capt. Richard Banks (Poplar Hill), he bequeathed all to Capt. Richard Banks & Richard Hatton. Date: 29 December 1665.

Francis Richardson, age 23, deposed the same.

24 February 1665. Mr. Richard Banks was granted administration on estate of James Oazey. Appraisers: William Tunnehill, John Cammell.
1F:48   Randall Henson to administer oath.

Notice to: Daniel Jenifer. Samuell Cresey (undersheriff to Mr. Adams) can't exhibit accounts on estate of William Robinson. Continuance granted.

Sampson Waring as guardian on behalf of Robert Brasseur (son of Benjamin Brasseur) was granted administration on estate of Robert Brasseur, Sr.
1F:49   Thomas Tovey & Robert Jarvis were found in contempt regarding the estate of Robert Brassieur.

Notice to: Daniel Jenifer. Mr. Waring to summon Thomas Tovey & Robert Jarvis. Sheriff Charles Brookes to summon Sampson Waring
1F:50   ...
1F:51   to take possession of the effects of

Court Session: <no date>

Robert Brasseur. Date: 27 February 1665.

1F:52 20 March 1665. Philip Calvert, Esq. was granted administration on estate of Capt. Nicholas Gwyther (St. Jerome's). Appraisers: William Calvert, Esq., Bryan Daley. Nicholas Young to administer oath.

1F:53 Inventory of Walter Jenkins. Date: 4 January 1664.

1F.54-55 ...

1F:56 List of debts: William Richard, Francis Barrens, Anthony Callaway, Thomas Hinson, Sr., William Standly, Henry Goat, William Davies, Morgan Williams, Ralph Ward & John Larrance, Francis Brooke, William Leeds, Peter Johnson, Joseph Wickes, Charles Steward, Mr. Henry Coursey. Legacies: wife & daughter, children. Amount: #72751. Appraisers: Morgan Williams, Josheph Wickes.

1F:57 Accounts of Walter Jenkins. Payments to: for wife & children. Amount: #25677.

1F:58 Gwy White administrator of John Brimston (CV) was granted discharge. Date: 2 January 1665.

1F:59 Inventory of Thomas Kempe.

Capt. Thomas Mannyng & George Peake exhibited will of Nic. Hammond, proved 20 March 1665/6. Executrix: Alice Hammond. Security: Sampson Waring. Appraisers: Sampson Waring, Tobias Miles.

1F:60 Petition on account of Mary Bateman executrix of John Bateman, Esq. by Tho. Truman & John Morecraft & Thomas Mannyng.

1F:61 Date: 6 April 1666.

16 April 1666. Jone Read relict of George Read was granted administration on his estate. Security: John Bougue. Appraisers: John Bougue, John Gittings, William Ennis, Andrew Robinson. Thomas

Court Session: <no date>
Truman to administer oath.

1F:62   Inventory of Bulmer Mittford (St. George's). Date: 20 December 1665. Appraisers: Henry Ellery, John Nicolls. Servant: John Brothers.

1F:63   List of debts: John Smith. Amount: #12623½. Items for Mrs. Fortune Mittford not appraised.

1F:64   Thomas Boudle administrator of Stephen Clifton vs. Tho. Sprigg attorney of Tho. Montfort (CV). Date: 11 November 1665. At September Court 1665, judgements cited: William Smith, William Muffett attorney for Richard Allen, Thomas Pagett. Signed: John Turvile (clerk). Thomas Pagett received of Tho. Bowdell.

Accounts of Thomas Boudell. Payments to: William Mountfort, William Smith (SM), Henry Keene, Thomas Glover, Tho. Mumford, John Turvile, Tho. Paggett. Date: 15 August 1665.

15 August 1665. Court. Attendees: Tho. Sprigg, Tho. Mannyng, Hugh Stanley, George Peake, Rich. Collett, William Dorrington, William Groome.

1F:65   Henry Keene vs. Tho. Bowdell. Mentions: estate of Dr. Clifton. Received of Thomas Bowdell. Signed: Henry Cane. Date: 4 April 1666.

15 August 1666. Court. Attendees: Tho. Sprigg, Tho. Mannyng, Hugh Stanley, George Peake, Rich. Collett, William Dorrington, William Groome.

1F:66   Thomas Glover vs. estate of Dr. Stephen Clifton. Received of Thomas Bowdell. William Smith (SM) received of Thomas Bowdell. Date: 1 November 1665. Signed: Ri. Smith. Received by William Moffitt from Thomas Bowdell. Date: 16 January 1665. Witness: Tho. Perey. Received of Thomas Boudell. Date: 17 January 1665. Signed: Tho. Mountfort.

Court Session: <no date>

1F:67
23 April 1666. Henry Meese was granted administration on estate of John Benbo. Security: Henry. Coursey.

1F:68

1F:69
28 April 1666. Augustine Herman exhibited inventory & accounts of John Brett (died at house of Augustine Herman, on 17 August 1664, Bohemian, BA). Accounts: Payments to: accountant, Robert Morgen, John Collett (high sheriff), Dr. Fisher, Dr. George Wheatley, John Brett, Abraham Morgan, Anthony Le Count, Brett Omale, John Meredith, Mr. Thomas Browning, Thomas Axell. Mentions: partnership with Henry Gutteridge.

26 April 1666. Randolph Hanson administrator of James Ouzen was granted continuance.

1F:70
Inventory of James Stroude. Amount: #7360. Appraisers: Guy White, Richard Bayley. Date: 24 April 1666.

Accounts of Thomas Darnell. Amount: #3680. Date: 25 April 1666.

1F:71
27 April 1666. Stephen Benson (CV) executor of Addam Stavely was granted administration on his estate. Security: Henry Mitchell (Clifts). Appraisers: Henry Mitchell, Joseph Hosley. Capt. Thomas Mannyng to administer oath.

1F:72

1F:73
To: Samuell Withers (AA) & George Puddington (AA). Re: Anne Grosse administratrix of Roger Grosse & her inability to travel. Said Samuell & George to administer oath to said Anne at her house. Date: 29 April 1666. Edward Lloyd on behalf of Anne Grosse relict of Roger Grosse (AA) was granted administration on estate of said Roger. Appraisers: Capt. Tho. Beesson, Capt. Thomas Burges, Thomas Taylor, Tho. Miles. Samuell Withers & George Puddington to administer oath.

Inventory of Mr. John Brett (died at house of Augustine Herman on 17 August 1665) by Mr. John Collett (high

Court Session: <no date>

1F:74 sheriff). Amount: #6595. Appraisers: Thomas Browning, Will. Savon. Date: 28 February 1665.

1F:75 Inventory of Anthony Willson. Date: 7 April 1666. Appraisers: Ablomar Martin, Richard Bayley. List of debts: IShmaell Wright, Thomas Sadches, William Berry, William King, John Pittes, Alexander Magruder. Amount: #5542.

1F:76 20 May 1666. Thomas Philips on behalf of Mary Overton (TA) petitioned for Seth Foster & Thomas Powell to administer oath to said Mary on estate of Francis Overton. ...

1F:77
1F:78
1F:79 Will of Robert Clarkson. Bequests: son Robert Clarkson "Horne Point" 300 a., daughter Elisabeth Clarkson 200 a. called "South Coatoid" (?), daughter Mary Clarkson 200 a. with Mr. John Collyer on Todd's Creek, wife Milkia Clarkson. Children are under age. Executrix: wife. Date: 10 March 1665. Witnesses: John Browne, William Davis, Jonathon Neale. Will proved on 22 May 1666 by John Browne & William Davis.

1F:80 22 May 1666. Richard Hill who married Milcah Clarkson relict of Robert Clarkson was granted administration on estate of said Robert. Samuell Withers & Robert Burle to administer oath. Appraisers: Cornelius Howard, Mathew Howard. Samuell Withers to administer oath.

1F:81
1F:82 Will of William Robeson. Bequests: son George land, son Charles, wife Zuzanna. Executrix: wife. Date: 20 January 1665. Witnesses: Daniell Johnson, William Price, Richard Randall. Will proved on 26 March 1666 by Daniell Johnson & William Price. Signed: Tho. Mathews, Francis Pope. Appraisers: Mr. Francis Pope, Mr. Thomas Baker.

Court Session: <no date>

1F:83	Inventory of Bartholomew Glevin by Mary Glevin (relict). Appraisers: Mr. Richard FitzAllen, Mr. William Heard. Date: 16 March 1665.
1F:84-85	...
1F:86	List of debts: Toby Wells, Mr. Lovilye, Mr. Dunch, Jonathon Hopkins, William Toulson, Anthony Sallaway, George Gouldhake, Jacob Brimington, Toby Wells by Thomas Hill. Amount: #54056.
1F:87	Inventory of Nicholas Hammond. Date: 13 April 1666. Mentions: chattel sold to James Thomson. Amount: #6290. Appraisers: Sampson Waring, Tobyea Miles.
1F:88	List of debts: Richard Young, Henry Mychell, Thomas Jones, William Ireland.
1F:89	Nuncupative Will of James Adwick (p, Herring Creek). Date: 7 December 1665. Bequests: eldest son William Adwick chattel on plantation of his brother John Walker at Piney Point, son John Adwick, wife Grace Adwicke. Executrix: wife. Overseer: Thomas Hinton. Said James died on 8 December. Witnesses: Adam Head, Sarah Frizell. Will proved on 25 May 1666.
	25 May 1666. Grace Adwick executrix of James Adwick was granted administration on his estate. Security: Adam Head. Appraisers: Robert Cadger, John Waghob. Thomas Dent to administer oath.
1F:90	Will of John Lumbrozo (Nunjemy). Date: 24 September 1665. Executrix: wife Elisabeth Lumbrozo.
1F:91	Bequests: Rebecca Lumbrozo, Edward Richardson 50 a. "Lumbrozo Distewy" (?) adjoining Richard True & Roger Dickeson, Overseers: Mr. Henry Addams (Portobacco), Mr. Luke Gardner (St. Clement's Bay),
1F:92	Mr. Edward Richardson (London). Witnesses: Edmond Lindsey, Robert Leeds. Thomas Allanson & John Browne for his now wife Elisabeth Browne late relict of John Lumbrozo (chyrurgeon, CH) was granted administration on his estate.

Court Session: <no date>

1F:93　Henry Adams & James Lindsey to administer oath. Appraisers: John Ward, Capt. Robert Troope. James Lindsey to administer oath.

30 May 1666. John Howard on behalf of Elisabeth Hill relict of William Hill was granted administration on his estate.

1F:94　Robert Burke & Samuell Withers to administer oath to said Elisabeth. Appraisers: Capt. John Norwood, William Hopkins.

1F:95　Will of William Hall (p, SM). Bequests: Ann Cage wife of John Cage the servant boy John Rowse, John Cage, Sr. Executor: said John.

1F:96　Date: 28 March 1666. Witnesses: William Hunt, Jonathon Marler (?). Will proved on 31 May 1666. John Cage (CH) was granted administration. Surety: Walter Beane.

1F:97　Appraisers: John Courts, Richard Morrice. Walter Beane to administer oath.

Inventory of William Robesson. Appraisers: Mr. Francis Pope, Thomas Baker. Date: 7 April 1666. List of debts: Thomas Allanson, Robert Taylor.

1F:98　Servants: Edward Richmond, Marke Clamton.

1F:99　Amount: #19240. Date: 10 May 1666.

Inventory of George Holdcroft. List of debts: Mr. Tho. Nottley, Mr. Robert Sly, John Pyper,

1F:100　Mr. Tho. Nottley for my Lord, Mr. John Foxhall, John Smith, Ranson Manfeild, Nicholas Kidmore, John Bynam, Mr. Luke Gardner, James Edmuns, Henry Shaddock. Mentions: Mr. Hufte. Signed: John Smith.

Capt. Thomas Mannyng exhibited oath of Henry Michell & Joseph Horsle, appraisers of estate of Adam Stavely, sworn 22 May 1666.

1F:101　Inventory of Adam Staveley. Amount: #4820. Appraisers: Jos. Horsley, Henry

Court Session: <no date>

Michell. Date: 22 May 1666.

1F:102 14 June 1666. John Cobreth, James Humes, & Robert Heigh were granted administration on estate of James Allen (CV). [His will was not allowed.] Will of James Allen. Bequests: John Cobreth & James Humes & Robert Heigh, Paul Ohoggan, Sarah Hume, John Bennitt, John Okeley. Date: 8 February 1665.

1F:103 Capt. Tho. Mannyng & George Peake to administer oath to administrators. Appraisers: Mark Claer, Tho. Sterling. George Peake to administer oath.

Administration of Sampson Waring on behalf of Rob. Brasseur on estate of Robert Brasseur was declared void.

1F:104 Tho. Tovey, Thomas Frost, & Thomas Smyth were granted administration on estate of said Robert. Security: John Troster, Charles Beavin. Appraisers: John Troster, Robert Heigh. George Peake to administer oath.

1F:105 Will of Robert Towe (CV). Bequests: wife Elisabeth Towe. Date: 24 November 1665. Witnesses: John Hollins, Nicholas Turner. Will proved on 23 February 1665.

1F:106 Jane Calvert now wife of Charles Calvert, Esq. (Lt. Governor) & relict of Henry Sewall, Esq. (Mattapennyent, CV)
1F:107 was granted discharge. Date: 20 June 1666.

22 June 1666. Philip Calvert, Esq. was granted continuance on estate of Nicholas Gwyther (St. Jerome's).

1F:108 Will of John James. Bequests: sister Elisabeth plantation "James Hill", servant Edward Thomas, sister Ann servant Moris Loyd, Ann Pereman servant to Samuell Withers, Elisabeth Hunt wife of Thomas Hunt, father-in-law William Toulson. Executor: said father-in-law. Sisters are under age & unmarried. Date: 26 November 1665. Witnesses: Samuell Withers, Thomas Frances. Will proved on

Court Session: <no date>

1F:109 26 June 1666 by Thomas Frances. Capt. William Burges & Tho. Taylor (AA) to prove will. William Toulson was granted administration on said estate. Security: Thomas Frances. Appraisers: Capt. William Burges, Tho. Taylor. Samuell Withers (AA) to administer oath.

1F:110 Will of Tho. Griffith. Bequests: wife Lucey Griffith 1000 a. on Susquehannah River (450 a. on north side "Mount Arakat" & 550 a. on south side "Alveys", Edward Helle his choice of 3 islands, Elisabeth Ward, sister Mary Saward & 2 oldest sons, Henry Hazellwood. Date: 20 April 1665. Witnesses: Lewis Stockitt, Rich. Loes. Will proved on 25 June 1666 by Lewis Stockitt.

1F:111 28 June 1666. Capt. Thomas Howell & Godfrey Bayley to administer oath to Henry Hazelwood as administrator on behalf of Lucey Griffith relict. Said relict is in VA "decripled". Security: Francis Wright. Appraisers: Henry Ward, Nathaniell Stiles. Capt. Thomas Howell to administer oath.

1F:112 Will of George Gouldsmith. To be buried on plantation by "my" children. Executrix: wife Mary Gouldsmith. Bequests: wife Mary Gouldsmith, son George Gouldsmith (under age 16) plantation after his mother's death, said George Negro Emmanuel (child),
1F:113 son & 2 daughters (under age 18), daughter Elisabeth 500 a. on Elk River ($\frac{1}{2}$ of 1000 a. taken up by my brother John Collett & myself) & 200 a. adjoining Mr. Richard Wright & 150 a.
1F:114 on Chaine Creek adjoining Mr. Charles James, daughter Mary 200 a. on Swann Creek called "Proctor's Hall" & 300 a. called "Surveyor's Point".
1F:115 Overseers: Mr. Samuell Gouldsmith (uncle), Mathew Gouldsmith (brother), Mr. John Collett (brother-in-law), Samuell Collett (cousin).
1F:116 ...
1F:117 Date: 12 April 1666. Witnesses: Sam. Gouldsmith, John Collett, Matt.

Court Session: <no date>

   Gouldsmith. Will proved on 20 July 1666 by John Collett.

1F:118
   21 July. Mary Gouldsmith executrix of George Gouldsmith was granted administration on his estate. Capt. Thomas Howell & Godfrey Bayley to administer oath. Appraisers: Godfrey Bayley, George Wells. Capt. Thomas Howell to administer oath.

1F:119
   John Foster (AA) was granted administration on estate of William Davies (p, AA). Security: Richard Hill. Appraisers: Cornelius Howard, Mathew Howard. Samuell Withers to administer oath.

   John Cobreth, James Humes, & Robert Heigh were granted administration on estate of James Allen. George Peake to prove said will by oaths of Samuell Crow & Thomas Hume (witnesses to will). Appraisers: William Innis, Andrew Robinson. John Browne & John Gittings to administer oath.

1F:120
1F:121
1F:122
   Will of William Browne (SM). Bequests: son John Browne, 2 children John & George Shaw & John Hopkins. 2 children to be educated by wid. Sherctcliff during minority. Overseers: John Warren, Edward Clarke. Bequest: Dr. James Poor. Mentions: Mr. Lloyd. Date: 27 February 1665. Witnesses: Peter Roberts, George Shaw, John Hopkins. Will proved on 28 July 1666 by John Hopkins.

1F:123
   Will of Macam Macenne. Bequests: son-in-law Padrick Hanson, daughter Katherine Hanson, 2 daughters-in-law Sara Ellins & Ann Ellens & son John Macenne. Witnesses: Alexand. Waters, Pasco Dunn. Date: 23 December 1665. Will proved on 27 March. Per John Dobbs who married Ann relict of Macam Macenne, witnesses are gone to England.

Court Session: <no date>

1F:124 27 July 1666. John Dobbs who married Annah relict of Macam Macenna (KE) was granted administration on said estate. Morgan Williams & Thomas Osburne to administer oath. Appraisers: Richard Blunt, Charles Steward. Thomas Osborn to administer oath.

Moses Stagett was granted administration on estate of Ruth Stagott relict of Tho. Stagott (KE) on behalf of Thomas & Mary Stagott (under age 21) children of said Ruth.

1F:125 Security: Richard FitzAllen. Appraisers: Richard FitzAllen, Richard Blunt. Capt. Robert Vaughan to administer oath.

2:1 28 July 1666. Will of Edmund Joy. Bequests: Thomas Martin "Hunts Mount", Jeremy Sudena & Dennis Meconnah. Witnesses: Patrick Suseman, Samuell Griffith. Will proved on 7 April 1666. Thomas Martin was granted administration on said estate.

2:2 Security: George Pascall. Appraisers: William Hunt, Robert Paca. Samuell Chew to administer oath.

Sampson Waring, guardian to Robert Brassieur, Jr. was granted administration on estate of Robert Brassieur, Sr. (uncle to said Robert). Date: 14 July 1666. The codicil bequeathed to Thomas Tovey, Thomas Frost, & Tho. Smyth.

2:3 Per John Cobreth (witness to codicil), said administration is revoked, and administration is granted to Thomas Tovey, Thomas Frost, & Thomas Smyth.

Samuell Withers exhibited oath of Cornelius Howard & Mathew Howard, appraisers of estate of Robert Clarkson (AA).

2:4 Inventory of Robert Clarkson (AA). Date: 2 July 1666. Appraisers: Cornelius Howard, Mathew Howard.

2:5-7 ...

2:8 Servants mentioned: Ewen Sacker (?), Mary More.

Court Session: <no date>

2:9	Samuell Withers exhibited oath of William Burges & Thomas Taylor, appraisers of estate of John James (AA). Inventory of John James.
2:10	...
2:11	Amount: #22099. Date: 5 July 1666. Randolph Handson exhibited oath of William Tunehill & John Camell, appraisers of the estate of James Oazey (SM).
2:12	Inventory of James Oazie. Date: 12 April 1666.
2:13	Mentions: tobacco copy of James Owsey. List of debts: Edmund Lyster. Amount: #1378.
2:14	Will of Capt. Robert Troop (CH). Bequests: goddaughter Elisabeth Theobalds of my herd with John Cane, Mrs. Elisabeth Harison wife of Mr. Joseph Harison & Mary Harrison daughter of
2:15	said Joseph, Mrs. Mary Lindsey wife of James Lindsey, Elisabeth Lindsey daughter of said James, Mary Lindsey daughter of said James, Stephen Mountague, goddaughter Elisabeth Theobalds plantation 200 a. & 100 a. adjoining,
2:16	Richard Harrison (son of Mr. Joseph Harrison) 150 a. bought of Mr. Thomas Allanson on John Ward's Creek & 100 a. "Troop's Supply" adjoining Henry Lylly in possession of John Lumbert, Mr. James Lindsey & James Macay 500 a. on Anacostine River,
2:17	John Browne & Thomas Allanson & Mary Lindsey (daughter of James Lindsey). Executors: Mr. Ignatius Cursina, Mr. Stephen Mountague.
2:18	Signed: Robert Troope. Witnesses: Nicholas Flin, Leo. Greene. Will proved on 1 August 1666 by Stephen Mountague. James Lindsey & Joseph Harrison to get oath of other executor. Ignatius Causine was not present.
2:19	Lindsey & Harrison also to swear witnesses Nicholas Fline & Leonard Greene. Said Mountague & Said Causine were granted administration. Appraisers: William Price, Nicholas

Court Session: <no date>

Emerson. James Lindsey to administer oath.

2:20   Will of Phillip Allenby (AA). Bequests: wife Jane Allenby & daughter Joyce Allenbie of Cochermenth (County Cumberland, ENG), Nathaniell Heathcoate (of same place).
2:21   Executor: said Nathaniell. Date: 12 October 1664. Witnesses: Tho. Bisson, John Hopkinson. Will proved on 3 August 1666.

2:22   3 August 1666. Nathaniell Heathcote was granted administration on said estate. Surety: Capt. Thomas Besson. Appraisers: John Ewens, Geo. Buschill. Richard Ewens to administer oath.

2:23   20 August 1666. Arthur Wright (KE) was granted administration on estate of John Jenkins (TA), as greatest creditor. Securities: William Coursey, Richard Woollman. Appraisers: Nicholas Braddaway, Robert Humphreys. Said Woollman to administer oath.

Mr. Samuell Withers exhibited oath of Capt. William Burges & Mr. Thomas Taylor, appraisers for estate of Roger Grosse (AA).

2:24   Inventory of Mr. Roger Gross by his administratrix Anne Grosse. Date: 2 August 1666.
2:25-27 ...
2:28   Mentions: 10 Negroes, 2 Negro children, 1 mulatto child, 3 English servants.
2:29   Amount: #190380. Signed: William Burges, Thomas Tailler.
2:30   Additional inventory. Amount (in money & plate): £214.17.4.

Inventory of John Lumbrozo. Appraisers: John Ward, Clement Theobalds. Date: 12 August 1666.
2:31   ...
2:32   Witness: James Lindsey.

22 August. Philip Calvert, Esq. petitioned for new appraisers on estate of Capt. Nicholas Gwyther (SM): William

Court Session: <no date>
Calvert, Esq., Bryan Daley, William Cole, Vincent Acthezon, William Lucas, Thomas Hooker.

2:33 Will of James Allen. Bequests: John Cobreath & James Hume & Robert Heighe, Paul Ohoggan, Sarah Hume, John Bennett, Samuell Crow, John Oackly. Date: 8 February 1665. Witnesses: Henry Perkone, Sam. Croe, Thomas Horne.

2:34 John Cobreth, James Humes, & Robert Heigh were granted administration on said estate. Thomas Mannyng & George Peake (CV) to administer oath. Inventory of James Allen (CV).

2:35 Appraisers: Thomas Sterling, Mark Clear. Date: 30 July 1666.

2:36 Expenses for use of Thomas Purnill & rest of orphans (SM). Date: 14 August 1664. Payments to: Mr. Sprigg, Robert Kingsberry.

2:37 Amount: #1000. Administrator: John Brooke (chirurgeon).

Inventory of Thomas Griffith (BA). Date: 17 August 1666.

2:38-39 ...

2:40 List of debts: Will. Begerlye, Edward Hagel.

2:41 Amount: #10023. Mentions: 2 patents for 1000 a. at Susquehannah River. Appraisers: Nath. Stiles, Henry Ward.

30 August 1666. Jone Read relict & administratrix of George Read was granted continuance.

Inventory of James Adwicks.
2:42 Date: 28 August 1666. Appraisers: Robert Cager, John Walker.

Inventory of William Adwick. Appraiser: John Walker.

2:43 Inventory of Robert Brassier. Amount: #9474. Appraisers: John Troster, Robert Heighe. Date: 28 June 1666.

2:44 Inventory of William Hall (p, SM) at house of John Cager. Date: 9 June 1666. Appraisers: John Courts, Robert Morris. Mr. Walter Beane administered the oath.

Court Session: <no date>

2:45 Servant: John Rowse. List of debts: John Smith, Humprey Warren, Thomas Simpson, Samuel Clarke, John Dowglas, Thomas Smoote, Robert Henley, John Pitts. Date filed: 1 September 1666. Additional inventory.

2:46 17 September 1666. Joseph Cunday (?) (AA) was granted administration on estate of John Jones. Security: Nathaniell Stiles. Appraisers: William Slayd, Sam. Allcock. Samuell Withers to administer oath.

2:47 Accounts of Bartholomew Glewin. Payments to: Mr. John Browne, William Read, John Vicar, Richard Tilghman, Mr. William Coursey, Mr. Thomas Hinson, John Sibrey, Ant. Callaway, Mr. William Hopkins, Mr. Cor. Howard, George Goldhauke, Tobias Wells, Mr. Raph Williams, James Browne, Mr. Rich. FittzAlley, Mr. Tho. Vaughan, Sarah Conner, Mr. Nicholas Pickitt, Mr. Henry Browne, Capt. William Burgess, John Hopkins, Philip & Sarah Conner, William Calvert, Esq., Ed. Loyd, Esq.

2:47l Amount: #56456. Signed: John Wright.

2:48 Inventory of Markeham Mekenne (KE). Appraisers: Mr. Richard Blunt, Charles Stuart. Date: 28 August 1666. List of debts: Anthony Callaway. Amount: #11939. Signed: Charles Stuard, Richard Blunt.

2:49 Will of Alexander Frissell. Date: 30 August 1666. Bequests: wife Sarah Frissell, daughter Rebecca Frissell. Witnesses: William Watts, Adam Head, Robert Page.

27 September 1666. Sarah Frissell was granted administration on estate of her husband Alexander Frissell (Herring Creek, SM). Thomas Dent to administer oath. Security: Stanop Roberts. Appraisers: Robert Cago, Stanop Roberts. Thomas Dent to administer oath.

2:50 Will of John Little (Hunting Creek, CV). Executrix: wife. Bequests: wife Mary

Court Session: <no date>

Little, Charles Calvert, Esq. (son of Lord Proprietor), William Bryan. Date: 16 September 1666. Witnesses: Hugh Standley, Joseph Tilly.

2:51 28 September 1666. Mary Little executrix of John Little was granted administration on his estate. Security: Hugo. Standley. Appraisers: Hugh Standley, George Peake. Capt. Thomas Manning to administer oath.

2:52 3 October 1666. Accounts of Bulmer Mittford. Administratrix: Fortune Mittford (widow, St. George's, SM). Amount of inventory: #12627. Payments to: Mr. John Nuthall, Mr. William Smyth, Mr. John Morecroft, Mr. John Lawson, James Young, Eli. Waddy. Amount: #2923.

2:53 Will of Joseph Edloe. Bequests: 2 sons Joseph Edloe & John Edloe. Overseers: William Lucas, Thomas Wright. Date: 3 July 1666. Witnesses: George Walker, Jane Wright.

2:54 26 October. Thomas Ward (St. Jerome's, SM) was granted administration on estate of Joseph Edloe, as greatest creditor. Surety: Lt. William Smyth. Appraisers: William Cole, Thomas Griffin. Thomas Dent to administer oath.

2:55 Will of James Forbes. Bequests: wife Margarett Forbes 100 a. on Choptank at head of Deviding Creek (TA) called "Wales". Executrix: wife. Mentions: Robert Blinchorne (St. Leonard's Creek), daughter Elisabeth Forbes. Servant: Joseph Williams. Date: 10 August 1666.
2:56 Witnesses: Robert Stapleford, David Davis. Will proved on 26 October 1666.

27 October 1666. Robert Blinckhorne, Jr. for Elisabeth Forbes (daughter & orphan of Margaret Forbes (dec'd) & relict of James Forbes (CV)) was granted administration on estate of James Forbes.
2:57 Surety: Robert Blinckhorne, Sr. Appraisers: John Hollins, Pratriack

Court Session: <no date>

Mullikin. Capt. Thomas Manning to administer oath.

29 October 1666. Margarett Hawkins (next of kin to Marmaduke Scott (dec'd)) petitioned that Ralph Hawkins (AA) be granted administration on his estate. Samuell Withers & Robert Burle to administer oath.

2:58 31 October. Stephen Montague was granted continuance on estate of Robert Troope (CH).

2:59 Will of Mark Manlove (p, Pocomoke, SO). Bequests: wife Elisabeth & children by her 500 a. on Pocomoke River, sons & & Christopher Manlove (all under age), Hannah Gilly & Richard Hackworth & his next son born being 3 of my grandchildren, sons John & Thomas, daughters Ann & Mary Manlove, sons William & Christopher & George & Luke & daughters Hannah & Abijah & Persy Manlove. Executrix: wife Elisabeth, son-in-law Richard Hackworth. Overseers: Mr. Steven Horsey, Mr. James Weeden. Date: 14 September 1666. Witnesses: William Greene, Will. Stevens.

2:60 5 November 1666. William Stevens (g, SO) on behalf of Elisabeth relict of Marke Manlove & Richard Ackworth was granted administration on said estate. Stephen Horsey & George Johnson to administer oath. Appraisers: Jeffery Mentiall, Edward Whaley. William Stevens to administer oath.

2:61 7 November. Edward Loyd, Esq. for Jane Knight relict of John Knight (TA) was granted administration on his estate. Appraisers: Andrew Skinner, James Scott. Richard Woollman to administer oath.

2:62 22 November. Edward Ayres who married Isabell Houldman relict of Abraham Houldman (p, BA) was granted administration on his estate. Capt. John Collier to administer oath.

Court Session: <no date>

Mr. James Lindsey & Mr. Joseph Harrison exhibited oath of Mr. Ignatius Causine & Mr. Stephen Mountague. Signed: James Lendsy, Joseph Harrison.

2:63 Accounts of George Holdcraft. Administrator: John Smith who married the relict. Date: 20 August 1666. Payments to: Thomas Nottley, Robert Slye, Henry Padock, John Foxhall, Luke Gardner, John Pyper, James Edmonds, Marmaduke Snow, Nicholas Skidmore, Vincent Mansfeild. Amount: #12028.

2:64 Inventory of Alexander Frizell. Date: 19 November 1666. Appraisers: Robert Cager, Stannop Roberts.

2:65-67 Inventory of Capt. Nicholas Gwither. Date: 4 March 1665. Appraisers: Esq. Calvert, Brian Daley. ...
2:68 Signed: Will. Calvert, Bryan Daley. Additional inventory. Date: 22 August 1666. Appraisers: William Cole, Vincent Atcheson.
2:69 Additional inventory. Date: 1 October 1666. Appraisers: William Lucas, William Cole. List of debts: Thomas Innis (SM), William Osbisson, Joseph Hackney.

2:70 Will of John Stevens. Date: 17 December 1665. Bequests: wife Ann Stevens. Witnesses: Richard Moy, Edward Powell. Will proved 19 September. William Thomas who married Ann relict of John Stevens was granted administration on his estate. Date: 13 November 1666. Security: Thomas Paine. Appraisers: Thomas Paine, William Cole.

2:71 10 December 1666. Anne Pinner relict of Richard Pinner (CH) was granted administration on his estate. Surety: George Harrise. Appraisers: Thomas Hussey, John Ward. Joseph Harrison to administer oath.

11 December 1666. Inventory of John Stephens. Appraisers: William Cole,

Court Session: <no date>

2:72   Tho. Payne.
       Signed: Tho. Paine, Will. Coale.

2:73   Inventory of John Jenkins. Date: 20
       August 1666.
       List of debts: Thomas Wilkinson.
       Appraisers: Nicholas Bradway, Robert
       Humfery. Before: Ri. Wollman. Amount:
       #5051. Filed on 22 October 1666.

2:74   Katherine Stephens relict of Robert
       Stephens (merchant, CV) was granted
       administration on his estate. Security:
       Richard Preston (CV). Appraisers:
       William Chaplin, Henery Sewall. William
       Groome to administer oath.

2:75   John Viccaridge who married Mary relict
       of Capt. Thomas Bradnox
       was granted discharge.

2:76   Thomas Brooke administrator of Walter
       Jenkin was granted discharge.

2:77   8 January 1666. Tobias Norton for
       Margarite Noubes on behalf of
       Bartholomew Herring orphan of said
       Margarite late wife of William Argent &
       relict of Thomas Noubes successor of
       Bartholomew Herring (dec'd) was granted
       administration on her estate. Security:
       William Groome. Appraisers: Arthur
       Ludford, James Godsgrace. Hugh Standley
       to administer oath.

2:78   Capt. Thomas Howell exhibited oath of
       Godfrey Bayley & George Wells,
       appraisers of estate of George
       Gouldsmith (BA). Inventory of Capt.
       George Gouldsmith. Date: 22 November
       1665.
2:79   ...
2:80   Servants: Peter Fookitt, Robert Jones,
       Robert Whitt, Suzanna Arrisbrooke, 4
       Negroes, 2 Negro children.
2:81   Amount: #110443.

2:82   Inventory of James Forbes. Appraisers:
       John Hollins, Patrick Mullican.
2:83   Amount: #8096. Signed: Patrick
       Mullican, Johannes Hollins.

Court Session: <no date>

2:84	Inventory of Capt. Robert Troope. Date: 25 August 1666. Servants: Edith, John Woodward, Hammon Morton (boy).
2:85	Filed: 1 December 1666. Appraisers: William Price, Nicholas Emanson.
2:86-88	Inventory of Capt. George Read (CV). Date: 4 October 1666. ...
2:89	Amount: #39689. Appraisers: John Gittings, William Simes. Signed: John Bogue, Andrew Robinson.
2:90	10 January 1666. Will of Tobias Bayly. Bequests: Thomas Oakeley 100 a. bought of Mr. Thomas Gerrard, wife of said Oakeley. Witnesses: Arthur Thompson, John Beard.
	19 January. Thomas Oakely was granted administration on estate of Tobias Bayley. Surety: Col. William Evans, Esq. Appraisers: Robert Joyner, (N) Ackillis. Col. William Evans, Esq. to administer oath.
2:91	Will of John Browne. Bequests: wife Elisabeth 100 a. out of 350 a. bought of Oliver Balf, brother Gerrard Browne & son John (under age) residue to land, servant Ann Lane.
2:92	Overseers: brother Gerrard, Mr. Stephen Mountague, Mr. John Wheeler. Date: 2 November 1666. Witnesses: Tho. Allanson, Edward Robarts.
	19 January 1666. Gerrard Browne (CH) was granted administration on estate of John Browne. Joseph Harrison & James Lindsey to swear Thomas Allanson & Edward Roberts. Security: Stephen Mountague.
2:93	Appraisers: James Macky, Roger Dickeson. James Lindsey to administer oath.
	George Coulton (p, CV) died at the house of George Beckwith. George Beckwith was granted administration on said estate.
2:94	Inventory of Mr. Richard Pinner. Amount: #13789. Appraisers: Thomas

Court Session: <no date>

Hussey, John Ward. Date: 16 January 1666.

2:95   Will of Mary Bateman (CV). Bequests: Philip Calvert, Esq. (Chancellor), Mr. Thomas Truman, godson John Gittings (son of John Gittings), Mary Boague, Susanna Henings, Mr. Knap, Elisabeth Cookey, John Boague, Negro Flora, daughter Mary Bateman. Overseer: Lt. John Boague. Date: 1 February 1666. Witnesses: John Stansley, Thomas Harcase. Will proved on 3 February 1666.

2:96   Inventory of Philip Allemby (AA). Date: 24 September 1666.
2:97   Amount: #7883. Appraisers: John Ewen, George Pascall. Rich. Ewen administered oath.

14 February 1666. Rich. FittzAllin vs. estate of John Elliott (KE) on behalf of Jane Elliott orphan of said John.

2:98   Inventory of Robert Stevens (CV). Date: 11 February 1666.
2:99   List of debts: John Foxell, Peeternell Chivers, George Richardson, James Collens, Henry Hooper, Sr., John Six.

Inventory of widow Stevens. Date: 11 February 1666.
2:100 Amount: 36063. Appraisers: William Chaplin, Henry Sewell.

Richard Wollman exhibited bond of Jane Knight (KE) relict of John Knight (TA).
2:101 Inventory of John Knight (TA). Appraisers: James Scott, Andrew Skinner. Date: 20 December 1666.
2:102 Mentions: Mr. Parker. List of debts: Nathaniell Chase, William Snaggs. Amount: #10680.

Inventory of Joseph Edloe. Date: 7 November 1666.
2:103 ...
2:104 Appraisers: William Cole, Tho. Griffin. Accounts. Payments to: Tho. Ward, William Smith, Lodwick Martin. Signed: Thomas Ward.

Court Session: <no date>

4 March 1666. Thomas Powell & Seth Foster were granted administration on estate of Francis Overson. Date: 30 June 1666.

2:105 Will of Thomas Pasey. Executrix: Jemima Long. Bequests: said Jemima wife of Robert Longe. Mentions: John Cootes, John Worland, servant Henry Hardey. Date: 3 November 1666. Signed: Thomas Pacey. Witnesses: W. Turner, Griffith Jenkins.

Col. William Evans was granted administration on estate of Tobias Bayley. Appraisers: Robert Joy, Peter Archilles. Date: 28 January 1666.

2:106
2:107 Thomas Bodell who married Jone relict of Stephen Clifton (CV) was granted discharge.

Accounts of John Jenkins. Administrator: Arthur Wright. Payments to: Edward Loyd, Mr. Taylor, Nicholas Broadway, Robert Humphrys.

2:108 5 March 1666. Mary Overton relict of Francis Overton was granted continuance. Some chattel is in VA.

Will of Henry Coler (merchant, Bristol City). Executors: sister Ann Jefferys (Dorsetshire), John Foyle. Bequests: John Neugwett & William Rosewill, John Foyle. Date: 4 March 1666/7. Witnesses: Jo. Horsley, George Seeling. Will proved for Henry Collier on 15 March 1666.

2:109 15 March 1666. John Foyle on behalf of Ann Jefferys was granted administration on estate of Henry Coller (CV). Bond: Joseph Horsley. Appraisers: Richard Hooper, Henry Hooper. Mr. William Groome to administer oath.

18 March 1666. Hopkin Davies (TA) was granted administration on estate of William Johnson (TA), as greatest creditor.
2:110 Security: John Pitts. Appraisers: John

Court Session: <no date>

Eason, Thomas Phillips. Thomas Powell to administer oath.

Edward Lloyd, Esq. exhibited bond of Arthur Wright administrator of John Jenkins (TA). Security: Henry Clay. Arthur Wright was granted discharge.

2:111 14 February 1666. John Boague overseer cited by Mary Bateman (CV) was granted administration on said estate for himself & on behalf of Mary Bateman, Jr. (daughter of said Mary).

2:112 Sureties: William Meares, Cuthbert Fenwick (CV). Appraisers: Richard Smyth, Thom. Sprigg. Thomas Truman, Esq. to administer oath.

2:113 Fortune Mittford administratrix of Bulmer Mittford was granted discharge.

2:114 Will of David Read (p, CV). Bequests: son-in-law John Hyott, wife (pregnant). Date: 16 November 1666. Witnesses: Samuel Copland, John Anderson, Edward Cowdery. Will proved on 22 March 1666 by Samuel Copeland & John Anderson.

23 March 1666/7. Mary Read relict of David Read was granted administration on his estate. Surety: William Bryan. Appraisers: Hugh Standley, Tobias Norton. William Groome to administer oath.

2:115 Inventory of Edmond Joy. Amount: #10423. Date: 16 August 1666. Appraisers: William Hunt, Robert Peca. Before: Samuel Chew.

Will of William Middleton. Bequests: Richard Rider 200 a. on Herring Creek, Mr. Randall Hanson for use of his son Richard Henson 300 a. on Potomack River, Mr. Richard Loyd for use of his son Richard Loyd, Mr. Randall Henson, Elisabeth Longlines chattel at Mr. Loyd, Samuel Mores, Richard Adams, John, Clement Hill. Executor: Mr. Andrew Henson. Date: 18 March 1665/6. Signed: William Midleton. Witnesses: Clement Hill, Christopher Ouldfeild, Samuel

Court Session: <no date>

Moris. Will proved on 28 March 1667 by Clement Hill & Samuel Moris.

2:116　Inventory of Marke Manlove (SO). Date: 31 January 1666.
2:117　...
2:118　Amount: #25888. Appraisers: Jeffery Minshall, Edward Wale. Additional inventory. List of debts: Rich. Bundicke, Emanuel Hall, Thomas Gilley, Mecom Thomas, Thomas Manlove, William Green, George Hoford, William Elwood.

2:119　Jemima Long was granted administration on estate of Thomas Percey (f. 104). Walter Bayne & William Marshall to administer oath.
2:120　Appraisers: James Walker, Jo. Douglas. Walter Bayne to administer oath.

1 April 1667. Henry Goodridge (g, AA) who married Katherine relict of Paul Kinsey (AA) was granted administration said estate. Surety: Anthon Calloway. Appraisers: Lewis Bayne, John Dixon. Richard Ball to administer oath.

Arthur Ludford exhibited will of William Burke (CV). Daniel Fisher affirmed said will. Date: 10 March 1666.

Inventory of Tobyas Bayley. Date: 13 January 1666. Amount: #6190. Appraisers: Robert Joyner, Mathew Tailler.

2:121　Inventory of Francis Overton. Appraisers: Thomas Vaughan, Richard Gurling. Date: 30 June 1666. Amount: #8080.

　　　Inventory of Mrs. Mary Bateman (CV). Date: 22 February 1666/7.
2:122-123 ...
2:124　English servants: John Burridge, Walter Thomas, Thomas Prichett, Robert Bendall, John Miles, 2 Negro men, Negro Flora, 2 Negro children, Negro Marea. Amount: #70223. Appraisers: Richard Smith, Thomas Sprigg. Additional inventory. Amount: #10290.

Court Session: <no date>

2:125 Accounts of John Brett at the house of Augustine Herman at Bohemia (BA). Date: 17 August 1665. Payments to: Augustine Herman & his man Maurice, Augustine Herman, Robert Morgan & his wife, John Collett (high sheriff), Dr. Fisher, Dr. George Whealey, cost of PoA to John Wright. Amount: #15602. Inventory. Appraisers: Thomas Browning, William Saffin. List of debts: relict of Aler Morgan, bill from Anthony LeCount to Bryan Omale. John Meridith, Thomas Aixell. Amount: #14464. Mentions: Henry Goodricke.

2:126 Will of John Davies (SM). Date: 24 January 1666.
2:127 Executrix: wife Mary. Bequests: son John Davies, wife (pregnant). Friends William Turbervill & Bryan Daley & brother John Harrinton to see my child/children brought up Roman Catholic. Servant: Richard Champhey. Witnesses: Mor. Jones, Bryan Daley, John Harenton. Mary Davies was granted administration on said estate. Date: 26 April 1667
2:128 per oaths of Morgan Jones & Bryan Daley. Security: John Harrington. Appraisers: Thomas Hughes, William Osbaston. William Calvert, Esq. to administer oath.

21 April 1667. John Worland affirmed the will of Thomas Percy exhibited by Jemima Long. Signed: Walter Beane, William Marshall.

2:129 Will of Lawrence Richardson (age some 60). Bequests: son Thomas Richardson, first-born Sarah Richardson, eldest son plantation, son John Richardson, youngest son Lawrence Richardson, daughter Mary Richardson,
2:130 2 youngest sons (under age 18) "Upper Tayton", youngest Elisabeth Richardson. Executor: son Thomas. Date: 1 October 1666. Witnesses: Row. Burghill, Abr. Dutton.

2:131 7 May 1667. Thomas Richardson was granted administration on estate of

Court Session: <no date>

Lawrence Richardson (AA). Samuell Withers & Robert Burle to prove will. Security: John Howard. Appraisers: William Crowtch, John Howard. Robert Burle to administer oath.

2:132 Will of William Stockden. Executor: Guy White. Bequests: Poor paid to Richard Preston or William Berry or John Webb, Thomas Wright land & servant John Mareday, John Mareday & John Davis, Mary Wright, Robert Wright, Margarett Wright, Sary Wright, William King, John Davis, Ishmael Wright, Guy White & Ishmael Wright. Date: 22 December 1666. Witnesses: John Gorge, Richard Woaker. Will proved 31 December 1666. Guy White was granted administration on said estate. Security: Daniel Clocker. Appraisers: Richard Bayley, Abdloe Martin. Thomas Sprigg to administer oath.

2:133 8 May 1667. Elisabeth relict of Thomas Williams (p, Wye River, TA) was granted administration on his estate. Bond: Lawrence Simons. Appraisers: James Scott, John Kennemont. Richard Woolman to administer oath.

2:134 Will of Richard Bennett, Jr. Bequests: wife Henerietta Maria Bennett, cousin John Langley 400 a. "The Folly" on Sassafras River. Executors: father Mr. Richard Bennett, wife's father Capt. James Neale, wife. Date: 29 January 1666. Witnesses: Daniel Silvaine, John Bristo. Will proved 6 May 1667. Henerietta Maria relict of Richard Bennett, Jr. was granted administration on his estate. Bond: Capt. James Neale. Date: 5 October 1667.

2:135 Lettice Lerry relict of Peter Lerry gave a PoA to James Thompson (CV). Date: 19 January 1666. Witness: Thomas Brooke.

2:136 Will of William Burke (p, Patuxent, CV). Date: 13 December 1666. Bequests: servant Arthur Nutthall, John Holshott servant to Mr. Pott, Mrs.

Court Session: <no date>

2:137 Elisabeth Pott, Elisabeth Pinter, Arthur Ludford. Mentions: John Pott. Executrix: Lettice Lerry wife of Peter Lerry. Witnesses: Arthur Ludford, Daniell Fisher.

Inventory of Mrs. Bateman. Date: 23 April 1667. Amount: #2080. Appraisers: Ri. Smith, Tho. Sprigg.

2:138 Gerrard Browne administrator of John Browne was granted continuance.

18 May 1667. Ann Hooper was granted administration on estate of her husband Robert Hooper (p, SM). Bond: William Smith (inholder, SM). Appraisers: Mr. Thomas Hatton, Mr. Thomas Harper. The Chancellor to administer oath.

2:139 Will of Edward James. Executors: Samuell Dobson & his wife Lucy Dobson. Bequests: my child then to children of said Samuell & Lucy.
2:140 Date: 14 August 1666. Witnesses: William Boarman, Thomas Darcy. Will proved 17 October 1666.

Inventory of Robert Hooper (SM). Date: 23 May 1667. Appraisers: Thomas Hatton, Thomas Harper.
2:141 Amount: #6190.

2:142 Will of William Boyss (p, Enemessicke, SO). Bequests: wife's sister Jane Bellamin
2:143 estate in Northampton Co. VA, John Barrett & Patrick Robinson their bills voided, Daniel Denahoe, William Willkinson, my only daughter Jane Boyss (under age 15) in custody of Robert & Ann Cattling.
2:144 Overseers: Richard Davis, William Davis. Executor: Robert Cattlin. Date: 19 January 1666. Witnesses: John Rhodes, Daniell Curtis, Patrick Robertson.

2:145 5 June 1667. Mr. Thomas Truman to prove wills of Richard Kirerne (?) & Morgan Guyanagh.

Court Session: <no date>

Robert Cattlin was granted administration on estate of William Boyss. William Stephens to prove will by swearing John Rhodes & Daniell Curtice.

2:146 Inventory of Margarett wife of William Argent & relict of Thomas Nobes successor of Bartholomew Herring. Date: 7 March 1666.
2:147 Amount: #5400. Appraisers: Arthur Ludford, James Godserosse.

Accounts of John Read. Administratrix: Margarett Gitting relict of said John. Payments to: Mr. Thomas Sprigg, John Pitts, Capt. Harwood, Joseph Hardy, Andrew Cooke, Stephen Clifton, Robert Tyler, William Stockdale for William Glanvile. Amount: #7831.

2:148 Will of James Barnaby (Monokin). Executrix: wife. Bequests: wife Mary Barnabe, son James Barnes, Jr. 200 a., daughter
2:149 Elisabeth Barnabe, daughter Rebecca Barnabe.
2:150 Son of age at 16; daughters at age 15. Mentions: John Whitehed (Northampton Co. VA). Overseers: Mr. Hugh Yeog, Charles Hall. Date: 26 January 1665. Signed: James Barnabe. Witnesses: Patrick Fleming, Robert Lewan.

2:151 28 May 1667. Court at Somerset Co. Attendees: Mr. William Stevens, Capt. William Thorne, Mr. James Jones, Mr. John Winder, Mr. George Johnson.

Mr. Hugh Yeo (Accomac Co.) & Patrick Fleming (SO) proved will of James Barnabe. Signed: Edm. Beauchamp.

2:152 10 June 1667. Randall Revell (g) for Mary Barnaby relict of James Barnaby (SO) was granted administration on his estate.
2:153 Appraisers: John Winder, Charles Bellard. Capt. William Thorne to administer oath.

Page 115

Court Session: <no date>

2:154 Ann Markum relict of John Markum, Sr. (p, SO) gave PoA to Mr. Randall Revell (g). Date: 11 April 1667. Witnesses: Edm. Beauchamp, Tho. Walley. Randall Revell was granted administration on said estate. Appraisers: William Jones, Thomas Bloys. George Johnson to administer oath.

2:155 Francis Barnes (inholder, KE) was granted administration on estate of Capt. John Odber (Chester River, TA), as greatest creditor. Date: 7 June 1667. Thomas Sowth to administer oath.

2:156 Appraisers: Thomas Snow, Antony Purse. Mr. South to administer oath.

2:157 John Stone (g, CH) was granted administration on estate of his brother Richard Stone (g, CH). Date: 11 June 1667. Security: William Calvert, Esq. Appraisers: Samuell Raton (?), Nathaniell Eaton. Joseph Harrison (g) to administer oath.

2:158 Inventory of Lawrence Richardson (AA). Servant: Gilbert Thurston (boy). ...

2:159 Mentions: 200 a., "Tayton" 280 a. Date: 29 May 1667. Amount: #6399. Appraisers: Will. Crouch, John Howard.

2:160 Inventory of orphans of Mr. Robert Cole. Amount: #15340. Before: Luke Gardner.

2:161 Payments to: Mr. Woodberry, Mr. Foxhall. Amount: #14431.

Walter King (merchant, Bristol) vs. estate of Richard Stone (CV). Date: 4 June 1667.

2:162 Will of William Eldridge (p, AA). Bequests: Samuell Lane & William Sifick 300 a. on Choptank Rivert, Samuell Lane chattel in hands of John Roberts. Date: 11 March 1665. Witnesses: Henery Benett, Robert Paca, John Burgis. Samuell Lane was granted administration on said estate. Date: 2 June 1667.

2:163 Samuell Chew & Richard Young to prove the will. Security: George Pascall. Appraisers: John Burridge, George

Court Session: <no date>

Pascall. Samuell Chew to administer oath.

28 June 1667. Anthony Calloway (p, KE) was granted administration on estate of Capt. John Odber (Chester River). Security: Edmond Barton. Appraisers: William Hemsley, Nathaniel Evett. Capt. Robert Vaughan to administer oath.

Hugh Stanley & his wife Dorothy & John Brooks (chirurgeon) to appear at Mattapony on 9 July to testify regarding the will of Stephen Yoe (CV).

2:164 Will of Stephen Yoe (CV). Date: 4 April 1666. Executrix: wife Ann Yow. Bequests: wife Ann, her son Henry & daughter Dorothy. Overseers: Mr. John Brookes (chirurgeon), Mr. Hugh Stanley. Witnesses: Hugh Stanley, Dorothy Stanley. Will proved on 9 July 1667 by Hugh Stanly & his wife Dorothy.

2:165 10 July 1667. Ann Yow relict of Stephen Yow was granted administration on his estate. Bond: William Adams, Michael Farmer (CV). Appraisers: John Brookes (chirurgeon), Michael Farmer. Tobyas Nortonn (g) to administer oath.

Inventory of John Browne (CH). Date: 15 June 1667. Amount: #1945. Appraisers: James Mackey, Roger Dickeson.

2:166 Accounts of John Browne. Administrator: Gerrard Browne. Date: 9 July 1667. Inventory amount: #1945. Payments to: Giles Glover, Walter Pake, William Smyth, Richard Randall. Amount: #5257.

2:167 Discharge was granted. Date: 16 July 1667.

2:168 Inventory of William Stockden. Appraisers: Abelor Martin, Richard Bayly. Date: 12 July 1667.

2:169 Signed: Richard Bayly, Abdelo Martin.

17 July 1667. Capt. Luke Gardner (g, St. Clement's Bay, SM) was granted administration on estate of Charles Alexander (joyner, SM). Appraisers: Richard Bennett, Thomas Bassett. William Bretton to administer oath.

Court Session: <no date>

2:170 7 August 1667. Margerite Wright relict of Ismaell Wright (CV) was granted administration on his estate. Security: Lt. William Smyth. Appraisers: Richard Bayley, Abdelo Martin. Tho. Sprigg to administer oath.

2:171 Inventory of Abraham Holdman (p, BA). Date: 4 June 1667. Appraisers: William Hollis, Joseph Gallion. Signed: John Collier.

2:172 Inventory of Marmaduke Scott (merchant, ENG). Administrators: Ralph Hawkins the elder, Ralph Hawkins the younger. Date: 6 July 1667. List of debts: James Foote, Mathew Clarke, Richard Hills, Robert Burle, James Southward, John Rockwell, William Neale. Amount: #3353.

Marriage license: John Cooper (CV) & Elisabeth Holland (CV). Date: 4 August 1666.

2:173 Inventory of William Hills (AA). Appraisers: Capt. John Norwood, William Hopkins. Date: 10 June 1667.
2:173! ...
2:174 List of debts: Ralph Salmon.
2:175 Amount: #19991.

Inventory of William Eldridge (AA). List of debts: Henry Benett. Date: 10 August 1667. Appraisers: John Burridg, George Pascall.

2:176 Will of Richard Wells, Sr. (AA). Date: 22 June 1667. Bequests: son Richard Wells plantation on Herring Creek called "Wells" 600 a. & "Little Wells" 100 a. adjacent to Mr. Anthony Sallway & "Wells Hill" 420 a., son George Wells 300 a. in BA bought of Capt. George Gouldsmith called "Planter Delight" & land on Gunpowder River "Wells Neck" 420 a., son John "Langford's Neck" on north side of Chester River (TA) 1500 a. bought of John Langford (g), son Robert Wells 350 a. "West Wells"
2:177 on Herring Creek, son Benjamin Wells

Page 118

Court Session: <no date>

2:178 "Benjamin's Choice" 280 a. west of land of Mr. Francis Holland on Herring Creek, daughter Martha wife of Mr. Anthony Salloway, daughter Ann wife of Mr. John Stansby (chirurgeon), daughter Mary wife of Mr. Thomas Stockett. Executors: 5 sons. Witnesses: Francis Stockett, Bonham Turnor, William Linckhorne. Will proved on 31 August 1667 by Francis Stockett & Bonham Turner.

2:179 3 September 1667. Richard Wells & George Wells were granted administration on said estate during minority of John, Robert, & Benjamin Wells. Appraisers (AA): Samuell Chew, Capt. William Burges. Tho. Taylor to administer oath. Appraisers (TA): Thomas South, James Ringould. Henry Coursey, Esq. to administer oath. Appraisers (BA): Capt. Thomas Howell, Godfrey Bayley. Capt. John Collier to administer oath.

2:180 Inventory of Charles Alexander. Appraisers: Richard Bennett, Thomas Bassett. Date: 23 July 1667. Amount: #1202.

2:181 Inventory of Ishmaell Wright. Appraisers: Richard Bayly, Abdlo Martin. Date: 23 September 1667. Land: 200 a. at Trasquakin, 225 a. at Patuxt., 300 a., plantation.

2:182 Amount: #38730.

2:183 Will of Richard Randall (CH). Date: 3 August 1667. Bequests: Mr. William Taylor (NE) to be paid by chattel at Mr. Anthony Bridges (VA) & at Stephen Mountague,

2:184 John Pinke (shoemaker, Boston, NE), church for maintenance of a Protestant minister 200 a. "The Addition" surveyed by Mr. Benjamin Rozer, John Robinson, Mr. Anthony Bridges, Thomas Cooper (servant boy) to Mr. Liddy Wilkinson (Northumberland Co. in Accomacke), Stephen Mountague, Mr. Joseph Harrison, father Richard Randall, Ann Randall. Executors: Mr. Joseph Harrison, Stephen

Court Session: <no date>

2:185 Mountague.
Witnesses: Samuell Harris, William Hillis.

24 September 1667. Stephen Mountague & Joseph Harrison were granted administration on said estate. Bondsmen: Ignatius Causeen William Allen.
2:186 James Lindsey to prove will, by oaths of Samuell Harris & William Hills. Appraisers: John Ward, John Munn.

Will of Hugh Kinsey (AA). Executrix: wife Margarett Kinsey.
2:187 Bequests: youngest daughter Elisabeth Kinsey then to Mary Humphreys, Sarah Clarke, grandchild Paule Kinsey
2:188 "The Wallnutt" on Middle Branch, grandchild Margarett Kinsey, Charles Gorsuch. Date: 6 May 1667. Witnesses: William Hare, John Malom.

2:189 22 September 1667. Margarett Kinsey relict of Hugh Kinsey (AA) was granted administration on his estate. Robert Burly to prove will. Appraisers: Henry Howard, William Timmes. Robert Burly to administer oath.

Will of Robert Cager (p, SM). Date: 10 August 1667.
2:190 Bequests: son Robert Cager (under age 21), daughter Dorothy wife of George Mounroe
2:191 ...
2:192 100 a.
2:193 ...
2:194 Overseers: John Lawson (g), Henry Hyde (g).
2:195 Witnesses: Thomas Hatton, Patrick Forrest, Evan Lewis. Will proved at Mattapenny on 5 September 1667
2:196 by Thomas Hatton & Patrick Forrest.

4 October 1667. John Lawson & Henry Hide were granted administration on said estate for use of orphans. Security: Patrick Forrest. Appraisers: John Waghop, William Watts. Mr. Thomas Dent to administer oath.

Court Session: <no date>

Richard Illinworth was granted administration on estate of John Garinier. Security: William Illinworth. Appraisers: Edward Skinner, Mathew Clarke. Mr. Robert Burle to administer oath.

2:197 Capt. William Smyth vs. estate of George Richardson (TA). Date: 3 October 1667.

8 October 1667. Walter Beane (g) was granted administration on estate of Arthur Turner (CH). Appraisers: James Walker, THomas Thorowgood. Francis Pope to administer oath.

10 October 1667. James Thompson (g) on behalf of Lettice relict of Peter Lerry (p, CV) was granted administration on estate of William Burke (CV). Tobyas Norton to administer oath. Security: James Thompson (g). Appraisers: Arthur Ludford, William Lowry. Hugh Stanley to administer oath.

2:198 Inventory of Thomas Percy (CH). Date: 15 May 1667. Appraisers: James Walker, John Dowglas. Administratrix: Jemima Long.
2:199-200 ...
2:201 Amount: #22848.

Inventory of James Barnaby (SO). Legacies paid: Mary Barnaby (relict),
2:202 James Barnaby, Elisabeth Barnaby,
2:203 Rebeckah Barnaby.
2:204 Additional inventory. Date: 31 July 1667.
2:205 ...
2:206 Appraisers: Charles Ballard, John Winder.

Inventory of Stephen Yeo. Date: 22 August 1667.
2:207 List of debts: Mr. Hugh Stanley, Michael Farmer, John Brooke (chirurgeon). Servant: Robert Hollyday. List of debts: John Bigger.
2:208-209 ...
2:210 Amount: #19015.
2:211 Appraisers: John Brooke, Michaell

Court Session: <no date>

Farmer.

	Will of Garrett Rutten (BA). Date: 8 March 1664.
2:212	...
2:213	Bequests: wife & children, eldest son Rutten Garrett.
2:214	Executrix: wife. Overseers: Mr. Francis Stockett, Mr. Thomas Stockett. Signed: Garratt Rutten. Witnesses: John Waterton, Robert Jones.
2:215	Will of Francis Wright (g, Clayfall, BA). Bequests: younger brother Raphaell Wright (Bovill, Parish of St. Andrew's, Clamorganshire, Wales) "Clayfall" (BA),
2:216	Jacob Clawson, Lewis Stockett, Edmond Cantwell, Francis Stockett, William Lyles,
2:217	brother Thomas Wright. Executor: brother Raphaell. Overseers: Maj. Gouldsmith, Maj. Thomas Howell.
2:218	Date: 25 July 1666. Witnesses: Geo. Wells, J. Waterton. Will proved on 12 March 1666 by George Wells & John Waterton.
	Inventory of Paule Kinsey (AA). Date: 22 June 1667.
2:219-220	...
2:221	Servants: Francis Dormand, Garrett Birkles, Richard Mascall, Hannah Morrice.
2:222	Amount: #15105. Appraisers: Lewis Brien, Warnar Shudall. Additional inventory. List of debts: Richard Phillips, Warner Shuall, Abraham Clarke, Richard Deaver, Joseph Cizell,
2:223	Alexander Mounteyne, John Tench, Richard Thurall, William Guinn. Amount: #21476. Accounts. Payments to: Capt. Norwood, Capt. Harwood, Thomas Marsh, John Aues, John Ewen, John Tench. Amount: #7960. Date: 18 December 1667.
2:224	Edmond Burton (KE) was granted administration on estate of John Elliott (KE). Security: Anthony Caloway (p, KE). Appraisers: Edward Hull, Anthony Kellaway. Capt. Robert Vaughan to administer oath.

Court Session: <no date>

2:225	Will of James Mulliken (p, Patuxon River, CV). Date: 18 August 1666.
2:226	...
2:227	Bequests: wife Mary Mullikin & children, son James Mullekin. Witnesses: William Murrah, Benjamin Granger. Will proved on 16 October 1667 by William Murray & Benjamin Granger.
2:228	18 October 1667. Mary Mullikin relict of James Mullikin (p, CV) was granted administration on his estate. Bond: James Williams. Appraisers: Richard Keene, Gwy White, George Beckwith. Mr. Thomas Sprigg to administer oath.
2:229	Daniel Jenifer (g) was granted administration on estate of John Nuttall (Crosse Mannor, SM). Date: 10 October 1667. Security: Capt. William Smith. Appraisers: Daniell Clocker, Thomas Innis.
2:230	Inventory of James Mullikin. Date: 27 October 1667. Appraisers: Geo. Beckwith, Gwy White.
2:231	30 October 1667. Richard Bayly (inholder, Patuxent River) was granted administration on estate of George Palmer (cooper, NE), as greatest creditor. Security: Capt. William Smith.
2:232	Appraisers: William King, Thomas Gannt. Thomas Sprigg to administer oath.
	Petition by Francis Pope regarding estate of Richard Smith. Arthur Tyrner is dec'd & John Hatch is overseer. Said Pope to remain administrator, with security William. Marshall. Date: 7 October 1667.
2:233-234	Inventory of Richard Stone (CH). ...
2:235	Amount: #18959. Appraisers: Samuell Eaton, Nathan. Eaton.
2:236	Inventory of John Davis (St. Jerome's).
2:237-238	...
2:239	List of debts: Jeremiah Harrington, John Reynolds. Amount: #11066.

Court Session: <no date>

2:240 Appraisers: William Asbeston, Thomas Hughes. Date: 14 June 1667.

2:241 Laus Deo 1667. Inventory of Mr. Richard Randall.

2:242 Servant: Thomas Cooper (boy). List of debts: Thomas Wharton, Thomas Robinson,

2:243 Roger Dickenson, Thomas Allanson, James Lee, George Thompson, John Tonkinson, Samuell Cressy, George English, Edmond Lyndsey, Nicholas Emanson, Mr. Richard Stone, Mr. John Stone, Mrs. Virlinda Stone, Mr. Thomas Stone, Mr. Thomas Mathews, Mr. Henry Adams, Stephen Mountague, Gyles Glover, Richard Boughton, Ignatius Causeene, William Hill, Samuell Harris,

2:244 Garrett Sennott, John Cane, John Lewger, Lawrence Little, Thomas Alkocke, Mr. James Lindsey, John Charman, James Macou (?), Robert Goodrick, Randall Fremen, Owen Jones, Mrs. Virlinda Burditt, John Lambert, Daniell Johnson, Edmond Lambert, John Robinson, Mr. Daniel Jenifer, George Harris, Mathias OBryan, George Mounroe.

2:245 Date: 7 October 1667. Appraisers: John Ward, John Munn.

2:246 Inventory of John Gammer (AA). Appraisers: Dedmoras Stenborgh, Mathew Clark. Date: 28 October 1667.

2:247 Amount: #4892.

2:248 Witness: Robert Burle.

2:249 Inventory of Hugh Kinsey (AA). Appraisers: Henry Howard, William Timmes. Date: 7 October 1667.

2:250-252 ...

2:253 Servants: Henry Morgan, John Maylam, William Hare.

2:254-255 ...

2:256 List of debts: Robert Parrett, estate of Paule Kinsey, David Jones, Nicholas Ruckeston, Even Swyer (?), Francis Pettitt. Amount: #34831.

2:257 Witness: Robert Burle.

2:258 Additional inventory. Land (on Patapsco River): 400 a. called "Kinsey", 100 a. called "Black Wallnutt".

Court Session: <no date>

2:259 9 November 1667. William Smith (SM) was granted administration on estate of George Richardson (TA). Security: Daniel Jenifer (carpenter, SM).

2:260 Inventory of George Palmer. Date: 7 November 1667. Appraisers: Thomas Gaunt, William King. Amount: #1570.

2:261 Elisabeth relict of Robert Brooke (CV) was granted administration on his estate. Appraisers: Tobyas Norton, John Tawny. Baker Brooke to administer oath.

Will of Martin Meckenny. Date: 23 November 1667. Executor: Edmund Lindsey. Bequests: Elisabeth Morne. Signed: Martin Mackennie. Witnesses: John Jenkinson, John Bond.

9 December 1667. Edmund Lindsey was granted administration on estate of Martin Mekenny. Appraisers: Clement Theobald, Thomas Baker. Henry Adams (CH) to administer oath.

12 December 1667. William Smith (inholder, SM) relinquished administration on estate of George Richardson (TA). Timothy Goodridge (TA) was granted administration. Security: John Edmundson. Appraisers: Simon Richardson, John Richardson. Tho. Powell to administer oath.

15 December. Appraisers: William Evans, Joseph Horsley. William Groome to administer oath. [No estate cited.]

2:262 Couden Marke was granted administration on estate of Thomas Willen (SM), as greatest creditor. Date: 12 December 1667. Appraisers: Thomas Wynn, Christopher Hall. Security: Nicholas Young (g).

Inventory of Capt. John Odber. Appraisers: William Hemsley, Nathaniell Evetts. Date: 17 August 1667.
2:263 ...
2:264 Amount: #4163.

Court Session: <no date>

2:265	Will of John Boage (CV). Bequests: godson
2:266	John Bigger, Jr., son-in-law Katherine Bradmore, Countryman Will. Mills & John Wright, wife Mary Boage land.
2:267	Executrix: wife. Date: 8 July 1667. Witnesses: John King, Hen. Cole.

17 December 1667.

2:268	Will proved by John King. Mary relict of John Boague was granted administration on his estate. Security: Thomas Sprigg. Thomas Truman, Esq. to prove will by oath of Henry Cole. Appraisers: Thomas Sprigg, John Bigger, Jr. Thomas Truman, Esq. to administer oath.
2:269	Will of William Champ (chirurgeon, SM). Date: 8 October 1666. Bequests: Fortune Medford, Elisabeth Forrest (eldest daughter of Patrick Forrest). Executrix: Fortune Medford. Signed: William Champe. Witnesses: Andrew Bashaw, Richard Berkitt.
2:270	Will proved on 13 December 1667 at Mattapenny. Fortune Metford (widow, SM) was granted administration on said estate. Security: Patrick Forrest. Appraisers: Henry Ellery, Patrick. Forrest. Thomas Dent to administer oath.
	Inventory of William Johnson. Appraisers: John Easson, Thomas Phillips. Date: 20 April. Mentions: John Slatter. Amount: #3630. Signed: Thomas Powell, John Eason, Thomas Philipps.
2:271	Inventory of Richard Wells, Sr. (chirurgeon, Herring Creek, AA). Date: 5 December. Appraisers: Capt. Thomas Howell, Godfrey Bayly.
2:272	...
2:273	Amount: £114.11.4. Additional inventory. Date: 28 November 1667.
2:274	...
2:275	Amount: #15577. Appraisers: Thomas South, James Ringgold. Additional inventory.
2:276-281	...

Court Session: <no date>

2:282 Amount: #132390. Additional inventory. List of debts: Mr. Richard Owen, Mr. Connoway, Mr. Richard Owen per Mr. Glover, cargo of the Baltimore per Mr. Barnaby Dunch,

2:283 cargo of Goulden Wheate Shiaff commanded by James Strong, Mr. John Stanly. Amount: #54145. Date: 10 December 1667. Appraisers: Samuell Chew, William Borgis.

2:284 31 December 1667. Estate of Francis Wright (BA) was committed to Maj. Samuel Goldsmith & Capt. Thomas Howell for use of Raphael Wright (brother of dec'd). Godfrey Bayly (BA) is to swear George Wells & John Waterton. Appraisers: James Frisby, John Vanheck. Godfrey Bayly to administer oath.

1 January 1667. Thomas Bowdell (CV) was granted administration on estate of James Adams (CV) for use of George, Isabella, John, Margarett, Phebe, James, & Elisabeth Adams (orphans of said James). Security: William Turner. Appraisers: Samuel Graves, Thomas Perry. William Groome to administer oath.

10 March 1667. Thomas Bowdell was granted continuance on said estate.

Daniel Jenifer administrator of John Nuthall (g, SM) was granted continuance.

2:285 Will of Rice Jones. Date: 31 December 1667. Bequests: wife Francis Jones (pregnant). Overseers: Mr. Thomas Nottley, Mr. Humprey Warren. Witnesses: Robert Gates, Robert Hunt, Samuell Dobson.

2:286 Inventory of Robert Cager. Date: 13 November 1667.
2:287 Amount: #37775. Appraisers: John Wahob, William Watts.

2:288 10 January 1667. Frances relict of was granted administration on estate of Rice Jones. Mr. Robert Sly to swear Samuell Dobson (witness). Appraisers: Samuell Dobson, Thomas Sampson. Mr. Robert Sly

Court Session: <no date>
to administer oath.

Henry Hide administrator of Robert Cager was granted continuance.

2:289 Will of Anthony Griffin. Bequests: daughter Lucie Griffin "Kingston", daughter Lucretia Griffin "Comb Hills", wife Jane Griffin. Date: 26 September 1667. Witnesses: Richard Foxun, Nicholas Stephenson.

20 January 1667. Henry Coursey, Esq. is to swear Richard Foxon (witness) & Jean Griffin relict of Anthony Griffin. Appraisers: Richard Jones, John Singleton. Henry Coursey, Esq. to administer oath.

Thomas Hynson & John Hinson (sons of Thomas Hynson, Sr.) were granted administration on his estate. Appraisers: Simon Carpenter, Philemon Loyd, William Hemsley. Henry Coursey, Esq. to administer oath.

Thomas South (g) was granted administration on estate of John Roise (?) (TA), as greatest creditor. Henry Coursey, Esq. to administer oath.

2:290 Will of Francis Trottin. Date: 7 January 1667. Bequests: Countryman Marke Cordea. Executor: said Marke. Witnesses: Henry Warren, Thomas Parsons. Will proved 16 January 1667.

26 January 1667. Marke Cordea (inholder, SM) was granted administration on estate of Francis Trottin (mariner, SM). Security: Richard Moy.

Inventory of Thomas Willin (husbandman, St. Jerome's). Date: 2 January 1667. List of debts: Lt. General, William Gringer.
2:291 Amount: #2017. Appraisers: Thomas Wynne, Christofer Hall.

Will of William Smith (innholder). Date: 18 December 1667. Bequests: Mary,

Page 128

Court Session: <no date>

2:292
Mr. John Morecroft. Executrix: wife. Mentions: brother Joseph & his son William. Overseers: Mr. John Morecroft, Mr. Thomas Nottley, Mr. Daniel Jenifer. Witnesses: William Harper, William Fardel. Will proved 8 January 1667.

2:293
Will of Thomas Addenbrooke (upholster, London). Date: 13 October 1667. Bequests: Thomas Ellees & William Adams, uncles & aunts Nicholas Addenbrooke & Roger Addenbrooke & Margrett Sherley & Johan Tayler. Executors: Thomas Ellees, William Adams. Witnesses: John Chambers, Nathaniell Umvin (?), Samuell Thompson. Thomas Ellees was granted administration on said estate. George Peake (g) to swear Samuell Thompson. Security: Sampson Warring. Robert Burle (AA) to swear John Dunch (commander of the Baltimore). Appraisers: Sampson Waring, William Simpson. Geo. Peake to administer oath.

30 January 1667. Robert Chisick was granted administration on estate of John Stantley (bricklayer, CV), as greatest creditor. Security: Richard Bayly. Appraisers: John Bigger, John Wright. Tho. Truman, Esq. to administer oath.

2:294
Will of William Smith proved by oaths of William Harper & William Fardel. Date: 31 January 1667.

1 February 1667. Elisabeth Story (CH) relict of Walter Story (CV) by Benjamin Rozer (g) was granted administration on his estate. Security: John Dowglas. Appraisers: Francis Pope, Humphry Warren. Mr. Henry Adams to administer oath.

2:295
Thomas Ward administrator of Joseph Edly was granted discharge.

5 February 1667. Joane relict of Thomas Smoote (CH) was granted administration on said estate. Security: Richard & William Smoote. Appraisers: Humphry Warren, Robert Henley (g). Francis Pope

Court Session: <no date>

2:296 — to administer oath.

John Smith who married Susanna relict of George Holdcraft (chirurgeon, SM) was granted discharge.

Will of Richard Pinner. Bequests: wife, 2 sons (under age 16) Richard & William Pinner land, Roger Cording (?) 80 a., Richard Roe & his wife Anne chattel to be paid from debts in Elisabeth River, cousin William Ellis & his 2 sons Philip & William.

2:297 Executrix: wife. Overseers: Francis Sawyer, William Ellis, Joseph Harrisson, Henry Adames. Date: 28 August 1666. Witnesses: William Ellis, John Digbey, Richard Rowe. Recorded in Lower Norfolk Co. 20 June 1667. Signed: John Okeham.

14 February 1667. Anne relict of said Richard Pinner (who died in VA) was granted administration on his estate. Security: Walter Pake.

Inventory of Robert Brook. Appraisers: Mr. Tobias Norton, Mr. John Tawny. Date: 23 November 1667.
2:298 Amount: #15043.

2:299 Inventory of William Boyss. Date: 15 October 1667. Appraisers: Daniel Curtis, John Rhodes.

2:300 List of debts: Thomas Deparkes, Patrick Robinson, Edward Dickeson, Joseph Hues, Stephen Horssi, Robert Cattling, William Davis, Thomas Davis. Amount: #19953. Accounts. Payments to: Jane Delamus her portion to her husband Thomas Manlove, William Kendall, John Rhodes, Edmund Beauchamp, Randall Revell, Thomas Cottingham, William Willkinson, Daniel Curtis, coffin for his wife, child's diet,

2:301 Patrick Robinson (legacy), Thomas Ball, George Johnson, William Willkinson, Patrick Robinson, Thomas Tull, Robert Cattling. Amount: #14439.

2:302 Inventory of Arthur Turner (CH). List of debts: William Hargust, Thomas Henshall, John Dunston, Capt. Hugh

Court Session: <no date>

2:303 Oneale, John Dunstone, Capt. Fendall, Mr. Robert Long. Amount: #12917. Date: 4 February 1666/7. Appraisers: Thomas Thorowgood, James Walker. Filed: 6 February 1667/8. Signed: Gualteri Bayne. Witness: Benjamin Rozer.

2:304 13 February 1667. Joseph Chope (?) (mariner, Devonshire, ENG) was granted administration on estate of John Esford (mariner, Devonshire, ENG). Security: John Vicaris. Appraisers: Robert Burle, John Welch. Samuel Withers to administer oath.

15 February 1667. Anne relict of Roger Grosse (merchant, AA) was administratrix on his estate. She married John Welch (g, AA). She is now deceased. Administration was granted to said Welch.

16 February 1667. Sibil relict of John Six (CV) was granted administration on his estate. Security: Richard Bayly. Appraisers: William Chaplin, Thomas How. William Groom (g) to administer oath.

2 March 1667. Virlinda Burditt relict of Thomas Burditt (CH) was granted administration on his estate. Security: Nathaniel Eaton. Appraisers: Tho. Stone, John Stone. Joseph Harrison (g) to administer oath.

2:305 Accounts of Bartholomew Glevin (KE). Administratrix: Mary Glevin. Amount of inventory: #54056. Mentions: 200 a. of land. Payments to: John Browne, William Read, John Vicars, Richard Tilghman, Mr. William Coursey, Thomas Hinson, Jonathon Sibrey, Anthony Calloway, William Hopkins, Cornelius Howard, Tobias Wells, Ralph Williams, James Browne, Richard FittzAlleyne, Thomas Vaughan, Sarah Conner, Nicholas Pickett, Capt. William Burgess, Jonathon Hopkins,
2:306 Philip & Sarah Conner, William Calvert, Esq., Edward Loyd, Esq., Thomas Marsh, John Wright, Richard Minton, Thomas Parsons. Amount: #58644. Signed: Mary

Court Session: <no date>

2:307 Wright (alias Mary Glevin). Mary Glevin (alias Mary Wright) administratrix of Bartholomew Glevin (chirurgeon, KE), now the wife of John Wright, was granted discharge.

2:308
2:309 Will of Charles Maynard (SM). Bequests: Ann land for self & 2 daughters Agnes & Elisabeth Maynard, Roman Catholic priest, wife Ann to receive servant Dennis Magrouder, Fran. Fitzherbert, Esq., Thomas Love (son of Judith Love), Peter Kempe. Executrix: wife. Overseers: Col. William Evans, Thomas Turner (St. Clement's Bay, g). Date: 2 May 1661. Witnesses: Thomas Turner, Bartholomew Philips, John Mecard.

2:310 Will of Alexander Hinderson. Bequests: Phillip Parker, godson John Bromfeild, godson Thomas Nichols. Executor: Nicholas Younge. Date: 28 January 1667. Witnesses: Abraham Rowser, Robert Wherell, Richard Rigll. Will proved on 24 March 1667 by Robert Worell.

6 April 1668. Timothy Goodridg administrator of Capt. George Richardson was granted continuance.

2:311 Inventory of William Champ. Date: 8 February 1667. Appraisers: Henry Ellery, Patrick Forest.

William Dorrington (g, CV) was granted administration on estate of Henry Sewall (merchant, CV). Appraisers: William Chaplin, Thomas Perry. William Groom to administer oath.

7 April 1668. Richard Tilghman (doctor of physeck, TA) was granted administration on estate of John Barret (TA). Appraisers: Richard Jones, John Singleton. Thomas South to administer oath.

2:312 Will of John Thurmar (CV). Bequests: daughter Ann Elwes & son Thomas Elwes, Capt. Samson Warren & his wife & his son Bassell Warren. Mentions: chattel

Court Session: <no date>

sold to William Worgin. Date: 4 April 1668. Witnesses: Richard Gibs, Francis Buckstone, Debera Edwards. Will proved on 10 April by Richard Gibbs & Francis Buckstone.

Inventory of James Adams. Amount: #5036. Date: 17 February 1667/8. Appraisers: Thomas Perey, Samuell Graves.

2:313 11 April 1668. Thomas Elwes (grocer, London) son-in-law to John Thurmar (CV) was granted administration on his estate. Security: Geo. Peake. Appraisers: John Troster, Robert Heigh. George Peake (g) to administer oath.

George Peake to swear George Munroe & Robert Heigh to prove will of Richard Collett (g, CV).

Inventory of John Boague (CV).
2:314 Servants mentioned: John Dylate, Mary Mitton, Jane Wharton.
2:315 Amount: #32260. Appraisers: Thomas Sprigge, John Bigger. Date: 20 February 1667. Additional inventory. List of debts: William Lille, Richard Stacie, Thomas Sedgwick, James Canedy, John Wright, James More, Nineon Bell, Alexander Magrowder, Peter Lamare. AMount: #10528. Mentions: land belonging to John Startup. Appraisers: John Bigger, John Wright.

2:316 Accounts of John Obder (TA). Administrator: Anthony Calloway. Amount of inventory: #4163. Discharge was granted.

26 April 1668. Sibil Six (alias Sibil Somerford) administratrix of her husband John Six was granted continuance.

2:317 Will of Henry Kent. Bequests: Dyana Kent, Ann Kent, Mary Kent, child of brother's wife, brother William Kent. Executor: brother William. Date: 24 February 1667. Witnesses: John Troster, James Humes.

Court Session: <no date>

21 April 1668. William Kent brother of Henry Kent was granted administration on his estate. George Peake to swear witnesses John Troster & James Humes. Security: James Cullines. Appraisers: John Troster, James Humes. George Peake to administer oath.

Hannah relict of William Simpsor was granted administration on his estate. Appraisers: John Troster, Robert Heigh. George Peake to administer oath.

2:318   Inventory of Thomas Smoot (CH). Appraisers: Humphrey Warren, Robert Henley. Date: 14 february 1667.
2:319-322 ...
2:323   Servants mentioned: Moses Tunnell, Anthony Emerson, Edward Chandler, Elisabeth Frances. Amount: #39875.
2:324   Filed on 24 April 1668. Administratrix: Joane Smoote.
2:325   Witnesses: Ben. Rozer, Humphry Warren.

2:326   28 April 1668. Nathaniell Stiles was granted administration on estate of William Orchard (BA). Appraisers: William Hollis, Thomas Overton. Capt. John Collier to administer oath.

2:327   Petronella Penelope Gouldsmith relict of Mathew Gouldsmith (BA) was granted administration on his estate. Security: John Collett. Appraisers: Maj. Samuell Goldsmith, John Collett. George Uty to administer oath.

2:328   Elisabeth Furbee relict of Benjamin Furbee (BA) was granted administration on his estate. Security: William Palmer. Appraisers: Maj. Samuell Gouldsmith, John Collett. George Uty to administer oath.

2:329   Nathaniell Uty executor of John Terre was granted administration on his estate. Security: Hans de Ringh. Appraisers: Maj. Samuell Goldsmith, John Collett. George Uty to administer oath.

Court Session: <no date>

2:330   27 April 1668. Petition by Capt. Thomas Stockett on behalf of Anthony Congee (p, AA). Warrant to Samuel Chew to bring Moses Groom & Henry Timberley to prove will of John Pert (AA).

          Will of Elisabeth Brewer (widow).
2:331   Bequests: sons John & William Brewer,
2:332   son William land on South River bought of Richard Tydings & 50 a. & Negro Peter & Mulatto Jeffery,
2:333   Anias Peirpoint & his brother Jabez, 640 a. on Wye River on Eastern Shore to be sold, daughter Rachell Negro Peter & Negro Suzanna,
2:334   Negro Inde (woman). Mentions: Mulatto Richard.
2:335   Overseers: Edward Selby, Nathaniell Heathcott, Henry Peirpoint.
2:336   Date: 6 March 1667. Witnesses: Michaell Pope, John Porter, Thomas Besson. Will proved on 22 May 1668 by Thomas Besson, Jr. before Thomas Besson.

          30 April 1668. Nathaniel Heathcoate was granted administration on estate of Elisabeth Brewer. Security: Henry Peirpoint. Appraisers: William Toulson, Robert Francklin. Capt. Thomas Besson to administer oath.

2:337   Inventory of Mr. Roger Gross. Date: 6 August 1666.
2:338-345 ...
2:346   Amount: £214.17.4. Appraisers: William Burges, Tho. Tailler. Accounts. Payments to: Samuell Lane, Richard Ewen, Tho. Manrow, Joh. Gundry, Samuell Chew, Robert Lloyd, for schooling John & Roger Gross,
2:347   Capt. Burges & Mr. Tayller. Amount: #8000.

          Inventory of John Bisco (SM). Administrator: Thomas Doxey who married the relict.
2:348-349 ...
2:350   Date: 12 February 1667.

          9 May 1668. Elisabeth relict of Thomas Leitchworth (CV) was granted administration on his estate. Security:

Court Session: <no date>

Thomas Sprigg. Appraisers: Thomas Bowdell, Arthur Ludford. Charles Brooke to administer oath.

2:351	Inventory of Walter Story. Appraisers: Francis Pope, Humphry Warren. Date: 18-19 February 1667.
2:352-354	...
2:355	Servants mentioned: Henry Barnes.
2:356	Amount: #132219.
2:357	List of debts: George English, Daniell Johnson, James Walker, Col. Foukes, Thomas Stone, Francis Pope, Edward Swan, Thomas Hustey, John Courtes, Walter Beane, Thomas Baker, Richard Wattson, Samuell Eaton,
2:358	Samuell Cressey, Edward Fillpott, William Hall, Henry Adams, William Marshall, Thomas Lomax, Thomas Mathews, Edmund Lindsey, Oliver Balte. List of debts: Jacob Petoson, Richard Whindell, Anthony Bridges, William Boyden, John Coffer, Abraham Rowse, Thomas Simpson, John Walton, Edward ORelly, And. Ward, John Clarke.
2:359	List of debts: John Douglas, Capt. Josias Fendall, William Love, Richard Chapman, Henry Moore, Robert Long, James Bewling, Humphery Warren. List of debts: Mrs. Virlinda Stone, Richard Stone, John Stone, William Nevill.
2:360	Will of Richard Collett. Bequests: wife Elisabeth Collett 200 a. "Susquehanna Point" bought of Robert Moore attorney for John Harris (son of William Harris (ENG)) & Henry Coursey who married relict of Richard Harris.
2:361	Date: 28 Janaury 1667. Witnesses: George Munrow, Robert Height. Will proved 28 April 1668.
2:362	16 May 1668. Elisabeth Collett relict of Richard Collett was granted administration on his estate. Security: John Stansby.
2:363	Will of Henry Ellery (St. George's River, SM). Bequests: Elisabeth Forrest (daughter of Patrick Forrest), Patrick Forrest ½ plantation, wife Elisabeth Ellery. Executor: Patrick Forrest.

Court Session: <no date>

2:364 Date: 15 April 1667. Witnesses: Marmaduke Semme, Walter Roules, Elisabeth Wockare. Will proved 16 May 1668.

2:365 18 May 1668. Patrick Forrest was granted administration on estate of Henry Ellery. Security: Thomas Hatton. Appraisers: John Nicholas, Thomas Hatton. Daniell Jenifer to administer oath.

2:366 19 May 1668. Ellinor Pickard relict of Nicholas Pickard (KE) was granted administration on his estate. Security: Mathew Read (g). Appraisers: Edward Burton, Anthony Calloway. Mathew Read (g) to administer oath.

2:367
2:368 Will of George Bussey. Bequests: wife Ann Bussey, children. Date: 17 April 1668. Witnesses: William Moffett, Francis Leigh. Will proved 19 May 1668.
2:369 Ann Bussey relict of George Bussey (CV) was granted administration on his estate. Security: Richard Cane. Appraisers: John Tawny, Tobias Miles. George Peake to administer oath.

Thomas & John Hinson administrators of Thomas Hinson were granted continuance. Date: 28 April.

2:370 22 May 1668. Thomas South was granted administration on estate of Anthony Purses (TA). Security: Simon Carpenter. Appraisers: Nathaniel Evitt, Edward Rogers. Symon Carpenter to administer oath.

2:371 Inventory of Mr. Thomas Hinson, Sr. (TA). Administrators: Thomas & John Hinson his sons. Date: 18 February 1667. Servants mentioned: Negro Dugo, Joseph, Robert Peek (boy), Ann Barly.
2:372-381 ...
2:382 List of debts: Thomas Hinson, John Hinson,
2:383 Edward Rogers, Anthony Purse, John Boule, Nathaniell Thornton, William Stockley,

Court Session: <no date>

2:384 Richard Pether. Mentions: Thomas Parker. Filed: 12 May 1668. Appraisers: Symon Carpenter, William Hemsley.

Inventory of Anthony Griffin. Date: 11 March 1667. Appraisers: Richard Jones, John Singleton.
2:385 List of debts: Henry Gott.
2:386 Amount: #10247.

2:387 Inventory of John Rice. Appraisers: John Hinson. Date: 14 May 1668. List of debts: John Bone, Richard Foxen, Thomas Hinson. Amount: #4510.

2:388 23 May 1668. Richard Perey brother of Mary Bateman (widow, CV) was granted administration on her estate. Her daughter Mary Bateman is in ENG. Lt. John Bouge was named as overseer; he is now deceased.

Moses Groom, age 19, & Henry Timberley, age 22, deposed that said Moses was at the house of Anthony Congue (Herring Creek, AA) when John Peart bequeathed all to said Anthony. Before: Samuel Chew. Will proved 18 May 1668.
2:389 Anthony Congue was granted administration on said estate. Date: 25 May 1668. Samuel Chew to administer oath.

26 May 1668. Marke Cordea (inholder, SM) was granted administration on estate of Thomas Andrews (p, SM). Appraisers: Barnaby Jackson, Peter Key.

Will of John Morgan. Executrix: only daughter Elisabeth Morgan. Overseer & guardian: brother-in-law Mr. William Coursey.
2:390 List of debts: Mr. Richard Tilghman, John Edmundson, Jonathon Hopkins, Simon Carpenter. Bequests: Simon Carpenter & his wife, Christopher Barnes. Date: 16 October 1667. Witnesses: William Hemsley, Robert Kent. Will proved 30 May 1668.

Court Session: <no date>

3:391	29 May 1668. William Coursey was granted administration on estate of John Morgain (TA). Security: Jonathon Hopkins. Henry Coursey, Esq. to swear William Kent (witness). Appraisers: William Hemsley, Stephen Tully. Henry Coursey, Esq. to administer oath.
3:392	Inventory of John Six. Appraisers: Mr. William Chapline, Thomas How.
2:393	List of debts: William Jones, John Tucker, John Hambleton, Henry Cox, Thomas Howton, Richard Meekins, John Harris, Abdelo Martyne, John Wattkins, Richard Moore, John Wattline, Thomas Bramble,
2:394	Henry Gough, Mr. Boteler, John Russell, William Lawrence, Robert Webb, Henry Johnson, Edward Norman. Amount: #8660.
2:395	Will of Francis Barnes (KI). Executrix: wife Isabell Barnes. Simon Carpenter to advise wife & children. Bequests: eldest son Thomas plantation, son Francis "Pett's Gift" & 100 a. on Lanckford Bay, grandchild Francis Stevens 125 a. bought of John Jenkins, daughters Mary & Dorathy.. Residue to aforesaid 4 children & Ailes Stevens. Date: last April 1667. Witnesses: Simon Carpenter, John Morgan.
3:396	Inventory of Robert Cager. Date: 16 March 1667. Amount: #6047. Additional inventory, given by Leonard Jones & Edward Chicken. Date: 16 March 1667. Appraiser: Henry Hyde.
2:397	Inventory of Martin Macheny. Amount: #5624. Appraisers: Thomas Bacer, Clement Theobald. Date: 7 February. Signed: Edmund Lindsey.
2:398	Inventory of Rice Jones. Date: 22 January 1667. List of debts: John Andrewes, Mr. Robert Sly, Vincent Manchfeild. Amount: #11580. Filed: 3 February 1667. Appraisers: Thomas Simpson, Samuell Dobson.

Court Session: <no date>

2:399   3 June 1668. Isab. Barnes was granted administration on estate of Francis Barnes (KI). Appraisers: John Wright, John Vicaris. Morgan Williams to administer oath.

2:400   John Warren & Edward Clarke overseers to William Browne (SM) were granted administration on his estate, for use of John & Mary Browne (orphans). Security: Thomas Covent. Appraisers: William Tettershall, Peter Mills. William Britten to administer oath.

Inventory of Henry Kent.
2:401-420   <do not exist>
2:421   List of debts: Thomas Jones, George Bussey. Amount: #10670. Appraisers: John Troster, James Humes. Date: 25 May 1668. Before: George Peake.

2:422   Accounts of Mrs. Mary Bateman. Administrator: John Boage (creditor). Payments to: Dr. Stansby, Edmund Hinchman, Pollard the cooper, Andrew Cooke, Dr. Peirce, Thomas Trayman,
2:423   Thomas Hillary, Walter Thomas, William Berry, servants from Mr. Foxhall,
2:424   John Burridge, Pricthard John & Robert,
2:425   Elisabeth Knap & Elisabeth Cooke (legacies),
2:424!   Mr. Jenifer. Further accounts. Administratrix: Mary Boage (administratrix of John Boage).
2:425!   Payments to: Mr. Abbington.
2:426   Amount: #32153. Date: 11 May 1668. Signed: Phip Calvert, Tho. Truman. Inventory delivered to Mr. Richard Perry. Date: 3 June 1668.
2:427-433 ...
2:434   Servants mentioned: Walter Thomas & John Berrudge, Thomas Pricthitt, Robert Bendall, John Myles, 2 Negro men & 1 Negro Flora (woman). Legatee: John Gittings.
2:435   List of debts: Andrew Cooke, William Berry, Mr. Preston, Chancellor.

2:436   Accounts of Robert Brookes. Payments to: Thomas Mountford, John Carye, Peter Sharpe, Tho. Brooke, William Evans, James Garner, William Bould, John Potts,

	Court Session: <no date>
2:437	John Ashcombe, Bridgett Bayes, Simon Reader. Signed: John Gittings. Additional accounts of Robert Brooke. Administratrix: Elisabeth Brooke. Payments to: Baker Brooke, Esq.,
2:438	John Gittings, Symon Reader,
2:439	John Potts. List of debts: Richard Marsham, Joseph Dawkins, James Price, George Alderson, Roger Brooke, James Veitch, James Thompson, Thomas Edwards. List of debts: James Veitch, Phillip Harrwood, Richard Drury,
2:440	Thomas Glover, William Graves, Richard Wadsworth, Thomas Houton, Charles Boteler, Demetrius Cartwright, William Wattson, Thomas Sherreden, William Herbert, David Browne, Peter Lamer, William Bryant, Andrew Dickeson, John Shinkeler, Edward Keene, William Berry, James Thompson. Additional inventory.
2:441	Amount: #33322.
	Inventory of Mr. Francis Wright (BA). Appraisers: James Frisby, John Vanhecke. Mentions: 500 a.
2:442-443	...
2:444	Amount: #85934.
2:445	Date: 22 April 1668.
	Inventory of Mr. Thomas Burditt.
2:446-448	...
2:449	Additional inventory at Accomacke.
2:450	Date: 14 May 1668. Appraisers: John Stone, Josias Lambert.
	Inventory of Mr. Thomas Addenbrooke. Date: 24 February 1667.
2:451-453	...
2:454	Appraisers: Samson Waring, William Simson. List of debts: Richard Ewen, Thomas Mills, Nathaniell Heathcoate, James Humes, Thomas Besson, John Cray, George Pascall, Robert Proctor, James Frizell. List of debts: Edward Cox, Anthony Demondidier, John Foster, Robert Love, Joseph Winslow, Thomas Waddy.
2:455	List of debts: Thomas Hinson, Joseph Wickes, Elisabeth Brewer, James Shaw, Richard Huggins, William Chandler, Robert Burle, Richard Ewen, Capt. Tully. List of debts: Thomas Bell, Henry Dabney, Morgan Williams, Thomas Spencer,

Court Session: <no date>

	Thomas Parsons, Dennis Maccounough, Ralph Hawkins. List of debts: Thomas Hinson,
2:456	Ralph Hawkins, estate of John S. Stone, Richard Preston. Amount: £279.15.1 & #48347. Signed: Thomas Elwes.
2:457	Inventory of Mr. John Thurmer. Date: 27 April 1668.
2:458-460	...
2:461	Amount: #17641. Appraisers: John Troster, Robert Heighe.
2:462	List of debts: Francis Hutchings, Capt. Waring, Henry Robinson, Roger Birch, Joseph Horsy, Patrick Allen, Walter Carr, Robert Towe, James Elton, William Sheares, William Freland, William Williamson, Thomas Lewis, George Blackiter, Edward Waring, Thomas Robinson. List of debts: Edward Lilly,
2:463	Francis Billingsley, Henry Mitchell. Amount: #35937. Signed: Thomas Elwes.
	Inventory of Elisabeth Brewer (widow). Date: 22 May 1668.
2:464-470	...
2:471	Amount: #45973. Appraisers: Robert Franklin, Will. Towlson. Before: Tho. Besson.
2:472	Will of John Browne. Date: 31 March 1668. Bequests: wife Mary Browne land, etc., then to William Hopkins for my daughter's son William Greene (under age 21),
2:473	my wife's daughter Alice Clarke, my daughter Mary Greene. Witnesses: William Hopkins, Edward Bransh, Thomas Browne.
2:474	<u>19 June 1668</u>. William Hopkins (AA) was granted administration on estate of John Browne (AA), during the minority of William Greene. Robert Burle to prove the will. Appraisers: William Crouch, Henry Cattline. Robert Burle to administer oath.
2:475	Mary Smyth executrix of estate of her husband (N) Smyth (SM) was granted continuance.

Court Session: <no date>

3:1	26 June 1650. Will of Rowland Haddaway, age 60. Date: 6 October 1667. Bequests: son Peter Haddaway land on Choptank Creek (TA), son George Haddaway 150 a. on Beare Creek on Patapsco River (BA), wife Ursula to bring up son George & daughter Margarett. Executrix: wife. Witnesses: Anthony Meayl, Richard Jones. Richard Gold who married Ursula relict of Rowland Haddaway (p, TA) was granted administration on his estate. Date: 25 June 1668.
3:2	Seth Foster to prove will by oaths of Anthony Meale & Richard Jones. Appraisers: Cuthbert Phelps, Richard Girdling. Said Foster to administer oath.
	Mattapany. 1 July 1668. Daniel Jenifer is current administrator of estate of John Nutthall (g, Cross Mannor, SM). Mentions: Thomas Sprigg who married Ellinor (daughter of said dec'd) & John Nutthall (son of said dec'd). Administration granted to said John Nutthall & said Thomas. Sprigg Nicholas Young appointed as guardian.
3:3	Mentions: James Nutthall (another son). Account of estate in hands of Daniel Jenifer. Payments to: Mary Smith executrix of
3:4	William Smith,
3:5-7	...
3:8	Mr. Thomas Allen,
3:9	Mrs. Clocker & her husband, Nicholas Rawlings,
3:10	John Macky, Rolls the taylor, executrix of Will. Champe, Robert Sly, William Lawrence, Marke Cordea,
3:11	Dr. Hough, William Calvert, Esq., the Chancellor. Amount: #20369. Signed: John Nutthall, Tho. Sprigg, Nicholas Young. Witnesses: Brian Jenifer, Cesar Wheeler.
3:12	4 July 1668. "Satisfactory inventory of said estate."
3:13	Appraisers: Thomas Innis, Daniell Clocker.

Inventory of Mr. Henry Sewall. List of debts: Michaell Cranly & Thomas Paggett

Court Session: <no date>

3:13½ for remainder of bill to William Scapes, John Tucker, John Salsbury, James Veitch, Michaell Collerton, William Reeves, Andrew Robinson, John Edmondson, Thomas Markin. Amount: #4710. Date: 11 June 1668. Appraisers: William Chaplin, Tho. Perey.

3:14 Will of John Lawson. Bequests: to be buried by wife, daughter Jean Lawson land & gift from
3:15 her godfather John Taylor, daughter Darcus Lawson then to children of Randall Hanson &
3:16 John Tunnehill, servant John Johns. Executors: Mr. Randall Hinson, Henry Hide.
3:17 <does not exist>
3:18 Witnesses: Richard Rider, Barbara Hanson. Randolph Hanson & Henry Hide (g) were granted administration on estate of John Lawson (g, SM) for use of Jane & Dorcus (orphans). Date: 2 July 1668. Appraisers: Richard Banckes, Thomas Bennett. Thomas Dent to administer oath.

3:19 Inventory of Henry Ellery.
3:20 Amount: #8406. Appraisers: John Nickall, Tho. Hutton. Date: 23 May 1668.

Inventory of James Adams. Administrator: Thomas Bowdell.
3:21 Amount: #2361. Appraisers: Thomas Perrey, Samuell Graves.

Inventory of William Browne. Appraisers: Mr. William Tettershall, Peter Mills.
3:22 Amount: #5610. Date: 18 July 1668.

14 July 1668. Thomas Oliver (shipcarpenter, KE) was granted administration on estate of Thomas Waddys (mariner, AA), as greatest creditor, for
3:23 Sarah (orphan). Appraisers: Thomas Linhecom, James White. Robert Burle (AA) to administer oath.

Court Session: <no date>

Inventory of Mr. John Nuthall (Crosse Mannor). Servants: Negro Peter & Negro Mary his wife, Charles Cavett & Elisabeth his wife & youngest child, Negro William, Negro Robert, Thomas, Mary (age 15), Sarah, Elisabeth, Richard,

3:24 Grace, Robert Large (English man).
3:25-26 ...
3:27 List of debts: Mr. Daniel Jenifer, Thomas Wynn, William Calvert, Esq., George Wright,
3:28 John England. Amount: £624.0.6. Date: 15 July 1668. Appraisers: Thomas Innes, Daniel Clocker.

Marke Cordea (innholder, SM) was granted administration on estate of Thomas Edwards (p, SM). Date: 13 July 1668. Security: Thomas Courtney. Appraisers: Thomas Wynne, Christopher Hall.

3:29 Inventory of Mr. Richard Collett.
3:30 ...
3:31 Servants: Mary Hubdon, Luke Porkeson (boy).
3:32 Amount: #26653. List of debts: Anthony Calloway, John Pearce, Nathaniell Heathcoate, John Anderton. Amount: #14876. List of debts: John Smith, George Richardson, Maharshalal Hasbazdier, Richard Deavor, William Wattson, Samue Goldsmith,
3:33 Henry Hare, Henry Hare on assignment from John Pitt, James Ringold, Thomas Vigris. Amount: #9116. List of debts: Tho. Andrews, Maj. Tho. Brooks, Richard Bennitt, Enoch Compt, Demetrius Cartwright, Charles Calvert, Esq., Philip Calvert, Esq., John Cobreth, Tho. Chanels, George Day, Edward Alberry, Edward Goad, Hugh Sherrwood, Francis Hutchinson, Henry Huff, John Holland, John Hambleton, Joseph Horsley, Major Ingram, Daniell Jenifer, William Kent,
3:34 William Lawrence, Edward Loyd, Richard Meekings, John Miller, Thomas Newman, Abraham Rouse, Francis Ringold, John Rapier, Percivall Read, John Smith, John Storrip, William Smith, Thomas Taylor, William Willett, John Wiseman. Amount: #10523. List of debts: Simon Carpenter,

Court Session: <no date>

3:35   Marke Cordea, John Edmondson, William Gray, Tymothy Goodridge, John Hockings, Francis Hopewell, John Jarboe, Thomas James, Tho. Losy, John Larkins, William Leeds, James Lewis, Edward Lee, Thomas Mitchell, Henry Mitchell, William Moffett, John Piggott, Benjamin Rozier, Capt. Thomas Stockett, Mathew Stone, William Stanley, Dr. Tilghman, Mr. Jerome White. Amount: #8312. Date: 10 July 1668. Appraisers: Tho. Taylor, John Halfhead.

3:36   Inventory of Anthony Purses. Appraisers: Nathaniell Evitts, Edward Rogers. Date: 13 August 1668.

3:37   List of debts: William Baggley, Richard Foxen.

3:38   18 August 1668. Anthony Congo administrator of John Pert took oath before Samuell Chew.

3:39   Inventory of John Peart (AA). Administrator: Anthony Conngo (AA). List of debts: Anthony Congo payable in Bristoll. Amount: £40.0.0. Signed: Anthony Gongo.

3:40-99 <does not exist>

3:100   Inventory of Mr. John Lawson (Popler Hill). Appraisers: Mr. Richard Banckes, Thomas Bennett. Date: 14 July 1668.

3:101-102 ...

3:103   List of debts: Philip Calvert, Walter Peake. Amount: #17815. Date: 5 September 1668.

3:104   Thomas Doxey who married Mary relict of John Biscooe (p, SM) was granted administration on his estate. Mentions (orphans): Thomas, John, Joseph, James, Jonathon, Hannah. Security: Richard Moy. Appraisers: Thomas Simmons, Joseph Brought. Capt. Nicholas Young to administer oath.

3:105   Inventory of Francis Barnes (KI). Administratrix: Issabella Barnes (relict). Appraisers: John Vicaris (g),

Court Session: <no date>

3:106 John Wright. Date: 22 July 1668.
3:107 ...
Servants: Andrew, Francis Ellis. List of debts: William Lacy, John Tassell, Rice Cookeman, William Head,
3:108 Thomas Ringold, Arthur Gum, George Yates, Nicholas Pickard, Anthony Purse, Thomas Hinson, Sr., Isacck Winchester. Amount: #85154. Signed: John Vicars, John Wright.

17 September 1668. William Hopkins administrator of John Browne was granted continuance.

3:109 Inventory of William Orchard Appraisers: William Hollis, Thomas Overton. Date: 15 July 1668. Amount: #3650.

3:110 Thomas Cooper (mariner, master of ship "John & Christian" at Patuxent River, of Bristoll) was granted administration on estate of Thomas Freeman (merchant, Bristoll). Security: Henry Hosier (merchant, Bristoll), Sampson Waring, William Hopkins (p). Appraisers (TA): Henry Hosier, John Richardson. Thomas Powell to administer oath. Appraisers (SO): Roger Woollford, James Davies. Capt. William Thorne to administer oath.

3:111 Randall Revell, age 57, deposed that Mr. Thomas Freeman was sick & desired that Mr. Cooper should look after his business. Date: 12 September 1668.

3:112 Account of orphans of Mr. Cotes. Date: 8 June 1668. Amount: #5576. Signed: Luke Gardnor.

3:113 10 October 1668. Will of John Taylor (CA). Bequests: son John Taylor 400 a. "Taylor's Folly", daughter Elisabeth Taylor 200 a. on Oyster Creek "Armestrong's Quarter", servant John Smith. Mentions: land at Trasquaking. Overseers: William Robson, Richard Hooper.
3:114 Witnesses: Richard Miller, Thomas Cobham, Godfry Cam. Will proved at

Court Session: <no date>

Mattapenny: 22 September 1668.

3:115 William Robinson & Richard Hooper were granted administration on said estate. William Robinson is overseer of
3:116 John & Elisabeth Taylor. Date: 23 September 1668. Appraisers: William Chaplyn, Richard Miller. Raymond Stapleford to administer oath.

3:117 Mr. Thomas Taylor (merchant) is a debtor to Francis Swanston. Accounts. Payments to: Mr. Thomas Taylor, Mr. Rowsby, John Creacroft. Amount: #1970. Date: 24 September 1668. Signed: Fran. Swanson.
3:118 Francis Swanston (chirurgeon, CV) was granted administration on estate of Thomas Taylor (merchant, London & CV). Security: James Shacklady, Appraisers: Christopher Rowsby, John Halfehead. Francis Anketill to administer oath.

Inventory of George Bussey. Appraisers: John Tawney, Tobias Mills. Date: 23 June 1668.
3:119-120 ...
3:121 Amount: #15116.
3:122 List of debts: Peter Lemall, John Biggs, Edward Armstrong, Walter Carr, Thomas Preston, Tobias Norton, Thomas Large, Numan Barber, William Reave, Robert Blinckhorne, William Mills, George Hardesty, Paul Bussey, Valentine Hudson, John Stansby, Gwy White, Nicholas Furms, John Leach, John Norwood, Josias Cooper, Griffen George, Andrew Marear, Thomas Towe, Thomas Kades, Isaack Marshall, Davy OBowen, John Winall, John Watkins, William Pritchett,
3:123 John Hollins, Thomas Jones, William Jones, Richard Moore, William Williams, Edward Cowdery, William House, William Chaplin, Joseph Mooreley, Patrick Due, Henry Coxe, Thomas Edwards, Charles Boteler, George Alderson, Mr. Ancton Comer, James Veatch, William Parker, Mathew Stone, Major Brookes, Peter Sharpe, Thomas Kemp, Thomas Mannyng, John Hance, Francis Spence, Arthur Ludford, John Panther, Thomas How, Henry Darnell, John Boage, William Smith (SM),

Court Session: <no date>

3:124 John Grammer, Stephen Venson, William Illingsworth, Richard Keene, Richard Bayley, William Herbert, Andrew Cooke, Mr. Staplefort, John Gittings, Cuthbert Phenix, Richard Webb, Peter Archer, Thomas Sprigg, George Whittle, Tobias Milles, James Tompson (Petuxent), Joseph Backer, William Adams, Joseph Tille, Joseph Horsley, William Bryant, Timothy Gunter, John Brooke, Robert Whittle, John Moreram, William Worging, William King, William Dorington, Thomas Perry, Samuell Taylor, Alexander Magrowder, Francis Billingsly, John Russell (Patuxent), William Enis, Demetrius Cartwright, Charles Brooke, Thomas Sherriden, Robert Brooke, Dr. Huffe, John Hambleton, John Rawlings, Thomas Pagett, Francis Brooke,

3:125 George Pake, Captaine Burges, Thomas Binckes, Richard Collett, Francis Leigh, Francis Swenfen, William Bold, Henry Robenson, Francis Dorington, Francis Gell, Raphaell Haywood, Hugh Stanley, William Stinett, William Barnett, Richard Freeman, Michaell Tawney, Henry Hooper. List of debts: John Welch, Arthur Thompson, William Gray, James Courtney, William Lizman, Robert Tow, Timothy Goodridge, James Elton, James Jolley.

3:126 List of bills: Richard Durin, William Turner, Robert Chisecke, Thomas Pagett, Neman Beale, Francis Swenfen, Thomas Tove, John Mason, John Saunder, William Barnett, Thomas How, Henry Mitchell, John Russell, Richard More, Samuell Goosey, Jeferry Sondford, James Cullins, Dr. Brookes, John Tucker, Thomas Boudle, John Skinkler, James Tompson. Amount: #30956.

3:127 Inventory of Capt. William Smith (SM). Date: 11 August 1667.
3:128-136 ...
3:137 Mentions: plantation on the Eastern Shore.
3:138 Appraisers: Daniell Clocker, Thomas Wynne.
3:139 Additional inventory. Amount: #206300.
3:140 List of debts: Robert Sampson, John Davis, Sr., Lodowick Martin, Robert

Court Session: <no date>

3:141 Corke, Thomas Harper, John Prowse, Thomas Wright, Daniel Devine, Thomas Ward, William Thomas, Bryan Daley, Thomas Andrewes, Richard Moy, Thomas Vaughan, Thomas Covant, William Watts, Francis Richardson, Joseph Hackney, Thomas Pritchard, Isaacke Bedlow, William Hampstead, William Pettipoole, Thomas Bryan, Abraham Rowse, Marmaduke Semme, Christopher Owen, Thomas Seamans, Nicholas Young, John Smith, Peter Watts, Daniel Grimes, William Cole, Thomas Hinton, John Benson, Mathias Decosta, John Garms, William Ososton, Richard Sleppey, William Hollingsworth, William Lucus, John Beale, Thomas Doxey, James Lewis, Evan Lewis, Thomas Hughes, William Bretton, Pope Alvey, Thomas Okeley, Joseph Brough, William Newport, George Walker, Walter Pake, Thomas Courtney, Dr. John Morecroft, John Brooke (chirur.), John Stansby (chir.), Charles Boteler, George Panther, John Davis, John Hambleton, Gwy White, Sibill Six, Thomas How, John Wiseman, Thomas Demery, Francis Swinfen,

3:142 George Beckwith, Richard Collett, Henry Pope, Dr. Stansbey, John Startup, Robert Tylor, John Rawlings, William Smiton, Sibill Six, Richard Collett & Francis Gunby, William Berrey, Henry Sewall, William Meere, John Grammer, Demetrius Cartwright, John Tucker, John Hollins, James Cullinnes, Thomas Frost, William Turpen, Thomas Pagett, Joseph Horsley, Henry Mitchell, Thomas Marshall, William King, William Moffett, John Perie, John Nevell, William Ireland, Robert Troop & Nich. Emanson & Thomas Allanson, Capt. James Neale, Capt. Hugh Oneale,

3:143 Morgan Jones, John Dustan, George Attkins, John Browne, Alexander Davis, Miles Chafe, Robert Taylor, John Wright, Nicholas Emanson, Benjamin Rozer, James Johnson, George Harris, Toby Wells, Izabella Barnes, Edmond Benton, Thomas Ingram, Ann Mott, Hubbert Lambert, Col. Lewis Stockett, Robert Peca, John Gray, Robert Lloyd, Anthony Gungo, Richard Hill, Henry Stockett, George Yate, Robert Burley, George Pascall, George Sanghier, Henry Goodrick & John Doppen,

Court Session: <no date>

3:144 Henry Goodrick, Richard Deavour, Thomas Vigris, William Stevens, George Smith, Jenken Price, George Mitchell, John Hillyard, John Anderson, Capt. William Thorne, David Jones, William Leeds, Timothy Goodridge, John Eason, Thomas Vaughan, Thomas Hinson, John Hunt, Joseph Inglsbey, Hopkin Davis, Miell Basey, Anthony Mayle, Robert Willen, George Watts, Thomas Lewis, John Anderton, Michaell Basey, John Pitt, Henry Parker, Isaack Winslow, James Ringold, Samuell Winsslow, Richard Bennett, Esq., Henry Ward, Godfrey Bayly, Augustine Herman, Roger Shacocke,

3:145 Philip Hollegar & George Wilson, James Jane, John Rhodes, Tho. Waley, Tho. Bloyse, William Stevens, Edmund Beachamp, Thomas Burditt, Robert Downes, Thomas Allanson, Tho. Mathews. Further list of debts: Zachariah Killam (?), John Gooding, Thomas Owen, William Williams, Edward Clarke, Robert Joyner, Capt. Richard Banckes, William Thelwall, William Tettershall, Pope Alvey, Daniel Smith, Thomas Simpson, Dr. Jasper Gnerin (?), James Bowling, Marke Phebo, Samuell Brorkers, Robert Prowse, Thomas Warner, William Hillingsworth, John Harrington,

3:146 Stanup Roberts, Robert Hatton, William Watts, Francis Moore, Robert Cager, Thomas Browne, Thomas Bennett, Edward Lee, Elias Beech, Robert King, Henry Warren, Daniel Clocker, Philip Luen, Thomas Dent, Philip Calvert, Esq., Thomas Cager, Peter Dagger, Jerome White, Esq., Robert Page, Walter Pake, Barnaby Jackson, William Calvert, Esq., William Kennady, Mr. Henry Hyde, Thomas Hinton, Nicholas Young, Richard Foster, John Nutthall, Sr., William Marlowe, Robert Grimes, William Champe, Henry Darnell, Thomas Melton, John Davis, Jr., Curtis Fletcher, Andrew Bashaw, John Lewling,

3:147 George Charlesworth, Percivall Read, John Williams, Dr. John Morecroft, Thomas Wynne, Richard Rustell, Francis Hill, Robert Jones, Thomas Beedle, Thomas James, Andrew Woodberry, Mr.

Page 151

Court Session: <no date>

3:148 Robert Slye, Lt. Col. Jarboe, John Reynolds, Thomas Hatton, Thomas Courtney, William Pettipoole, Joseph Brough, James Lewis, Henry Mathews, Mathias Decoster, Capt. Luke Gardner, John Wynne, Thomas Ward, Thomas Hughes, Will. Lawrence, Thomas Griffin, Thomas Lampen, Thomas Vaughan, John Prowse, George Marshall, Henry Pennington, Thomas Loker, Martin Kirke, Henry Smith, Daniel Devine, William Black, Thomas Mitchell, George Gooding, Thomas Wattkins, Leonard Greene, Nicholas Salsby, Edmond Lister, John Mathewes, John Camell, William Cole, Thomas Payne, James Edmonds, John Archer, Robert Macklyn, Peter Mills, Randall Hanson, Thomas Lomax, George Walker, William Newport, George Charlesworth, Peter Carwardine, John Davis, Jr., Richard Lloyd, William Asbiston, Walter Hall, Col. William Evans, William Cattland, Robert Hatton, John Blomfeild, John Wayhopp, John Nutthall, Marmaduke Semme, Robert Corke, John Charlesworth, Thomas Melton, Henry Banister, Thomas Clarke, Mrs. Bateman,

3:149 George Read, John Elly, Patrick Mulleken, Mr. Broome, John Read, Hugh Johnson, Thomas Perie, Patricke Hinderson, William Bradley, George Bussey, John Potts, Richard Smith, Edward Isaack, Edward Richardson, Edward Perren, Thomas Preston, James Veitch, Raphaell Haywood, Stephen Benson, John Hamblton, Mathew Smith, Isaack Abraham, Christopher Humphreyes, Francis Hutchings, John Grammer, Valentine Hudlestone, Edward Armstrong, John Pollard, Thomas Booth, Thomas Studd, Andrew Cooke, Christopher Rowsby, Thomas Pagett, Mathew Stone, Hugh Stanly, Thomas Tovey, Robert Tylor, William Kent,

3:150 William Meare, Sampson Waren, William Gray, Dr. John Stansby, William Chaplin, Henry Sewall, Richard Bayley, Richard Meekins, William Moffett, Dr. Swanston, John Halfehead, Henry Hough (chirurgeon), William Groome, Demetrius Cartwright, Mr. Thomas Truman & uxor, William Berry 80, Charles Boteler, Peter

Court Session: <no date>

3:151 Bayward, John Pattin, Alexander Standish, doctor of the ship "Walsingham", Abdelo Martin, William Dorrington, John Brooke, Jr., Thomas Sprigg, John Gittings, Thomas Mannyng, Joseph Horsley, Raymond Staplefort, Katherine Stevens, William Brooke, Richard Collett, Thomas How, Thomas Taylor, Thomas Allibane, Walter Greene, George Aldridge, William Storey, John Wattkins, Francis Richardson, Samuell Sewall, Thomas Barbery, Thomas Bowdle, Thomas Sherriden, Dr. John Pearce, Lt. General, James Walker, Arthur Turner, John Hatch, George Thompson, Francis Fookes, Edward Scounn, James Bowlin, Bartholomew Coates, Thomas Hussey, Richard Stone, John Lewger, George Harris, Dr. Thomas Mathews, Samuell Crostley, Mrs. Long, Benjamin Rozer, Capt. Hugh Oneale, Richard Broughton, Capt. Josias Fendall, Richard Randall, John Sharman, Francis Pope, Stephen Mountague, Jonathon Marler, John Dowglas, Edmund Lindsey,

3:152 Col. Gerrard Fooke, Henry Adams, William Marshall, Mr. Goodrick, Walter Beane, George Newman, Dr. Richard Tilghman, Roby Wells, Moses Stagwell, John Wright, Thomas Marsh, Robert Lloyd, Robert Bennett, Edward Ayres, Robert Peca, Henry Perpoint, Richard Foster, Paull Marsh, Thomas Stockett, Richard Ewen, Cornelius Howard, John Burridge, John Webster, Thomas Thurstone, John Ewen, Thomas Vigris, Nathaniell Heathcott, Capt. Thomas Stockett, Anthony Mayle, Stephen Gearing, Joseph Inglesbey, Mr. Woollman, Alexander Maxwell, John Miller, Robert Wellen, Jonathon Browne,

3:153 Andrew Skinner, Edward Roe, Henry Tripp, Thomas Markin, John Morgan, John Scott, John Barnes & Tho. Homper, Richard Cottmer, Miell Basy, David Dale, Henry Coursey, Esq., James Ringold, Thomas Lewis, Henry Parker, Seth Foster, Christopher Oldfeild, John Anderton, Timothy Goodridge, John Edmondson, John Pitt, Richard Booker, Col. Nath. Uty, Richard Bennett, Esq., John Collett, Mary Games, Richard Lewes, George

Court Session: <no date>

3:154 Willson, Charles James, Francis Moore, John Vanhacke, Jacob Michaelson, Randall Revell, Edmond Beauchampe, Jenkin Price, Samuell Long, William Coleburne, Richard Stevenson, John Anderson, John Avery, Nehemiah Coventon, Thomas Clarke, Thomas Kerney, William Stephens, Robert Jones, John Garner, Mr. Mees, James Howbacke, Joseph Harcott, Thomas Wharton, John Raven, James Hawly, John Fountaine, John Smith, Justinian Gerrard, Richard Helding, James Petekin, Anthony Linton, John Foxall, George Wale, William Denly, Mr. William Shacerly, Mr. Robert Starr. Further list of debts: Henry Keene, William Argent, William Price, John Booth, Francis Browne, John Merryweather, Thomas Heylens, Henry Hare,

3:155 Jacob Michaelson, Francis Riggs, Cornelius Verroff, John Powick, Vincent Acheson, Gilbert Anderson, Dr. John Percefor, John Smith. Further list of debts: John Hopewell, Francis Taylor, Francis Carpenter, Henry Roch, Paul Jacob, William Morgan, William Thornbury, Barnaby Edly, Mr. Warding, John Lumbrozo, Thomas Bradley, Mr. Tydder, James Jolly, Thomas Haylens, Robert Skinner, William Price, Thomas the tincker, Christopher Walter, Governor of Delaware, Mr. Hopkins, Mr. Robert Williams, William Smith, Mr. Trippen, William Jennyngs, Mr. Foster, Thomas Martyn,

3:156 Mr. Selleck, Mr. Witherall, Mr. Vaughan, Mr. Brundally, Thomas Markum, Henry Butler, Mr. Turner, Mr. Tuck, Mr. Clement, John Demery, John Jones, Tho. the Governor's seaman, Thomas Ireton, Thomas Ashbrooke, Robert Ratcliffe, Hugh Nash, Mathew Goldsmith, Lawrence Simmons, Thomas Meere, John Knapp, Nicholas Bentley, Thomas Haynes, Henry Clay, Jeremyah Wytherell, Mr. Woodbury, Thomas Hanck, James Price, Dr. Hacke, David Anderson, Mr. Wells, Francis Towneley, Richard Sherrin, William Argent, John Dangly, Henry Osterlin, William Nevell, Maximilan Pinson, John Carrington, Thomas Middleton,

Court Session: <no date>

- 3:157 Isaack Bedlow, John Balley, Samuell Pricklow, Edward Hoskins, Joseph Gardner, John Merryweather, William Price, John Booth, Samuell Sloper, Joseph Gunnery, David Jones, Thomas Frost, Abraham Rowse, John Smith, Accoliah Bridges, Cornelius Verroof, Thomas Willen, Mr. Gard (?), Alexander Davis, John Hopkins, John Carpenter, Thomas Sherredin, Thomas Hatton,
- 3:158 Katherine Stevens (administratrix of Robert Stevens), Nicholas Gwither, Richard Collett for bill in hands of John Halfehead,
- 3:159 Thomas Bradley, Thomas Perrey (VA), William Price. Amount: #717236. Accepted by: Mary Jenifer (alias Mary Smith).
- 3:160 Inventory of William Simson. Amount: #4373. Appraisers: John Troster, Robert Heighe. Date: 6 June 1668 before George Peake.
- 3:161 10 October 1668. Rebecca Burton relict of Edmond Burton (KE) was granted administration on his estate. Appraisers: George Goldhacke, Mathew Read. Capt. John Vicaris to administer oath.
- 3:162 Will of Thomas Bull. Bequests: son Thomas Bull, wife. In case of her death & that of my son John, estate to be divided between her children by her previous marriage & my father, brothers, & sister. Executors (on behalf of my son): brother-in-law Samuel Lucas (baker, Dower) & John Marsh (woolcomer, Dower) in ENG, Mr. Walter Beane & Mr. John Coates & Mr. John Bowles in MD.
- 3:163 Date: 15 August 1668. Witnesses: Mewell Hussey, Stephen Tully, Joseph Horton. Will proved on 29 September 1668 by Mewell Hussey & Joseph Horton.
- 3:164 21 October 1668. Walter Beane, John Courts, & William Boules were granted administration on estate of Thomas Bull (ENG, MD). Appraisers: Nehemiah Blackston, Thomas Lomax (g). Humphry Warren (g) to

Court Session: <no date>

administer oath.

3:165 Inventory of John Taylor.
...
3:166 Amount: #24870. Appraisers: William Chaplin, Richard Miller.

3:167 Inventory of John Terry. Date: 2 September 1668. Amount: #2130. Signed: Sam. Gouldsmith.

3:168 Inventory of Benjamin Furby. Date: 2 September 1668.
3:169 Amount: #7640. Signed: Sam. Gouldsmith.

3:170 Inventory of Mathew Gouldsmith. Date: 2 September 1668. Mentions: 200 a. Amount: #19596. Signed: Sam. Gouldsmith.

3:171 Inventory of Rowland Haddaway (TA). Appraisers: Cuthbert Philips, Richard Girdling. Amount: #11396.

3:172 Inventory of Thomas Taylor (merchant). Appraisers: Christopher Rousby, John Halfehead. Date: 21 October 1668. Amount: #821.

3:173 Accounts of Rice Jones. Payments to: for wife, John Cane, Samuell Dobson, Mr. Thomas Gerrard, John Foster, Mr. Hall, John Smith. Amount: #10211.

3:174 30 October 1668. Lodowick Williams was granted administration on estate of William Thompson (BA), as joint partner. Surety: William Osborne. Appraisers: William Osborne, William Hollis. Capt. John Collier to administer oath.

3:175 3 November 1668. Henry Hawkins (TA) was granted administration on estate of William Snaggs (TA). Appraisers: John Scott, Francis Bellus. Mr. Richard Woollman to administer oath.

3:176 Elisabeth Barber relict of Luke Barber (Phizitian, SM) was granted administration on his estate.

Court Session: <no date>

3:177   11 November 1668. James Thompson (g, CV) was granted administration on estate of Robert Philips (CV), as greatest creditor. Appraisers: John Harris, Edward Pirke. Charles Brooke (g) to administer oath.

3:178   Will of Thomas Martin (p, Herring Creek, AA). Bequests: daughter Mary Martin plantation 200 a., daughters Mary Martin (under age 16) & Sarah Martin (under age 16). Executors: Jeremiah Guleman, Marke Clare. Mentions: servant Edward Mason.

3:179   Date: 26 March 1667. Witnesses: Nathan Smith, John Sollers. Will proved on 11 May 1668 by Nathan Smith. Will proved on 12 May 1668 by John Sollers.

3:180   Marke Clare (carpenter, AA) was granted administration on said estate. Security: Joseph Chew. Appraisers: Joseph Chew, John Covell. Samuell Chew (g) to administer oath.

19 November 1668. Mary Clarke relict of Mathew Clarke (p, AA) was granted administration on his estate.

3:181   Appraisers: Richard Mosse, Richard Ellingsworth. Robert Burle to administer oath.

Will of William Dawson (p, TA). Date: 19 December 1666. Bequests: son William Dawson

3:182   all tobacco due in VA, daughter Jane, Anthony Cox (son of Joseph Cox) 100 a., Samuell Abbott (son of Samuell Abbott) 100 a., daughter Joyce, son Anthony Dawson & Samuell Abbott, son Anthony Dawson. Executor: son Anthony Dawson. Witnesses: Edward Roe, John Richason, John Ingrum.

3:183   Will proved on 21 July 1668 by Edward Roe & John Richardson.

Inventory of Mr. Thomas Letchworth.

3:184   ...
3:185   Amount: #13823. Appraisers: Arthur Ludford, Tho. Boudell. Mentions: wife of Mr. Letchworth, John Potts, his son (unnamed).

Court Session: <no date>

3:186	Inventory of John Biscoe (SM). Date: 15 October 1668. Appraisers: Joseph Brough, Thomas Seaman. ...
3:187	List of debts: Bryan Daley, Richard Moy, Martin Kerke, Henry Pennington, Daniel Deeme, Fobber Roberts, John Stephens, Robert King. Amount: #21405.
3:188	Inventory of Edmond Burton (KE). Date: 12 November 1668.
3:189	List of debts: Francis Morlin. Appraisers: George Gouldhawk, Maty Read.
3:190-191	Inventory of Mr. Thomas Bull. Appraisers: Mr. Thomas Lomax, Nehemiah Blackiston. ...
3:192	List of debts: Peter Roberts, Mr. Thomas Lomax, James Walker, Edward Swann, Edward Philpott, Alexander Simpson, Thomas Gibson, Edward Knight, Alexander Smith, John Court, John Richards, James Lindsey. List of debts: Mr. William Marshall,
3:193	Mr. Walter Beane, John Court for George Holmes, Richard Morris, James Johnson, Benjamin Rozier. Amount: #34783.
3:194	5 December 1668. Accounts of Arthur Turner (CH). Administrator: Walter Beane (CH). Amount of inventory: #12917. Payments to: accountant,
3:195	Francis Pope, Robert Yates, James Bowling, Benjamin Rozer, James Walter, Thomas Throughgood, John Morris. Amount: #12890.
3:196	Witness: Humphry Warren. Date allowed: 8 December 1668.
3:197	Said Walter Bayne granted discharge.
3:198	Inventory of John Jones (AA). Appraisers: Henry Stockett, William Slade. Date: 3 October 1666. Servant mentioned: Roger Roberts. List of debts: Stephen Whiteman, Ralph Masley, George Collens, William Price, William Saffnie, Richard Leake, Peter Jones.
3:199	Amount: #7916. Accounts. Administrator: Joseph Gundry (merchant, AA).
3:200	Payments to: Joseph Gundry, John Norwood, James Rigby, Richard Leake,

Court Session: <no date>

3:201 Peter Jones, Stephen Withams, William Saphines, Ralph Masley, George Collins, Capt. Stockett. Amount: #8000. Discharge was granted.

3:202
3:203 10 December 1668.
Edward Beetle (BA) was granted administration on estate of Garratt Rutten (BA). Appraisers: Mr. John Collett, Henry Haslewood. Capt. Howell to administer oath.

3:204 Oliver Hollaway son of Oliver Hollaway (AA) was granted administration on his father's estate. Security: Mr. John Morecroft. Appraisers: John Norwood, Mathew Howard. Robert Burle to administer oath.

3:205 Inventory of George Richardson (TA). Administrator: Timothy Goodridge. Servants mentioned: Miles Waterline (boy), Jeane Crispen. Amount: #11050. Jacob Francis deposed.

3:206 List of debts: Thomas Powell, (N) Chatterline, George Watt, Thomas Clarke, John Ferson & Bartholomew Mills, Jonathon Coventrey, John Engrum, Gabriell Bartle, George Anderson, Francis Armstrong. Signed: Simon Richardson, John Richardson.

3:207 Amount: #2000. Date: 25 February 1667. Appraisers: Will. Ewen, Jos. Horsley.

3:208 13 December 1668. Continuance was granted to Tym. Goodridge on estate of George Richardson (TA).

Accounts of Thomas Leitchworth (CV). Administratrix: Elisabeth Leitchworth (widow, CV). Amount of inventory: #13823.
3:209 Payments to: Charles Boteler. Amount: #1616.
3:210 Date: 14 December 1668.

3:211 29 December 1668. John Hitchinson (CH) was granted administration on estate of John Allen (merchant, CH), as greatest creditor. Security: Thomas Mathewes. Appraisers: Henry Adams, Ignatius Causeene. Thomas Mathewes (g) to

Court Session: <no date>
administer oath.

3:212 Will of John Hopper (p). Date: 20 December 1668.
3:213 Executrix: wife Dorothy. Bequests: wife, Nathaniell Padifitt, Elisabeth Tipping the younger, John Hilton. Overseers: Patrick Forrest, John Macky.
3:214 Witnesses: Curtis Fletcher, Sam. Dickinson, William Howell. Will proved by Samuell Dickeson & William Howell on 28 January 1668.

3:215 3 February 1668. Richard Lloyd was granted administration on estate of John Hopper. Security: Patrick Forrest. Appraisers: George Macall, Peter Watts. Mr. Thomas Dent to administer oath.

3:216 Robert Blinckhorne the younger (son of Robert Blinckhorne the elder (dec'd)) was granted administration on his estate. Appraisers: Joseph Horsley, John Nevill. William Groome to administer oath.

3:217 Thomas Cooper administrator of Thomas Freeman was granted continuance. Date: 26 December 1668.

Inventory of Mathew Clarke. Date: 30 January 1668. Appraisers: William Slayd, James Lyle.
3:218 ...
3:219 Mentions: my brother William Meriken. Amount: #28183. Appraisers: William Sleed, James Kyll.
3:220 Oaths administered to: Mary Clarke administratrix of her husband Mathew Clarke (AA); William Slayd & James Lyle in lieu of Richard Mosse (ill) & Richard Ellingsworth (left county). Date: 29 January 1668. Signed: Robert Burle.

3:221 Mary Vaughan relict of Robert Vaughan (KE) was granted administration on his estate. Appraisers: Toby Wells, Arthur Wright. Morgan Williams to administer oath.

3:222 15 February 1668. Mary relict of Henry Franckain (CH) was granted

Court Session: <no date>

administration on his estate. Security: Richard Fooke. Appraisers: John Ward, Francis Thortine. Zachary Ward to administer oath.

Inventory of William Thompson. Appraisers: William Hollis, William Osbourne. Date: 14 December 1668. Amount: #4070.

3:223 Will of George Black (St. George's). Executrix: wife Ann Black. Overseers for wife & children: Patrick Forrest, John Mockey. Bequests: Harbert Howman, John Mackey. Date: 18 November 1668. Witnesses: Curtis Fletcher, William Greene. Will proved by Curtis Fletcher & William Green on 11 February 1668.

Inventory of Thomas Martin. Appraisers: John Cobreth, Joseph Chew.
3:224 ...
3:225 Amount: #24162. Signed: Joseph Chew, John Cobreath.

3:226 Will of William Evans (SM). Bequests: pastor of Roman Catholic church at New Towne, goddaughter Mary Mansell (under age 21), godson William Green (under age 21), wife Elisabeth Evans. Executrix: wife. Witnesses: James Martin, Will. Asiter.

1 April 1669. Margarett Burridge relict of John Burridge (g, AA) was granted administration on his estate. Appraisers: Henry Stockett, Thomas Meech. Samuel Chew (g) to administer oath.

Inventory of Mr. Thomas Freeman (merchant, Bristoll). Appraisers: James Davis, Roger Woolford. Capt. William Thorne had administered oath.
3:227 ...
3:228 Mentions: Mr. Revell. Servant mentioned: Dennis Holland.
3:229-230 ...
3:231 Signed: Roger Wolford, James Daves. Additional inventory. Appraisers: Henry Hosier (Bristoll), John Richardson (p). Thomas Powell had administered oath.

Court Session: <no date>

3:232   Amount: #44146. Found in the hands of John Edmondson. Signed: John Edmondson, Will. Hopkins.

3:233   List of debts: Thomas Cooper.

Will of George Renolds (Brittons Bay). Bequests: wife Dorothy "Fox" 100 a., Thomas Covent,

3:234   wife "Bennitt's Purchase" 100 a. & "Tomson" 100 a. Executrix: wife. Overseer: Col. Evans. Date: 11 January 1668. Signed: Geo. Reynolds. Witnesses: John Browne, Thomas Bennet, Robert Joyner.

3:235   Will of Francis Armstrong (TA). Date: 18 February 1668. Bequests: son Francis Armstrong land near John Edmondson, son Philemon Armstrong land at fork at head of my creek & "Armstrong's White Marsh" 200 a., daughter Elisabeth Armstrong "Bette's Cove" & land on St. Michael's River, daughter-in-law Cornely Abrahamson land adjoining the fork, William Bennett,

3:236   mother-in-law, wife Francis Armstrong plantation. Overseers: William Hemsley, William Bennett. Executrix: wife. Witnesses: Patrick Browne, Francis Churchyard. Will proved by Francis Churchyard & William Hemsley on 13 October 1669.

Inventory of John Barnes (TA). Appraisers: Richard Jones, John Singleton. Date: 29 July 1668.

3:237   List of debts: Henry Clay, Mr. William Coursey administrator of John Morgan. Signed: R. Tilghman. Amount: #4922.

3:238   Inventory of John Morgan. Appraisers: Stephen Tully, William Hemsley. Date: 26 June 1668. List of debts: John Edmondson, Jonathon Hopkinson, William Denby. Amount: #12340.

Inventory of Henery Frankrume (CH). Appraisers: John Ward, Francis Thorntine. Mr. Zachary Wade had administered oath. Date: 3 March 1668.

3:239   List of debts: William Allen, Mr. Allenson, Francis Thorntine, Thomas

Court Session: <no date>

3:240　　Bayley. Amount: #1080. Signed: Francis Thornton, John Warde.

10 May 1669. Timothy Goodridge administrator of George Richardson was granted continuance.

3:241　　Inventory of Robert Blinckhorne.
3:242　　Amount: #25090. Date: 27 March 1669. Appraisers: Jos. Horsley, John Nevell.

Inventory of George Richardson. Administrator: Timothy Goodridge.
3:243　　Amount: #5400. Appraisers: John Richardson, Simond Richisson.

Inventory of William Snaggs. Appraisers: Francis Bellows, John Scott. Date: 8 November 1668.
3:244　　List of debts: Daniell Walker. Amount: #3502. Date filed: 7 April 1669.

3:245　　Inventory of John Hopper.
3:246　　List of debts: Mr. Nettles, Mr. Vanswaden. Appraisers: George Mackall, Peter Watts.

3:247　　Inventory of Capt. Robert Vaughan (KI). Appraisers: Arthur Wright, Tobias Wells. Date: 22 February 1668.
3:248　　Amount: #46112.
3:249　　Additional inventory. List of debts: Thomas Linstead, Roger Baxter, Richard Pether. Amount: #7393. Additional inventory. List of debts: William Herd, Andrew Anderton, John Grimston, John Spurdance. Amount: #2229.

Inventory of Thomas Edwards. Appraisers: Tho. Wynne, Christopher Hall.

3:250　　William Moffett vs. William Dorrington administrator of Henry Sewall. Date: 3 June 1669.

3 June 1669. Rebecca Davis relict of Edward Davis (TA) was granted administration on his estate. Surety: Christopher Denning. Henry Coursey (g) to administer oath. Appraisers: Tho.

Court Session: <no date>

South, Richard Tilghman. William Coursey (g) to administer oath.

4 June 1669. John Bennett was granted administration on estate of John Parr (CV). Surety: John Ramsey. Appraisers: Robert Height, John Toster. George Peake (g) to administer oath.

3:251 Will of William Coale (p, St. Jerome's, SM). Date: 21 March 1669. Bequests: daughter Sarah Beech wife of Elias Beech, wife Sarah Coale, sons Richard & William & John & Charles & daughter Mary Coale.

3:252 Executrix: wife. Witnesses: Thomas Paine, Tho. Griffin. Will proved by Thomas Griffin on 17 July 1669 before John Blomfeild. Sarah Cole was granted administration on estate of William Cole. Security: Thomas Griffin. Appraisers: Thomas Griffin, Henry Penington. Nicholas Young to administer oath.

Inventory of John Burridge.
3:253-254 ...
3:255 Mentions: widow. List of debts: William Brougham, William Powell, John Evens, Will. Pierce, Sam. Pellinger, Joseph Morely, James Maxell, Edw. Parrish, Gerrard Hopkins, Tho. Ramsey, Will. Taylor, Tho. Morris (CV), Rich. Baily, Geo. Parkall, Sam. Lane, Sam. Thornbury, John Duall, Alexander Humphry, Rich. Skey, Tho. Ford,
3:256 Tho. Jones, William Connaway, John Hawkins, Tho. Morris (on the Ridge), Will. Alder, John Gunn, Will. Gunnell & James Jagger, John Hillen, Tho. Tully, Rich. Newell, Rich. Devom, Will. James, Hen. Timber, Lionell Pawly, Charles Bevrm (?), Fra. Stocket, Evan Davis, Sam. Garland, Arthur Brisco, Geo. Simmonds, Tho. Watkins, Fra. Hutchinson, John Larkin, Rich. Bedworth, Hen. Darnell, William Harris, Rob. Smith, Edw. Allily, John Watkins, Rich. Arnold. Amount: #26387. Date: 18 June 1669. Appraisers: Henry Stockett, Thomas Meech.

Court Session: <no date>

3:257 Will of William Parrat (Tridhaven, Choptank River, TA). Bequests: wife Ann Parrat, sons (under 21) William Parrat & Henry Parrat & George Parrat & Beniamin Parrat, wife "Marsh Point" then to sons George & Benjamin, son William land at Oxford & "Reserve" 1500 a., son Henry "Poppins Gaye" 500 a. on Petuxon River, sons George & Benjamin "Wharton" 1000 a on north side of Chester River.

3:258 Executors: son Will. Parrat, brother Isaac Abraham (of Miles River). Date: 14 March 1668. Witnesses: John Richarson, Simond Richardson, James. Will proved by John Richardson & Simon Richardson on 22 May 1669 before John Blomfeild. William Parrett (son of William Parrett) relinquished administration. Date: 21 May 1669. Witnesses: John Blomfeild, Rich. Moy. Isaac Abrahams was granted administration on estate of William Paratt. Appraisers: Richard Woollman, Edward Roe. Thomas Powell to administer oath.

3:259 Will of William Elleyeatt. Bequests: son William Elleyeatt, Mary Staggall the chattel that was her mother's, Thomas Staggall, Thomas Taylor, John Browne & his wife Margrett, Robert Kent, sister Mary Midwinter (living at Horsie Down). Overseers: James Riggby, Thomas Taylor, John Browne, Robert Kent. Date: 2 7th Month 1668. Witnesses: John Foard, Edward Sparks. Administration granted on 24 July 1669. Appraisers: Arthur Wright, Toby Wells. John Vicaris to administer oath. Will of William Elliott was proved by Edward Sparkes on 19 October 1669 & by John Ford on 2 November.

3:260 Inventory of Edmon Burton. Date: 2 August 1669. Amount: #12695. Appraisers: Arthur Wright, Edward Hull.

12 July 1669. Margarett relict of Marke Brunfeild (SM) was granted administration on his estate. Security: Thomas Hughes. Appraisers: Thomas

Court Session: <no date>

Hughes, William Abestone. Nich. Young (g) to administer oath.

3:261 Will of Richard Blunt (g, KI). Bequests: sons Samuell & Richard, son Josias, daughter April, daughter Grace Hill, wife Ann, sons Robert & Thomas, sons Samuell & Richard plantation as long as their mother's a widow, sons Josias & Robert 200 a. on Petapseco River, the Blind Man, daughter Rebeccah.
3:262 Executrix: wife. Date: 17 August 1669. Witnesses: William Milles, Disboro Bennett.

Will of John Ewen (AA). Date: 6 April 1669. Bequests: servants Michell Repland & Samuell Robarts, wife Sarah Ewen. Witnesses: Joseph Mosley. Capt. William Burges (AA) to cause will to be proved. Date: 4 October 1669.

Will of John Parr. Bequests: Martha Peake, Johanna Peake, George Peake, mother Mary Peake,
3:263 Henry Viney, Katherine Peake, son of John Ramsey, John Bennett, Rice Griffin. Witnesses: Abraham Clarke, John Cable. Will proved on 24 July 1669.

7 May 1669. Rebecca relict of Edmond Burton (KE) was granted administration on his estate. Appraisers: Edward Hull, Arthur Wright. Mathew Read (g) to administer oath.

Frances Armstrong was granted administration on estate of Francis Armstrong (TA). Security: William Hemsley. Appraisers: Daniel Walker, Thomas Booker. Richard Woolman (g) to administer oath.

Will of William Catlyne. Bequests: Mrs. Elisabeth Barbier chattel due from Mr. George Munroe & Mr. Walter Hall,
3:264 Thomas Covey & Mrs. Elisabeth Barbier & Gregory Rouse & William Gater, James Paddison, Luke Barbier, Joshua Guibert, Henry Taylor. Date: 1 February 1667. Witnesses: Gregory Rouse, William Gater. Will proved on 19 May 1669.

Court Session: <no date>

3:265
Will of James Martin (St. Clement's Bay, SM). Date: 3 August 1669. Bequests: wife Ann "Edinborough" & "Ralley" then to son James Martin (under age 16) & daughter Ann Martin (under age 16), son James "Cole Parke" 150 a. Mentions: Charles Maynard & his sister Elisabeth Maynard & his sister Agnes Maynard, Peter Mills. Overseers: Mr. Thomas Notley, Mr. Walter Hall, Mr. John Shanks, Peter Mills. Witnesses: David Driver, George Bancke, Peter Evers, Peter Mills. Will proved by David Driver & Peter Mills on 4 September 1669.

4 September 1669. Anne relict of James Martin was granted administration on his estate. Security: Peter Mills. Appraisers: John Jordaine, William Rosewell. Robert Slye (g) to administer oath.

3:266
Will of James Edwards (soyer, Tradaven Creek, TA). Bequests: William Parratt. Mentions: servant John Dollby. Date: 7 June 1668. Witnesses: Richard Sixbe, James Doud. William Parratt assigned all rights to Isack Abrahams. Date: 23 August 1669. Witnesses: Richard Sixbe, James Doude. Will proved on 25 August 1669.

3:267
Will of Thomas Cheeke. Bequests: Henry Merest, Mrs. Legate, Mrs. Thorowgood, Mr. Robert Massey & Thomas Thorowgood. Executors: Mr. Robert Massey, Thomas Thorowgood. Date: 16 August 1669. Witnesses: John Hodgson, Sr., Adam Banckes. Will proved on 11 September 1669. Robert Massey & Thomas Thorowgood were granted administration on said estate. Appraisers: Tobias Fendall, John Hodgson. Humphry Warren (g) to administer oath.

21 August 1669. Isaac Abrahams was granted administration on estate of James Edwards. Appraisers: William Sheares, Simon Richardson. Thomas Powell (g) to administer oath. Security: Thomas Skillington.

Court Session: <no date>

3:268 Mary Elliott widow of William Elliott (KI) was granted administration on his estate. Date: 21 May 1669. Appraisers: Arthur Wright, Edward Hull. Robert Dunn (g) to administer oath.

1 September 1669. Garret Vansweringeen was granted administration on estate of William Thellwell, as greatest creditor. Appraisers: Daniel Clocker, William Gringoe. Security: Marke Cordea.

Will of Francis Bullock. Bequests: Mr. William Crouch (upholsterer, Bishopsgate St., Devonshire House, London) for use of my mother Mrs. Jean Bullock, servant Winifred Massey. Executors: John Hatch, Robert Rowland (CH).

3:269 Bequests: Mathew Brookes. Date: 1 July 1669. Signed: Francis Bullocke. Witnesses: Walter Davis, Richard Lowder. Will proved on 28 September 1669. John Hatch & Robert Rowland were granted administration. Appraisers: Robert Henley, Walter Davis. Humphry Warren (g) to administer oath.

Will of John Elis (KI). Bequests: son John Elis land on Kent Island, daughter Elisabeth Elis 170 a. on Great Choptank River near Henry Willchurch & land on St. Michael's River bought of Charles Hulinworth, daughter Mary Elis land bought of Charles Hulinworth on St. Michael's River.

3:270 John Elis (age 8 on 29 July next), Elisabeth Elis (age 12 on 1 February next), Mary Elis (age 3 next November). Overseers: William Eylett, Richard Blount, Charles Hulinworth, Alexander Maxwell. Date: 1 October 1668. Witnesses: Robert Martin, William Mountique. Will proved on 6 November 1669 before Will. Hambleton.

Inventory of Robert Burtton. List of debts: Edward Leake, William Suchole, Henry Hudson, Edward Hull, John Martin, John Tassell, Capt. John Vickeres. Amount: #7940. Date: 15 September 1669. Appraisers: Arter Wright, Edward Hull.

Court Session: <no date>

3:271 Inventory of William Elliott (KI). Appraisers: Arthur Wright, Edward Hull. Date: 8 October 1669. Amount: #18500.

3:272 2 October 1669. Ann Blunt was granted administration on estate of Richard Blunt (KI). Appraisers: John Vicars (g), Robert Dunn. Thomas Osborn (g) to administer oath.

Isaac Winchester was granted administration on estate of John Winchester (KI). Appraisers: Tobias Wells, Morgaine Williams. Robert Dunn (g) to administer oath.

15 October 1669. Ann relict of Gerrard Fowkes (CH) was granted administration on his estate. Appraisers: Richard Fowke, Thomas Thorowgood. Henry Adams (g) to administer oath.

30 September 1669. John Blackiston son of George Blackiston (g, SM) was granted administration on his father's estate. Appraisers: Luke Gardner, Richard Foster. Robert Sly to administer oath.

3:273 Inventory of Mr. Georg Blackstone. Appraisers: Capt. Luke Gardner, Richard Foster. Date: 11 October 1669.
3:274 Amount: #14881. Witness: Elisbath Fenwicke.

2 November 1669. Margarett Miles relict of Thomas Miles (AA) was granted administration on his estate. Appraisers: John Welch, Joseph Chew. Samuel Chew (g) to administer oath.

17 October 1669. Margarett Brumfeild widow of Marke Brumfeild was granted continuance.

3:275 19 October 1669. Mary Elliott administratrix of William Elliott (KI) was granted continuance.

John Meggison was granted administration on estate of Gregory Mudge (KE).

Christopher Rousby vs. estate of Hugh Stanley (CV). Caveat.

Court Session: <no date>

3:276 Will of Emanuell Drue (AA). Bequests: 2 sons Thomas Drue (under 21) & Samuell Drue land. Mentions: James Rigbey, daughter Elisabeth (under age 16), daughter Martha (under age 16), Mr. Francis Stockett, Mrs. Elisabeth Strong. Executors: William Stead, Ralf Hawkins, Jr. Robert Burle & Richard Moss to assist. Date: 3 August 1669. Witnesses: Olliver Halloway, Mary Turner.

3:277 Will of Ralph Hawkins, Sr. (AA). Bequests: wife Margrett Hawkins to receive servant Andrew, son William Hawkins, son Ralph Hawkins & son William Hawkins plantation. Executors: 2 sons. Date: 19 September 1669. Witnesses: William Neale, Joseph Hawkins.

John Morecroft vs. estate of William Lane. Caveat.

3:278 8 November 1669. Thomas Truman, Esq. to prove will of Hugh Stanley by oaths of Roger Blackhurst & Margarett Weeks.

Will of Thomas Haukings. Bequests: son Thomas Haukings ½ land on Poplie Island, Margrett Hull (daughter of Edward Hull), wife Elisabeth Haukings residue. Overseers: Capt. Robert Vaughan, Mr. Henry Carline, Mr. Seth Foster. Date: 2 October 1656. Witnesses: Edward Hull, Greshom Cromwell. Codicil: Bequests: Mr. Seth Foster. Will found among papers

3:279 of Thomas Hawkins (dec'd). Son Thomas Hawkins left ¼, ¼ to wife of Seth Foster, other ½ to said Foster by deed dated 1654. Date: 19 April 1669.

Will of Hugh Stanley (CV). Executrix: wife Dorithy Stanley. Bequests: wife then to brother John Stanley then to his 2 sons John Stanley & Edward 200 a. & 50 a. in Pocomoke,

3:280 brother John Stanley, Sebyna Frances Jacob. Date: 30 July 1667. Witnesses: John Owen, Margret Wikes, Roger Blackhurst. Will proved by Roger

Court Session: <no date>

3:281 Blackhurst & Margret Wikes on 26 November 1669. Signed: Tho. Truman.

3:282 Will of Robert Perkins (p, Portobacco, CH). Date: 30 December 1668. Executrix: wife Anne Perkins. Bequests: wife, Mrs. Jane Waghob wife of Mr. Archbald Waghob, wife's son Patrick Forrest, Thomas Corker. Witnesses: Bartho. Coates, Thomas Corker, Clement Theobald.

3:283 Inventory of Mr. Thomas Cheeke. Mentions: 22 books. Appraisers: Josias Fendall, John Hodgson.

3:284 List of debts: Mr. Thomas Notley, Mr. Benj. Rozer, Capt. Ashton (VA), John Winscomb (VA), Mr. Robert Perce (chyrurgeon). List of debts (in VA): John Axton, Robert Collinion, Richard Thorpe, Joseph Vendall, John Pleasants, Oliver Balts, David Jones, Thomas Smith, John Withers.

3:285 Will of John Lewger (CH). Date: 26 November 1669. Bequests: sons John Lewger & Thomas Lewger "St. Barbarys Manner" 1000 a., daughter Elisabeth Lewger 300 a., wife Martha Lewgar. Overseers: Thomas Galley, John Ward. Witnesses: Thomas Galley, George Lodge. Will proved 9 December 1669.

3:286 Inventory of Edward Davis. Date: 1 July 1669. Appraisers: Thomas South, Richard Tilman.
...

3:287 Will of Hatton Bond (Clifts, CV). Date: 28 February 1667. Bequests: wife Sarah Bond. Witnesses: Elisabeth Savege, Walter Pilkinton. Will proved at Mattapenny on 23 October 1668.

2 October 1669. Citation to Mary Elliott administratrix of William Elliott (KE).

Court Session: <no date>

3:288 Will of Henry Catlen. Bequests: 3 girls of Abraham Dasen, Robert Godgon, Jr., 2 twins of James Smith, Volentine Horner (under 21) 50 a. Residue: children of brother & sister in ENG. Executor: Edward Sealsbey. Overseers: William Crouch, William Hopkins. Codicil: Bequests: Robard Tylers Frances.

Walter Lane received of William Calvert, Esq. 1/5th of money from chest on board Speedwell of London. Date: 30 December 1669.

3:289 Inventory of chest on Speedwell of London. Date: 21 December 1669.

Inventory of John Parr. Amount: #4102. Date: 10 July 1669. Appraisers: John Troster, Robert Heighe. Before: Peake George

3:290 20 November 1669. Margreat Myles took oath for her husband's estate. Before: Sam. Chew.

10 November 1669. Mr. John Walsh & Mr. Joseph Chew took oath as appraisers of estate of Tho. Miles. Before: Sam. Chew.

Mrs. Anne Fouke administratrix of Mr. Gerrard Fouke took oath for his estate. Date: 26 October 1669. Before: Henry Adams.

17 November 1669. TA Court. Present: Mr. Ri. Woleman, Mr. Tho. South, Mr. Phi. Steevenson, Mr. Sy. Carpender, Mr. William Hambleton, Mr. William Coursey, Mr. Ja. Ringould, Mr. Tho. Hinson, Mr. Tho. Powell, Mr. Jona. Sibery.

Orders vs. estate of Fran. Armstrong (TA): William Younge, William Richardson, Robert Harwood, Edward Roe, William Hemsley, John Edmundson, Mr. Richard Tilghman, Sam. Winslow, Jona. Hopkinson,

3:291 John Pitt, Mary Dickinson, Joseph Sone, William Charlton, Richard White, John Briges, Ralph Dowsey.

Court Session: <no date>

3:292	Accounts of Francis Armstrong. Executrix: Frances Armstrong. Amount of inventory: #38044. Payments to: William Young, William Richardson, Robert Harwood, Edward Roe, William Hemsley, John Edmondson for Richard Preston, John Edmondson for William Tetherly, John Edmondson, Rich. Tilghman, Samuel Winslow, Jonathon Hopkinson, John Pitt, Mary Pickenson, Joseph Sone, William Charleton, Richard White, John Briggs, Ralph Dawsey, Major Ingram. Amount: #55248. Discharge was requested.
3:293	Attachment to estate of Richard Richarbie (mariner, London, dec'd). Date: 1 October 1668. Items in hands of John Edmondson. Mentions: Thurston Withnall (notary, merchant, London). Signed: William Scorey (notary). Witnesses: Robert Barton, Solomon Allen. Before: Spencer Hales, Edward Worrill.
3:294 3:295 3:296 3:297	Will of Richard Preston (Patuxent). Date: 16 September 1669. Bequests: son James Preston (if living, to come to MD) plantation on Patuxent River until grandchild Samuell Preston come to age 21 & "Neglect" 200 a., son James Preston (if he return from ENG) "Barren Island" on Eastern Shore, daughters Rebeckah & Sarah Preston "Horne" on Great Choptank River bought of Walter Dench (if they die without issue, to son James Preston, then to 2 kinsmen James & John Dorsey), said John Dossey 500 a. at head of Little Choptank River (1/3rd already given to Ralph Dossey), William Tick (Dutchman), Edward Norman (overseer), Thomas Brockson, William Purnell, George Hawes (if he comes from ENG), 2 grandchildren William & James Berry, grandchild Rebeckah (no surname given), kinsman James Dossey, daughter-in-law Margaret Preston, son James Preston ½ money sent for by James Conneway, Thomas Preston (Clifts), Isaac Hunt, William Harper. Residue: 3 children: James, Rebeckah, Sarah. Overseers:

Court Session: <no date>

3:298
William Berry, Peter Sharpe (KE), Thomas Taylour (KE), John Meares (Clifts). Signed: Ri. Preston. Witnesses: Enoch Coomes, George Deulin, Thomas Peake, William Jones. Codicil: Dated: 2 December 1669. Witnesses: Thomas Peake, George Deulin, William Jones. Will proved by George Deuline & William Jones on 8 January 1669.

Certificate that William Berry (p, Patuxent, CV) married Margaret Preston widow of Richard Preston. Date: 8 January 1669.

William Hambleton exhibited the oath of Robert Martin & William Mountagne, affirming the will of John Ellis (KE, dec'd). Date: 6 November 1669.

3:299
3:300
Inventory of William Coles.
...
Amount: #14594. Date: 30 November. Appraisers: Tho. Griffin, Henery Penington.

Inventory of Francis Armstrong. Appraisers: Daniel Walker, Thomas Booker. Date: 20 October 1669.

3:301
Inventory of John Winchester (KE). Appraisers: Morgan Williams, Tobias Wells. Date: 12 November 1669.

3:302
3:303
...
List of debts: Christopher Barnes, Capt. William Leads, John Wright, Mathew Masson. Further list of debts: John Laurence. Further list of debts: Williams Heeds, John Dobe, Alexander Walter, Capt. Jacob Brimington, Henery Downes, Tobias Wells, John Vickiricus, John Wright, Abraham Holt, Richard Browne, Isaack Winchester, Mathew Masson. Further list of debts: William Pledg, Charles Steuard, Peter Scale, Alexander Maxfeild.

3:304
William Justice, Esq. (London) executor of John Benbow (citizen, groser, London) gave PoA to Henry Coursey & Christopher Rowsbey (merchants, MD) to recover from Nathaniel Uty, Esq.

Court Session: <no date>

3:305 Before: Tim. Brigge (notary).
Witnesses: Humfry Brigge, Rob. Morris,
Tim. Brigge, Jr.

Additional inventory of William Wyott.
Date: 13 October 1669. Appraisers:
Arthur Wright, Edward Hull.

Inventory of Marke Bromfield (SM).
3:306 List of debts: William Calvert, Esq.
3:307 Appraisers: Tho. Hughs, William
Asbestone.

Frances Armstrong relict of Francis
Armstrong was granted administraton on
his estate. Appraisers: Daniel Walker,
Tho. Booker. Date: 4 November 1669.
Signed: Ri. Wollman.

3:308 Accounts of Richard Stone (CH).
Administrator: John Stone. Payments to:
Jerimiah Dickison, Walter King, William
Allen, John Hichinson, Tho. Allcocks,
Mr. Robert Slye, Tho. King, Mr.
Jenifer, accountant, brother Mathew
Stone. Amount: #23264. Discharge was
granted. Date: 16 January 1669.

3:309 22 November 1669. William Stead & Ralph
Hawkins were granted administration on
estate of Emanuel Drue for the orphans
of the dec'd. Appraisers: William
Neale, Robert Parnaphee. Robert Burle
to administer oath.

Will of Ralph Hawkins, Sr. (AA) to be
proved.

26 November 1669. Mary relict of John
Vicaris (g, KE) was granted
administration on his estate.
Appraisers: John Wright, Thomas
Osbourne. Robert Dunn (g) to administer
oath.

One of the appraisers of the estate of
Robert Blunt (KE) is dec'd. New
appraisers: Mathew Read, Morgan
Williams. Thomas Osborne to administer
oath.

Court Session: <no date>

3:310 Ann Perkins relict of Robert Perkins (CH) was granted administration on his estate. Security: Bartholomew Coates. Appraisers: Clement Theobalds, Bartholomew Coates. Henry Adams (g) to administer oath.

1 December 1669. Thomas Fisher was granted administration on estate of Robert Atkins (CV), for use of Thomas Ellis (merchant, Bristoll). Security: Sampson Warring. Appraisers: Sampson Warring, John Staymes. George Peake (g) to administer oath.

3:311 Accounts of Thomas Freeman (Bristoll). Administrator: Thomas Cooper. Date: 4 June 1669. Amount of inventory: #16814 by Roger Woolford & James Jones in hands of Rendell Revell (Manokin, SO); #1731 by Henry Hooper & John Richardson in hands of John Edmondson (Choptank, TA); #44146 in hands of John Edmondson (Choptank, TA); #148696 in hands of the Governor; #49716 in hands of said Revell. Payments to: Henry Hosier & John Staymes, Richard Atkins, Thomas Whitup, Richard Bayley, Rendell Revell, Thomas Gant, Edmond Beachamb, George Johnson, Jenkin Price, Mr. Sampson Warren & William Hopkins.

3:312 Amount: #262354. Discharge was granted. Date: 16 January 1669.

3:313 Inventory of Robert Brookes. Appraisers: Mr. Tobias Norton, Mr. John Tawney. Date: 23 November 1667.

3:314 Amount: #15043. List of debts: Richard Marsham, Joseph Dawkins, James Price, George Alderson, Roger Brookes, James Vitch, James Thompson, Thomas Edwards. Amount: #4368. Further list of debts: James Vitch, William Graves, Charles Boteler,

3:315 William Herbert, David Brown, William Bryant, Edward Keene, William Berry, James Thompson. Amount: #1779. Accounts. Payments to (per CV Court): Thomas Sprig, Thomas Brooke, Charles Brooke, William Bolds, James Garner, John Ashcomb, William Evans, John Carey, Peter Sharpe. Payments to: Rob. Brookes

Court Session: <no date>

3:316 (due in his lifetime), fees to fetch Baker Brooke, Esq. to give oath to Elisabeth Brooke & the appraisers, John Gittings, Simon Read, John Pots, Reymond Staplefort. Amount: #28532. Bills & Accounts attached by Major Brooke (sheriff) for John Avery. Date: 19 September 1668: James Vitch, Phillip Harwood, Richard Drury, Tho. Glover, Richard Wadsworth, Thomas Howeton, Demetrius Cartwright, William Watson, Thomas Sherriden, Peter Lames, Andrew Dickason, John Shinkle, James Thompson. Amount: #4910. Account passed. Before: William Calvert. Date: 22 July 1669.

3:317 Will of William Chaplin (p, Patuxent River). Date: 9 December 1669. Bequests: daughter Elisabeth Chaplin plantation on Eastern Shore, son William Chapline (under age 16) plantation that I live on, daughter Mary Chapline, wife Mary Chapline,

3:318 kinsman Richard Hopper (CV), John Webb. Overseers: John Webb, Richard Hopper. Witnesses: John Brooke, Richard Tubman, Rd. Rainer, John Holliway. John Webb relinquished overseership. Date: 5 January 1669. Will proved by Richard Tubman & John Holloway on 8 January 1669.

3:319 Will of Nicholas Young (g, SM). Bequests: wife Elisabeth Young land at Cedar Point (CH), wife all rights to "Fresh Pond Neck" (St. Michael's Hundred, SM) bequeathed to me by my son-in-law Edward Parker. Executrix: wife. Date: 11 January 1669. Witnesses: H. Warren, Rob. Carville. Will proved by Robert Carvill on 29 January 1669.

3:320 Will of Edward Parker (St. Innagoes Mannor, SM). Bequests: father-in-law Nicholas Young "Fresh Pond Neck", mother land at Cedar Point (CH), brothers Samuell (under age) & Phillip "Parker's Land" (BA) 800 a., sister Elisabeth, Mr. Michael Foster debt due of John Nicholls if "I die a true Roman Catholic".

Court Session: <no date>

3:321 Overseers: father-in-law Nicholas Young, kinsman William Bretton. Date: 3 January 1669. Witnesses: Nicholas Solby, Richard Ridgell, William Gifford. Will proved by Richard Ridgell & William Gifford on 29 January 1669.

3:322 Will of William Thorne (Manokin, Eastern Shore). Bequests: John Richards "South Petherton" 100 a., said Richards to remain in service of wife Winifred Thorne until he is 21. Residue: wife. Executrix: wife. Overseers: Mr. George Johnson, Mr. James Jones. Date: 12 February 1665. Witnesses: Tho. Meech, Roger Woolford, Edward Southrins.

3:323 Will of Marke Phepo (St. Michael's Hundred, SM). Bequests: my children Phillip Land & Thomas Land & William Land, Bryan Dayley, Jr. "Phepo's Fort", Thomas Keyton, Richard Russell, John Stocks, John Mathews, Constant Daniell. Executor: Bryan Daley. Date: 19 January 1669. Witnesses: Tho. Paine, Will. Abbestone. Will proved 8 February 1669.

3:324 Will proved by Thomas Paine on 9 February 1669. Appraisers: Thomas Doxey, George Marshall.

3:325 Will of Abdaloe Martin (p, CV). Bequests: eldest daughter Elisabeth Martin (under age 21), daughter Mary Martin, daughter Sarah Martin. Executor: Mr. John Peerce (chirurgeon). Mentions: gift to children from Emperour Smith. Date: 25 May 1668. Signed: Abdeloe Martin. Witnesses: Fran. Swanstone, Ralph Wells. Will proved by Francis Swanstone on 5 June 1669. Will proved by Ralph Wells on 14 December 1669. Before: John Blomfeild.

3:326 Inventory of Capt. John Viccaris. Appraisers: John Wright, Thomas Osborne. Date: 28 December 1669. Mentions: 700 a. on Chester River, "Broadoake" 500 a. Amount: #37380. List of debts: Augustin Harman, William Stanley, Edmond Mustian, John Webster, Thomas Collins, William

Court Session: <no date>

Plead, Mr. Ringold, John Treckson, John Bowles, Henry Gott, Thomas Hinson, Thomas Phillips, Richard Howard, Francis Armstrong, Tobias Wells, Capt. Howell. Amount: #8103.

3:327 Further list of debts: Ezechiell Croscombe, Major Ingram, Mathias Peterson, Roger Baxter, Vallentine Suthrine, Henry Dawnes, Thomas Baxter, James Ringold, Joseph Hopkins, John Wright. Further list of debts: Peter Scale, (N) Winchester, John Martin, Robert Humphryes.

Inventory of Mr. John Hitchenson. Appraisers: Mr. Henry Adams, Mr. Ignatius Cusseene. Date: 7 January 1668.
3:328 Amount: #9440. Date: 1 February 1668. Signed: Henry Adams, Ignatius Cousins.
3:329 List of debts per John Allen (administrator): Mr. Fran. Pope, Tho. Baker, John Mills, Sander Smith, Richard Rowe, Thomas Baker, Jacob Peeterson, Bartholomew Coale, James Mechie, John Smart, Mr. Harrison, Robert Downes. Amount: #13059.

Inventory of James Edwards. Appraisers: William (N), Richardson Simon.
3:330 List of debts: Richard White, Robert Jenkinson, Henry Lam, William More, James Shacklady, Edward Wincles, Edward Roe, Anthony Dawson, Robert Jinkinson, John Dolby, Hopkin Davis, Clement Seales, William Hill. Appraisers: William Sheries, Simon Richeson. Debt to Isaac Abrahams & William Parrot.

Inventory of William Parrot. Date: 5 July 1669.
3:331 ...
3:332 Amount: #27451. List of debts: Isaack Abrahams, Francis Whitewell, John Richardson. Debts from the estate: John Clemens, Michaell Taylour,
3:333 Obadiah Jenkins. Appraisers: Ri. Woolman, Edward Roe. Legatees: wife Anne Parrot, son William Parrot, son Henry Parrot, son Benjamin. Servants: John Keyes, Richard Sixby, James Dowd, Alice Bevin, John Rively.

Court Session: <no date>

3:334 Further inventory. Amount: #3027.

4 December 1669. Dorothy Stanley widow of Hugh Stanley was granted administration on his estate. Appraisers: Edward Keene, Samuell Goosey, James Godscrosse. Thomas Truman (g) to administer oath.

3:335 9 December 1669. Martha Lucar relict of John Lucar (f. 284) was granted administration on his estate. Appraisers: Richard Fowke, Francis Thornton. Zachariah Wade to administer oath.

18 December 1669. William Crouch & Christopher Rowles to appraise estate of John Browne. Robert Burle to administer oath.

11 December 1669. Walter Lane son of William Lane (Galloway, IRE) was granted administration on his estate. Appraisers: Garret Vanswearing, George Manwaring.

4 January 1669. Edward Selby was granted administration on estate of Henry Catlin. Robert Burle to prove will.

3:336 Appraisers: James Smith, Mathew Howard. Robert Burle to administer oath.

8 January 1669. Francis Staunton (merchant, London) was granted administration on estate of Christopher Walter (TA). Bondsmen: Richard Moy, Jenkin Price. Appraisers: Robert Smith, Bryan Omaile. William Coursey (g) to administer oath.

22 January 1669. Edward Howard (CV) was granted administration on estate of John Murraine (CV). Bondsman: William Groome. Appraisers: John Cobreath, Mathew Clare. George Peake (g) to administer oath.

29 January 1669. Elisabeth Young (widow) was granted administration on estate of Edward Parker. Bondsman:

Court Session: <no date>

Robert Carvill (g). Appraisers: Robert King, Thomas Pearce. William Bretton (g) to administer oath.

3:337   7 February 1669. William Steevens (g) to prove will of William Thorne (Manokin). Appraisers: Thomas Bloyce, John Shipway. William Steevens to administer oath.

12 February 1669. Alexander Maxwell (TA) was granted administration on estate of John Ellis (KI). Bondsmen: John Wright, John Mitchell. Appraisers: John Ellickson, Thomas Bright. Mathew Reade (g) to administer oath.

10 February 1669. Patrick Hall (AA) was granted administration on estate of James Maxwell. Bondsmen: James Humes, Thomas Knighton. Appraisers: Richard Wells, Jeremiah Swillivant. Samuell Chew, Esq. to administer oath.

11 February 1669. Elisabeth Davis relict of Hopkin Davis (TA) was granted administration on his estate.
3:338   Bondsmen: Anthony Male, John Edmondson. Appraisers: Thomas Vaune, Hugh Sherwood. Thomas Powell (g) to administer oath.

Mary Chaplin relict of William Chaplin was granted administration on his estate. Bondsmen: Richard Hooper, Francis Swinson. Appraisers: Henry Hooper, Sr., William Groome, Richard Smith, Demetrius Cartwright. Thomas Brooke (g) to administer oath.

Will of Gilbert Corner. Bequests: son Job Corner "Chestnut Point" 200 a. Overseers: Thomas Pope, wife Ellinor Corner. Date: 20 October 1669. Witness: Richard Ambrose. Will proved 5 March 1669.
3:339   Mrs. Martha Lugar, Richard Fowke, & Francis Thorntine took oath. Date: 29 December. Signed: Zachary Wade.

Inventory of Capt. James Martin (St. Clement's Bay, SM).
3:340   Amount: #25771. Date: 1669.

Court Session: <no date>

Appraisers: Will. Rosewell, John Jordaine.

Inventory of Mr. John Lewger (CH). Date: 29 February 1669. Appraisers: Richard Fowkes, Francis Thorntine. Accounts.

3:341 Will of William Lewis (p, TA). Date: 23 September 1669. Bequests: Wenlock Christison, Henry Wilcocks, wife Sarah Lewis plantation & "Sarah's Neck", John Webster (servant), daughter Sarah "Boston Clifts" 680 a. on Great Choptank River bought of Samuell Winslow & "Mounthope" 300 a. on Island Creek on Chester River demanded of Ralph Fishborne, daughter Mary 450 a. on Nanticoke River & 200 a. on Chester River at Corseick Creek, wife "Lewis" 100 a. on Michael's River adjoining Thomas Emerson.

3:342 Executors: Henry Wilcocks, William Southeby, Thomas Taylour (KE), John Pitt (Tredavon). Witnesses: George Collison, Ralph Fishborne, George Clandman, John Burrows. Will proved by George Collison & John Boroughs on 12 March 1669.

Inventory of Richard Blunt (KE). Appraisers: Mathew Reade, Morgan Williams (g). Date: 30 December 1669.

3:343 Amount: [torn]. List of debts: Lt. Ninian Beale, Tobias Appleford, Hopkin Davis, Richard Pether, Cornelius Monteague, Constant Perey, John Winchester, Jr., John Winchester, Sr., Edward Hull, Richard Morris, John Mecoakin, Richard Nash, Alexander Nash, John Stevens, John Lawrence, Richard Browne, Tobias Appleford, Charles Steward, Richard Draver, Capt. John Viccaris,

3:344 [torn-7 entries], [torn] Burton, Henry Downes, Henry Howard, John Cooper, William Bishop, Alexander Waters, William Hemsley, Christopher Denny, John Alexson, Alexander Townson, William Gammack, Arthur Ginn, William Rodwell, estate of John Ellis, the County. Amount: #14398. Additional list of debts: Mr. Witham, William Milles, Peter

Court Session: <no date>

Scale, John Tassell, Robert Tallent.
Amount: #1286.

4A:1   2 October 1669. Citation regarding administration of estate of William Elliott (KE). John Browne by his attorney Thomas Knighton vs. William Lawrence who married Mary relict of dec'd by their attorney Robert Carvile, lately William & Mary by John Morecroft. Date: 21 June 1670. "No recipeatur quia not venit ad diem."

4A:2   28 March 1670. Daniel Jenifer attorney for William King who married Margarett (alias Margarett Wright) administratrix of Ishmael Wright vs. John Morecroft for Jesper Allen who married Mary (daughter of said Ishmael). Summons to said Margarett King.

28 May 1670 at CV. Joseph Horsley summoned to exhibit will of James Cullams.

4A:3   25 June 1670 at SM, before William Calvert, Esq. Allen & ux vs. King & ux. Richard Bayly, Guy White, John Meriday, & Thomas Hewse summoned.

Browne vs. Lawrence & ux.

30 July 1670. SM, before William Calvert, Esq. Browne vs. Lawrence & ux. Will of William Elliot to be void. Said Mary granted administration on the estate.

4A:4   Allen & ux. vs. King & ux.   Caveat.

Browne vs. Lawrence & ux.   Caveat.

Allen & ux. vs. King & ux.   Caveat.

4A:5   27 August 1670 at SM, before William Calvert, Esq. Jesper Allen & Mary Allen vs. William King & Marg. King. Richard Bayly, Guy White, & Judith Cooper to be interrogated. John Meredith also to be interrogated.

Court Session: <no date>

4A:6 6 September 1670 at SM, before William Calvert, Esq. Jesper Allen & Mary vs. William King & Marg. King. John Meredith deposed.

4A:7 ...

4A:8 2 December 1670. Love Mathews widow of John Mathews to show cause why administration of his estate should not be granted to Joseph Brough the principle creditor.

10 December 1670. James Chesholm vs. estate of Thomas Jones. Caveat.

Thomas Sprigg (CV) to exhibit account of estate of Sarah orphan of Thomas Belcher.

16 December 1670. Mr. Robert Sly to exhibit nuncupative will of Daniell Johnson.

4A:9 2 January 1670. Richard Ewen vs. Samuel Lane (g, AA) who married Margaret relict & administratrix of John Burridge (AA). Summons.

5 January 1670 at SM, before William Talbot, Esq. John Morecroft attorney for Elisabeth Johnson widow of Daniell Johnson exhibited nunucpative will of her husband. Robert Sly argued that it should be void. Mr. Jacob Peterson to remain on the land leased from said Daniell.

21 January 1670. Robert Sly ordered to deliver all chattel of the estate of Daniell Johnson to Elisabeth Johnson (relict) for use of the orphan.

Thomas Sprigg was to appear with accounts of Sarah orphan of Thomas Belcher.

4A:10 Said Sarah to be delivered to John Sewell (CV) & his wife Ellinor (both godmother & nurse to said Sarah).

30 January 1670. Raymond Stapleford (DO) to exhibit account of chattel that he has of the estate of Richard Miller.

Court Session: <no date>

11 February 1670. Richard Gorsuch (Choptank, TA) was granted continuance on estate of Thomas Stone.

8 March 1670. Richard Bayley (CV) vs. estate of George Aldridge. Caveat.

18 March 1670. Henry Hosier (CV) vs. estate of John Webster (merchant, TA). Caveat.

25 March 1671. Nath. Garret (SM) to produce an account of estate of Thomas Poore (merchant). Caveat.

4A:11 4 May 1671. James Garret (CV) vs. estate of Richard Johnson. William Kent, Henry Anderson, & Elisabeth Howard to exhibit will of said Johnson.

Will of Richard Johnson. Bequests: Dyna Bagby, Ann Kent, Mary Kent, Grace Humes.

19 May 1671 at SM, before Sir William Talbot . William Kent, Henry Anderson, & Elisabeth Howard brought in will of Richard Johnson & attested to it. Said Richard constituted James Garret as executor.

4A:12 Daniell Jenifer (g, SM) was granted administration on estate of Capt. William Smith (innholder, SM). Date: 24 December last. Estate was unadministered by Mary Jenifer his late wife & lately Mary Smith executrix of said William. On the same day, said Daniell was granted administration on estate of said Mary Jenifer.

4A:13 Continuance granted.

29 August 1671. Richard Moy creditor to estate of William Wenham vs. Thomas Hopkins who married Alice widow of said William. Said Hopkins declared he would not administer the estate. Administration granted to said Richard.

7 September 1671. Marke Cordea creditor to estate of Thomas Covant vs. Mary Covant widow of said Thomas. Caveat.

Court Session: <no date>

15 September. William Hopewell, age 32, deposed that he served Mary Covant with the subpoena.

11 October 1671. Mr. Henry Adams stated that most of the estate of Georg Manwaring was in debt.

4A:14 Mary Burton administratrix of Edward Burton (KE) was granted administration on his estate. Oath was administered by John Wright.

4A:15 18 December 1671. John Wright administrator of John Lawrence was granted continuance.

4 January 1671. John Damrell administrator of John Hawkins (BA) to show cause why the administration should not be granted to Robert Hawkins (brother of dec'd).

4A:16 John Pott, Arthur Ludford, & Phillip Harwood to testify as witnesses to will of Bartholomew Herring (CV), who bequeathed all to William Muffett (CV). Said William has not received the bequest.

4A:17 25 March 1671. Walter Carr & Arthur Brisco (AA) vs. estate of James Foote (AA). Caveat.

29 March 1671. John Parker (merchant, CV) vs. estate of Francis Pyne (KE). Caveat.

7 June. Samuell Hatton attorney for Thomas Hatton vs. estate of John Hatton (merchant). Caveat.

Nathaniell Heathcot executor of John Brewer administrator of John Hatton (merchant) to show cause why administration of said Hatton should not be revoked.

10 July 1672. Edw. Gowdree (CV) petitioned for administration on estate of Edward Cooke (dec'd).

Court Session: <no date>

John Bigger (CV) petitioned for administration on estate of John Bigger.

4A:18 10 July 1672. John Anderson (CV) to render an account of the estate of Robert Cobathwaite. William Johnson to be summoned.

7 October 1672. Roger Baker vs. Richard Ladd & ux administratrix of (N). Horsley. Caveat.

20 October 1672. Mr. Thomas Notley vs. administrator of John Parker. Caveat.

4A:19 The estate of John Hatton (merchant) was administered by John Brewer (now dec'd). Elisabeth Brewer (widow of said Brewer) is also now dec'd. New accounts to be rendered. Date: 23 October 1672.

25 October 1672. Abraham Roades (SM) vs. estate of John Parker. Caveat.

4A:20 Edward Cowdry (CV) to render accounts on estate of Edward Cooke. John Bigger administrator of John Bigger to render accounts on said estate. John Anderson administrator of Robert Coperthwayte to render accounts on said estate. Subpoena to said Edward Cowdry, John Bigger, & John Anderson. Date: 14 November 1672.

Henry Addams & Thomas Mathews (g) executors of George Manwaring were granted continuance.

4A:21 Edward Cowdry, John Bigger, & John Anderson to render accounts on estates of Edward Cooke, John Biger, & Robert Cobertwait. Date: 13 February 1672.

William Berry to appear regarding executorship of estate of John Parker.

10 May 1673. Roger Shehee (SM) to appear to prove will of Richard Russell (SM). Humphry Lunbrey (CV, one of the witnesses) to also appear.

Court Session: <no date>

	16 May 1673. John Bigger, Jr. (CV) to render accounts on estate of John Bigger, Sr. (CV).
	William Berry (CV) executor of John Parker did not appear. William Dare is attorney for William Eriste & Co. (merchants of Dorchester) & other creditors.
4A:22	Administration granted to said Dare. Tho. Notley (g) & Abraham Rhoads also to appear. Security: Tho. Rynolds (Clifts).
	last October 1673. Samuell Hatton administrator of John Hatton vs. Nathaniell Heathcote administrator of (N) Brewer. Caveat.
4A:23	Nathaniell Heathcote administrator of Elisabeth Brewer (widow) responded:
4A:24	John Brewer (AA, dec'd) had administration on estate of John Hatton. Bondsman: Francis Holland (AA).
4A:25	John Brewer made said Elisabeth Brewer his executrix. Said Elisabeth made her will on 6 March 1667 & appointed Edward Selby & Henry Perrpoint as overseers & the care of her children John & William Brewer (under age).
4A:26	Said Edward & Henry refused. Amount of inventory: #45923.
4A:27-28	...
4A:29	Accounts of Elisabeth Brewer (widow). Amount of inventory: #45923. Payments to: accountant, William Harriss, Thomas Besson, Henry Perepoint, Mr. John Welsh, Richard Tideings, William Miles, Edward Selby, John Foster, William Cross, Robert Lloyd, Mr. Thomas Ellwis, John Larkin, Mr. Thomas Tailor, John Grey, Francis Johnson, Mr. Rich. Cutt, Capt. William Burgess, Tho. Plumer, Robert Wilson, Francis Williams, Capt. Burgess, Mr. Withers, John Gray, Dr. Porter, Amos Perrepoint, Jade. Amount: #44176. Mentions: John Hatton. Date: 4 November 1673. Administrator: Nathaniell Heathcote.
4A:30	Godfrey Bayley assigned chattel to Joseph Wickes. Date: 1 June 1660.

Court Session: <no date>

Witness: William Hemsley.

	Seth Foster to the Company merchants. Date: 15 October 1663. Inventory. List of debts: Mr. Seth Foster, Mr. John Hatton. Further inventory.
4A:31	List of debts: John Eason, James Rigby, Richard Cheyney, Mr. Broadnox, Mr. Foster,
4A:32	Mr. Richard Blunt, Richard Woollman, Tho. Tolly, Mr. Stile for Thomas Odonell. Amount: #7148.
	Inventory of John Hatton. Date: 10 August 1663. Administrator: Mr. Seth Foster. Mentions items bought of Edward Savage at the Adam & Eve Cannon Street dated 6 December 1662.
4A:33	Mentions items bought of Thomas Stringer. Amount: £10.4.8. Mr. Tobya Michell to pay to Capt. Samuell Pensax.
4A:34	Samuell Hatton administrator of John Hatton answer to Nathaniel Heathcote administrator of Elisabeth Brewer (widow). Mentions: John Brewer administrator of John Hatton, bond by wife of Francis Holland (AA). Said Brewer made inventory of the estate on 30 July 1663, appraised by Roger Cross & William Burgess. Amount: #65419.
4A:35	List of bills: John Walters, William Davis, William Neale, John Jones, Robert Parker,
4A:36	Gresian Crumwell, Mary Broadnox, William Hunt, Thomas Daniell, John Collier, Robert Tyler, Richard Blunt, William Plaucleg.
	2 February 1673. John Blomfeild (g, SM) to render account of estate of Dr. Luke Barber (g, Mechans Hall, SM) to Joshua Guibert (administrator of dec'd).
4A:37	9 March 1673. William Yorke (BA) who married Anne relict of John Collier (BA) executor of James Stringer to render accounts of both estates.
	3 April 1674. John Troster (p, CV) vs. estate of John Foster (CV). Caveat.

Page 189

Court Session: <no date>

8 April 1674. William Melton (CV) creditor vs. estate of John Foster (CV). Caveat.

11 April 1674. John Edmondson vs. Thomas Vaughan administrator of John Leaven (merchant, TA). Caveat.

4A:38 Samuell Goldsmith (g, BA) & Thomas Howell (g, BA) were bound to the Lord Proprietor on 21 April 1674 & committed to chattels & debts of Francis Wright (BA, dec'd) & until Raphael Wright the executor makes a true inventory. Witnesses: Godfrey Bayley, T. Sallmon. Bond was assigned to Margarett Tenry (?) the second administratrix of said estate. Date: 11 June 1674.

4A:39 18 June 1674. Sheriff (BA) to summon Henry Haslewood (BA) to render accounts of estate of John Collett.

Sheriff (CV) to summon Edward Keene (CV) to render accounts of estate of Henry Refue.

Sheriff (AA) to summon Susanna White (AA) to render accounts of estate of James White.

Sheriff (TA) to summon Thomas Vaughan (TA) to render accounts of estate of John Leaven.

Sheriff (BA) to summon Thomas Armiger (BA) to render accounts of estate of Francis Trippe.

Sheriff (CV) to summon Mich. Higgen (CV) to render accounts of estate of William Dreure.

4A:40 26 June. Luke Gardner (sheriff, SM) exhibited oath to Edward Fitzherbert & Caleb Baker executors of William Hattoft with security: Garret Vansweringen. Also to John Barnes executor of Walter Walterlin the other security.

Court Session: <no date>

1 July. Sheriff (CH) to summon Robert Henly & John Worland to exhibit accounts of estate of John Harrington. Administrator is Samuel Cressey.

9 July. Sheriff (TA) to summon William Hemsley to exhibit accounts of estate of James Wood (chirurgeon, Wapping, ENG). Also to James Clayland to render accounts of chattel received from said estate. Also to William Jones for charges (dec'd died at house of said Jones). Administrator is Nathaniell Lamphigh.

4A:41   10 July 1674. Sheriff (CV) to summon Joan Tyler relict & administratrix of George Read to render accounts on said estate.

13 July 1674. Sheriff (SM) to summon Thomas Pinck (SM) to render account of estate of Samuell Neall. John Barnes to testify.

17 July 1674. George Wells (BA) one of the executors of Samuell Goldsmith to render accounts of said estate.

23 July. Sheriff (CH) to summon Henry Adams & Thomas Mathews to render accounts of estate of George Manwaring.

Per Kenelm Cheseldyn, Ignatius Caussin (g, coroner of CH) to summon John Allen (CH) to exhibit an inventory of estate of Nicholas Solsby (CH) & accounts of estate of William Jackson (CV).

4A:42   5 August. Sheriff (CH) to summon Samuell Cressey executor of John Harrington to exhibit an inventory of said estate.

Sheriff (SM) to summon Jane Wright widow & executrix of Thomas Wright (St. Jerome's Hundred) to exhibit an inventory.

Sheriff (SM) to summon Marck Cordea (g) administrator of John Brookes to render accounts.

Court Session: <no date>

Sheriff (SM) to summon Sara Russell relict & administratrix of Richard Russell (St. Michael's Hundred) to render accounts of said estate.

Sheriff (TA) to summon Richard Wollman to render accounts of estate of Charles Masters.

Sheriff (TA) to summon Philemon Lloyd to render accounts of estate of Henry Hawkins.

4A:43 Sheriff (AA) to summon Thomas Tourner executor of Thomasin Stinchcombe widow & executrix of Nathaniell Stinchcombe to render accounts of said estate.

Sheriff (AA) to summon Robert Burle & Thomas Marsh executors of Ralph Williams to render accounts of said estate.

6 August. Robertt Ridgely for William Ponning & Thomas Smart (merchants, Bristoll) vs. Edward Fitzherbert & Caleb Baker executors of William Hattoft. Caveat. Mentions: Humphry Barecroft (dec'd).

4A:44 ...

4A:45 11 August. Sheriff (AA) to summon Thomas Roper to render accounts on estate of Okey Roulands.

Sheriff (KE) to summon Arthur Wright to render accounts on estate of Joshua Meriton.

Sheriff (CH) to summon Thomas Wackfield to render accounts on estate of Jonathon Marler.

Sheriff (SM) to summon William Clew & John Smallpeece to render accounts on estate of John Reynolds.

4A:46 Sheriff (DO) to summon Hester LeCompte widow & executrix of Anthony LeCompte to render accounts on said estate.

Sheriff (KE) to summon John Wright to render accounts on estate of John

Court Session: <no date>

Boulton.

Sheriff (CV) to summon James Humber to render accounts on estate of Cornelius Rogers.

Sheriff (CV) to summon Mary Hooper to render accounts on estate of Richard Hooper.

Per John Bowling administrator of John Carraway (BA), sheriff (BA) to summon Francis Petit to show cause for detaining chattel.

4A:47
18 August. Inventory of George Manwaring. Executors: Thomas Mathews, Henry Adams. List of exceptions to the inventory, including debt from Capt. Neale & Edmund Linsey, bills in the hands of Thomas Wyn.

21 August. Sheriff (CV) to summon Mary Hooper to render accounts of estate of William Hopkins.

Sheriff (CH) to summon Elisabeth Harrison to render accounts of estate of Joseph Harrison.

Sheriff (CH) to summon Francis Wyn to render accounts on estate of William Marshall.

Coroner (CH) to summon John Allen to render accounts of estate of William Jenkson.

4A:48
Sheriff (CV) to summon William Chandborne who married relict of Richard Foxon to render accounts on said estate.

27 August. Charles de la Roche (SM) vs. estate of William Head (KE). Caveat.

Sheriff (KE) to summon Thomas Marsh to render accounts of estate of Ralph Williams.

31 August. Sheriff (CH) to summon John Bowles to render accounts of estate of Capt. William Butting.

Court Session: <no date>

Sheriff (CH) to summon John Bowles to render accounts of estate of Margery Buttin (alias Bowles) his wife.

4A:49 1 September. Sheriff (BA) to summon George Wells one of the executors of Samuell Goldsmith to render accounts on said estate.

Sheriff (BA) to summon Henry Haslewood to render accounts on estate of John Collett

Sheriff (BA) to summon Thomas Armiger to render accounts on estate of Francis Trippe.

Sheriff (AA) to summon Susanna White to render accounts on estate of James White.

Sheriff (CV) to summon Michael Higgnen to render accounts on estate of William Diveare.

Sheriff (TA) to summon Vincent Atcheson to render accounts on estate of Thomas Snow.

4A:50 Sheriff (SM) to summon Jonathon Squire to render accounts on estate of John Morecroft

Sheriff (AA) to summon Damorus Wyatt to render accounts on estate of Nicholas Wyatt.

Coroner (CH) to summon John Allen to render accounts on estate of Nicholas Solsby.

8 September. John Grammer (CV) vs. Samuell Graves of "Perryneck" formerly belonging to Thomas Perrie. Caveat.

Per John Dowling (BA) administrator of John Carraway, sheriff (BA) to summon Francis Petit (BA) to report regarding chattel of dec'd.

25 September 1674. At Court held at St. John's on 12 September, the bond passed

Court Session: <no date>

by executors of William Hattoft is to be delivered to the Attorney General, & Mr. Robertt Ridgely is to be the interim Attorney General.

2 October. Sheriff (KE) to summon Elisabeth Head widow & executrix of William Head to prove said will.

3 October. Sheriff (TA) to summon John Browne to provide an inventory for estate of Wardner Shudall (DO).

	18 September. Robertt Crossman creditor to estate of George Manwaring vs. executors of said estate. Came Henry Adams & Thomas Mathews (gentlemen) executors of George Manwaring. Answer to exceptions of Kenelm Cheseldyn.
4A:52	Answer made regarding the wearing apparel of his servants to be appraised by Mr. Henry Warren & Mr. Temperance Britton. Answer made regarding the debts of Capt. Neale & Edmund Lindsey.
4A:53	Answer made regarding bills in hands of Thomas Wyn.
4A:54	...
4A:55	9 October. Sheriff (SM) to summon Hester Cordea relict & executrix of Anthony LeCompte (DO) to render accounts of said estate.
4A:56	16 October 1674. John Ingram & Michael Miller creditors vs. John Wright administrator of (N) Boulton (KE). Caveat.

19 October. Mich. Miller creditor vs. estate of William Head (KE). Caveat.

26 October. Capt. John Quigley vs. estate of Thomas South. Caveat.

27 October. Sheriff (KE) to summon Michael Miller to render accounts on estate of Henry Lamb.

Sheriff (KE) to summon John Currer to render accounts on estate of his brother John Curer, Sr. (grocer, London).

Court Session: <no date>

Sheriff (TA) to summon John Browne to render an inventory of estate of Warner Shudall (BA).

4A:57 John Quigley vs. estate of Thomas South. Ruling: case dismissed. Rich. Tilghman & Joane Colleck were granted administration on said estate.

28 October. Sheriff (AA) to summon Elisabeth Warner executrix of James Warner & Abraham Chilld & John Jacobe (witnesses) & William Hopkins & Johanna Seuell (evidences against) to testify to said will.

16 October 1674 at SM. Samuell Hatton administrator of John Hatton vs. Nath. Heathcoate administrator of John Brewer administrator of John Hatton. Caveat.

4B:1 21 February. Cornelius Howard (AA) exhibited papers of Nicholas Wyatt dated 10 December 1671 & exhibited in court in 1673 by Damaris widow of said Nicholas as his last will & testament:

4B:2 Bequests: to only son Samuel a bare plantation. Richard Warfield (AA) & Edward Dorsey can provide other information regarding the revocation of the will.

30 August 1675. Ellen Hall, age 22, deposed that she was a servant to Nicholas Wyatt (SS) in 1673 & she was at the house of said Nicholas when he died. He was loving to his wife. Mr. Cornelius Howard made the will for said Nicholas on 10 December 1671. Date: 10 August 1675. Witness: Samuell Chew.

4B:3 Sarah Cooper, age 22, deposed that she was at the house of Robertt Gudgion (AA) & they discussed the will of said Nicholas. Date: 10 August 1675. Witness: Samuell Chew.

Mary Welsh, age 30, deposed that she was at the house of Nicholas Wyatt her father-in-law a day or two after Cornelius Howard wrote the will of said Nicholas. The deponent heard Mrs.

Court Session: <no date>

Cleggatt ask said Nicholas about his will. Date: 20 August 1675. Witness: Samuell Chew.

4B:4 10 August 1675. Robertt Goodwin came into the court & refused to take the oath & to answer questions. Nicholas Sheppeard did likewise.

Mary Evens, age 30, deposed that she was present when Cornelius Howard wrote will for Nicholas Wyatt that he would give his son Samuell Wyatt his plantation & his daughter chattel. Mrs. Wyatt & Mrs. Clagett both questioned said Nicholas. Edward Dorsey cross-examined said Mary.

4B:5 Date: 15 August 1675. Witness: Samuell Chew.

16 November 1675. Sheriff (CH) to summon Edward Maddox who married the relict of Henry Franckam to render accounts on his estate.

Sheriff (AA) to summon John Webster administrator of Roger Groce unadministered by the relict to render accounts on his estate.

17 November 1675. Sheriff (AA) to summon Mary Whelock widow of Edward Wheelock to prove the will of said Edward.

4B:6 Sheriff (AA) to summon John Teuge, Jr., Thomas Hooker, & Joshua Shaller (witnesses to the will of John Hawkins) to prove said will.

19 November 1675. James Holland & Luther Wilmer creditors vs. estate of Robertt Harrod. Caveat.

30 November 1675. Sheriff (KE) to summon Vincent Atcheson to render accounts on estate of Thomas Snow.

Sheriff (KE) to summon Elisabeth Head widow & executrix of William Head to render accounts on his estate.

Court Session: <no date>

4B:7   6 December 1675. Sheriff (AA) to summon John Groce, Richard Snowden & his wife Elisabeth (late Elisabeth Groce), Roger Groce, William Groce, & Francis Groce (orphans of Roger Groce) to render exceptions to accounts by John Welsh who married Anne relict of said Roger.

8 December 1675. Charles de la Roche (inholder, SM) creditor vs. estate of William Lucas. Caveat.

Charles de la Roche (inholder, SM) creditor vs. estate of William Baker. Caveat.

9 December 1675. Sheriff (CV) to summon Roger Brookes (g), et. al., to testify on cancellation of will of William Singleton (CV).

4B:8   17 December 1675. William Coursey (g, TA) to summon Robertt Markline, Jr. to prove will of Robertt Markline, Sr. Ralph Blackhall wrote said will.

29 December 1675. Mark Cordea (g) creditor vs. estate of Charles de la Roche (SM). Caveat.

Thomas Griffin (p, SM) creditor vs. estate of Peter Eure (SM). Caveat.

31 December 1675. Francis Blanch (SM) to summon Elisabeth de la Roche (SM) widow & executrix of Charles de la Roche (inholder) to prove his will.

4B:9   14 January 1675. Robertt Cager, Jr., nephew & next-of-kin, vs. estate of William Cager (SM).

Capt. John Quigley (SM) creditor vs. estate of Charles de la Roche (inholder, SM).

19 January 1675. Abraham Rhoades (SM), next-of-kin, vs. estate of Francis Duckson (CV).

9 February 1675. John Edmundson (TA) creditor vs. estate of Robertt Harwood

Court Session: <no date> (TA).

12 February 1675. Sheriff (AA) to summon William Farguson administrator of Thomas Phelps to render accounts of his estate.

4B:10   14 February 1675. Sheriff (AA) to summon Damaris Bland relict of Nicholas Wyatt to render accounts on his estate.

19 February 1675. John Groce received of Mr. John Welsh (AA). Witnesses: Richard Snowden, Thomas Knighton.
- Chattel. Date: 5 January 1673.
- Bills: Edmundson & Pitts, William Taylor, Edmund Coxe, Dennis Mecconnak, Jasper Flambert, William Smith, Nathaniell Clese, William Jones, Richard Deavor, John Winchester, Thomas Bradle & William Nesfolde. Date: 14 February 1673/4.

4B:11
- 5 patents for 2350 acres, belonging to estate of his father Roger Groce. Date: 29 August 1672.
- Chattel, per Court of the Eastern Shore. Date: 3 December 1672.
- Chattel. Date: 6 December 1673.
- Chattel. Date: 18 November 1672.

4B:12
- Chattel. Date: 18 November 1672.
- Chattel, per Court of the Eastern Shore. Date: 8 December 1672.
- Currency of England. Date: 28 March 1674.

4B:13
- Negroes (unnamed). Date: 18 November 1672.

21 February 1675. John Edmundson (merchant, TA) vs. estate of Capt. John Carre. Caveat.

22 February 1675. Sheriff (AA) to summon John Groce, Richard Snowden, Elisabeth Snowden (late Elisabeth Groce), Roger Groce, William Groce, & Francis Groce (orphans of Roger Groce (AA, dec'd))
4B:14   to render exceptions to accounts of John Welsh in right of his wife Anne.

Court Session: <no date>

29 February 1675. John Moll (merchant, Delaware) vs. estate of Capt. John Carre (CE). Caveat.

3 March 1675. Morgan Jones vs. estate of Charles North. Caveat.

Benjamin Mansfield (SM) by his attorney Kenelm Cheseldyn vs. estate of Richard Foster (SM). Caveat.

4 March 1675. John Baker (inholder) creditor vs. estate of Dianna James widow of Abell James. Caveat.

4B:15   Sheriff (SM) to summon Mary Goff widow & administratrix of Col. John Jarbo to render accounts on his estate.

14 March 1675. Sheriff (CV) to summon Edward Turner executor of William Singleton to confirm will. Also to summon Roger Brooke (g).

6 December 1674 at Pope's Freehold. Before: Philip Calvert, Esq. John Welsh (g, AA) by Robert Ridgely vs. John Groce, Richard Snowden & Elisabeth his wife (late Elisabeth Groce), Roger Groce, William Groce, & Francis Groce (orphans of Roger Groce (AA)). Said Roger died on 1 November 1665. Anne Groce is the widow & administratrix.

4B:16   Said Anne married John Welsh on 9 June 1666.

4B:17   ...

4B:18   20 March 1675. Sarah Francis (AA) relict & administratrix of John Shaw to render accounts on his estate.

4 April 1676. Thomas Notley (g, SM) vs. Mary Goff relict & administratrix of Col. John Jarbo. Caveat.

5 April 1676. Sheriff (CV) to summon Jasper Allen administrator of John Martin (merchant, Barbadoes) to render accounts on estate of Mathew James (merchant, Barbadoes, dec'd).

Court Session: <no date>

6 April 1676. Clement Haly (SM) to summon Casiya White widow of Rowland White to appear for administration on his estate.

George Parkes (g, CV) vs. estate of Andrew Higgs (CV). Caveat.

4B:19 Henry Jowles (CV) vs. estate of Andrew Higgs (CV). Caveat.

Okey Rowland vs. estate of John & Mary Sicely (AA, both dec'd). Caveat.

10 April 1676. John Edmundson (merchant, TA) vs. estate of Peter Syndewood (DO). Caveat.

John Codasck vs. estate of Edward Roe (TA). Caveat.

13 April 1676. William Sims vs. William Dare (merchant) administrator of John Parker. Caveat.

15 April 1676. Capt. Quigley vs. estate of Robertt Williams (TA). Caveat.

4B:20 17 April 1676. John Hall (g, CV) to summon Richard Ladd (g) to render accounts on estate of George Beckwith.

19 April 1676. Edward Gunnell (CE) for Edward Blake & Micaiah Perry & Thomas Lane (merchants, London) vs. estate of John Turpinne (BA). Caveat.

Sheriff (CE) to summon Arthur Carleton administration of Thomas Carleton to render accounts on his estate.

25 April 1676. Thomas Rowdell (CV) vs. estate of Richard Bromale (CV). Caveat. Mentions: relict.

Sheriff (AA) to summon Elisabeth Sparrow & Salomon Sparrow executors of Thomas Sparrow to render accounts on his estate.

4B:21 Sheriff (AA) to summon John Larkin administrator of William Powell to

Court Session: <no date>
provide an inventory of his estate.

Edward Englis (merchant) vs. estate of John Turpinne (BA). Caveat.

3 May 1676. Sheriff (BA) to summon Capt. Samuell Boston to render accounts of the estate of Capt. George Goldsmith unadministered by Mary Boston relict & executrix of said George & to render accounts of said Mary.

Sheriff (BA) to summon Thomas Overton to render accounts of the estate of Bernard Uty.

Sheriff (BA) to summon Mary Stansby daughter & executrix of Johanna Spry to render accounts of her estate.

4B:22 Sheriff (BA) to summon George Wells executor of Samuell Goldsmith to render accounts on his estate.

8 May 1676. Sheriff (CE) to summon Samuell Stiles to render accounts on the estate of Thomas Salmon.

Sheriff (CE) to summon John Ward to render accounts on the estate of Nicholas Tovey.

26 May 1676. Sheriff (CV) to summon William Dare administrator of John Parker to render accounts on his estate.

30 May 1676. Sheriff (CE) to summon Abraham Stran, William Southersby, William Pierse, & Richard Thornton executors of George Wilson to accept or reject the administration on his estate.

4B:23 Sheriff (CE) to summon widow of William Chadborne to appear for granting of administration on his estate.

17 June 1676. Sheriff (CV) to summon Roger Brooke executor of Edward Keene to answer complaint of Susanna Keene (widow of the dec'd).

Court Session: <no date>

Sheriff (CV) to summon William Dare administrator of John Parker to pass accounts.

20 July 1676. Sheriff (AA) to summon Alice Roper relict & administratrix of Jarvis Morgan to render accounts.

Sheriff (AA) to summon Lewis Blangey to render accounts on estate of James File.

22 August 1676. Sheriff (BA) to summon John Ireland (chirurgeon) to exhibit why his administration of the estate of Margret Penroy (CE) should not be revoked & granted to Kenelm Cheseldyn.

4B:24 24 August 1676. John Cage vs. estate of Charles Gregory (SM). Caveat.

25 August 1676. Edward Man (merchant, TA) on behalf of William Orchard & Co. (merchants, Poole, ENG) vs. estate of Margret Penroy (CE). Caveat.

Per Marmaduke Semms, William Watts (SM) to summon Jonathon Clerk to show why he detained chattel of the estate of Samuell Dickeson (SM).

31 August 1676. Sheriff (TA) to summon Peter Sayer & Frances his wife administratrix of the estate of Henry & Frances Morgan (TA, both dec'd) to render accounts & to show why his (Peter's) bond & that of William Coursey should not be assigned to John Rowsby who married Barbara (daughter of the dec'd).

4B:25 4 October 1676. Sheriff (BA) to summon John Ireland (chirurgeon) administrator of Margret Penroy (CE) to exhibit why his administration should not be revoked & granted to Kenelm Cheseldyn (greatest creditor).

Sheriff (CH) to summon John Cage to show why his administration on estate of Charles Gregory (chirurgeon) should not be revoked & granted to Capt. John Allen (greatest creditor).

Court Session: <no date>

12 October 1676. Sheriff (TA) to summon James Sedgewick, as only relation, to appear for granting administration on the estate of Capt. Miles Cooke.

Evan Carew (SM) to summon Mathias Gerrardy (Dutchman) to give evidence concerning the estate of Abell James.

4B:26 14 October 1676. Michael Miller vs. estate of Thomas Barnes (KE). Caveat.

Sheriff (KE) to summon Patrick Gordon to prove will of Peter Harrison (KE).

14 November 1676. William Hanman (mariner, Bristoll) vs. estate of William Worgan (DO). Caveat.

William Younger (SM), as next of blood by marriage to mother of the dec'd, vs. estate of Richard Cole (SM). Caveat.

4B:27 20 November 1676. Elias Beeche (SM) to summon Thomas Griffin, Thomas Raile, & Grace Willen to give evidence regarding the estate of Richard Cole (SM).

29 November 1676. Henry Mathews (TA) to summon Henry Hosier & John Bowles (KE) to render accounts on the estate of Walter Spencer.

Edward Man vs. Jonathon Loggins (TA) administrator of Richard Walters. Caveat.

Thomas Carlisle & John Watson (SM) summoned to answer to Samuell Leadbeather (merchant) attorney of Cadwallader Jones (merchant) & to exhibit an inventory of the estate of John Cunningham.

4B:28 1 December 1676. Edward Manne (merchant, TA) vs. estate of Jonathon Eaton (KE). Caveat.

Edward Man (merchant, TA) vs. estate of Arthur Wright (DO). Caveat.

Court Session: <no date>

Edward Man (merchant, TA) vs. estate of Thomas Earle (TA). Caveat.

John Pitt (merchant, TA) vs. estate of Thomas Earle (TA). Caveat.

John Edmundson (merchant, TA) vs. estate of Thomas Earle (TA). Caveat.

3 December 1676. Leonard Greene (SM) to summon William Watts administrator of Thomas Cager to render accounts on his estate.

5 December 1676. Alexander Younger (SM) to exhibit why administration should not be granted to Sarah Beeche on the estate of her brother Richard Cole.

4B:29 7 December 1676. Sheriff (SM) to summon Marke Cordea to render chattel of the estate of John Baylie to his administrator Stephen Murty.

8 December 1676. Sheriff (SM) to summon Alexander Younger & Sarah his wife to render guardian accounts of the orphans of William Cole.

Edward Man (merchant, TA) greatest creditor vs. estate of John Ingram (TA). Caveat.

21 December 1676. Sheriff (SM) to summon Marmaduke Semms to render accounts on the estate of Abell James.

28 December 1676. Sheriff (CV) to summon John Halfehead, Jr. administrator of John Halfehead, Sr. to render accounts on his estate.

4B:30 29 December 1676. Sheriff (AA) to summon Capt. Richard Hill administrator of James Rawbone to exhibit an inventory of his estate.

Garret Vansweringen (SM) vs. estate of Capt. Miles Cooke (mariner, ENG). Caveat.

Court Session: <no date>

5 January 1676. Henry Rider (SM) creditor vs. estate of William Lucas. Caveat. Francis Lucas is executrix.

Joseph Edloe (SM) creditor vs. estate of William Lucas. Caveat. Francis Lucas is executrix.

4B:31 16 January 1676. John Saunders (merchant, Bristoll) creditor vs. estate of Luke Greene (CH). Caveat.

20 January 1676. Sheriff (SM) to summon Marke Cordea to render chattel to Stephen Murty administrator of John Bayley.

27 January 1676. John Atkin (SM) to summon Petter Watts & Daniel Clocker executors of Daniell Clocker, Sr. to render accounts on his estate.

3 February 1676. Sheriff (CV) to summon George Lingen
4B:32 executor of Thomas Cox to exhibit why Henry Cole should not possess the chattels of the dec'd, per letter from the relict (now in ENG).

John Baker (inholder, SM) vs. estate of Vincent Atcheson (KE). Caveat.

15 February 1676. John Atkins (SM) vs. estate of William Jenkins (CV). Caveat.

17 February 1676. William Coursey (TA) vs. estate of Disborough Bennet (g, KE). Caveat.

4B:33 Henry Coursey (TA) vs. estate of Disborough Bennet (g, KE). Caveat.

John Moll (DE) vs. estate of Vincent Atcheson (KE). Caveat.

20 February 1676. Dr. John Stansby creditor vs. estate of John Barret (BA). Caveat.

21 February 1676. John Allen (CH) creditor vs. estate of Charles Gregory (CH), unadministered by John Cage (CH,

Court Session: <no date>

dec'd). Caveat.

4B:34
12 March 1676. Sheriff (SM) to summon Anne Fisher relict & administratrix of William Burges to render accounts on his estate.

14 March 1676. Sheriff (SM) to summon Thomas Potter executor of George Marshall (SM) to render accounts on his estate.

15 March 1676. Sheriff (SM) to summon Mary Goffe relict & executrix of Lt. Col. John Jarboe to render accounts on his estate.

4B:35
18 April 1677. Sheriff (AA) to summon Thomas Francis administrator of John Shaw to render accounts. Estate unadministered by Sarah Francis wife of Thomas Francis & relict & administratrix of said John.

19 April 1677. Elisabeth Phippes relict & executrix of George Dundasse (SM) summoned to render accounts.

20 April 1677. Sheriff (CE) to summon Edward Inglish (merchant) administrator of Roger Thorpe (merchant, London) to render accounts on his estate to George Parker (CV) attorney for Ralph Fortly (London).

4B:36
23 April 1677. Mary Clements executrix of John Clements (TA) creditor vs. estate of William Cannons (merchant, TA). Caveat.

Sheriff (CV) to summon Roger Brooke (g, CV) executor of Edward Keene to render accounts on his estate.

Sheriff (BA) to summon Thomas Preston executor of Thomas Arminger to render accounts on his estate.

4B:37
Sheriff (TA) to summon Mary Briges widow & executrix of Richard Briges to render accounts on his estate.

Page 207

Court Session: <no date>

24 April 1677. Mary Clemens executrix of John Clemens (g, TA) vs. estate of Thomas Earle (TA). Caveat.

25 April 1677. James Guthrey (CV) vs. estate of Richard Wadsworth, Jr. (CV). Caveat.

4B:38   3 May 1677. Sheriff (CV) to summon Mary Griggs relict & executrix of Richard Keene to render accounts on his estate.

4C:1   16 May 1677. Sheriff (SM) to summon Richard Edelen executor of Samuell Cressey (CH) to render accounts on his estate.

Sheriff (SM) to summon Garret Vansweringen (St. Mary's City) administrator of William Baker to render accounts on his estate.

4C:2   Sheriff (CV) to summon Rebecca Brooke widow & administratrix of John Brooke (CV) to render accounts on his estate.

Sheriff (SM) to summon Roger Digins sole surviving executor of William Bourke to render accounts on his estate.

21 June 1677. Sheriff (DO) to summon Anne O'Bryan widow of Denis O'Bryan to show why administration should be committed to Henry Harris principle creditor.

4C:3   Henry Harris creditor vs. estate of Denis O'Bryan (BA). Caveat.

22 June 1677. Sheriff (AA) to summon Alice Skidmore widow & executrix of Edward Skidmore to show why she retains the will from probate.

11 July 1677. William Ball (Rapahanock, VA) vs. estate of his son Richard Ball (g, Patapsco, BA). Caveat.

4C:4
4C:5   14 August 1677. Sheriff (CE) to summon the following to render accounts:

- Edward Inglish administrator of John

Court Session: <no date>

- Allen, unadministered by John Vanheck.
- vidua Blunt executrix of Richard Blunt.
- Arthur Carlton administrator of his brother Thomas Carlton.
- Henry Ward administrator of Abraham Coffin.
- Henry Ward administrator of Richard Gore (merchant, Barbadoes).
- John Browneing (merchant) administrator of John Gilbert.
- Edward Inglish administrator of William Hewett, unadministered by John Turpin (BA).
- John Howell executor of his father Thomas Howell.
- Anne Nash relict & executrix of Richard Blunt who was administrator of William Howard.

4C:6

- Richard Whitton executor of Richard Leake (BA).
- Martha Shaw relict & executrix of Thomas Middlefield.
- Thomas Hacker executor of John Powell.
- Nicholas Shaw administrator of his brother William Shaw (TA), unadministered by Joyce Shaw (widow of said William).
- John Howell only executor at age of John Vanheck.
- William Peerce administrator of George William during executor's minority.
- Peternella Oldfield relict & executrix of Capt. John Carr.
- Jane Crouche widow & executrix of John Crouche.
- Henry Ward (g) administrator of Daniell Glover.
- Elisabeth Morgan widow & executrix of John Morgan.
- Capt. Edmund Cantwell (DE) administrator of Daniell Mackary.

4C:7

- Bennet Morgan widow & administratrix of Robert Morgan.
- Sarah Poole widow & executrix of John Poole.

Court Session: <no date>

4C:8

Sheriff (SO) to summon the following to render accounts:

- Anne Ackworth executrix of Richard Ackworth.
- Thomas Walker executor of William Morgan.
- Robert Richardson administrator of John Teage.
- William Steevens administrator of Macona Thomas.
- William Steevens administrator of Macon Thomas.
- Henry Boston the son administrator of Henry Boston, Sr.
- Arnold Parrimore executor of John Parrimore.
- vidua Shills executrix of Thomas Shills.

4C:9

Sheriff (DO) to summon the following to render accounts:

- Katharine Mountague vidua & administratrix of Henry Mountague (TA).
- Jane Raven widow & administratrix of John Raven.

4C:10

- Elisabeth Skinner widow & administratrix of Thomas Skinner.
- William Dorsey administrator of John Wigfield.
- Henry Hooper, Jr. administrator of Henry Hooper, Sr.

4C:11

Sheriff (BA) to summon the following to render accounts:

- James Mills sole remaining executor of Capt. Samuell Boston, who was administrator of William Boughton.
- Miles Gibson administrator of Abraham Clarke, unadministered by Sarah (widow).
- James Denton administrator of Thomas Daniell.
- James Mills executor of Capt. Samuell Boston, who was administrator of Capt. George Goldsmith, unadministered by Mary Boston relict & executrix of said

Court Session: <no date>

- George. Also the estate of said Mary.
- Richard Simms administrator of Roger Hill. Executor is an infant under age.
- James Mills administrator of Robert Maddock.

4C:12
- Miles Gibson executor of John Newton.
- Dr. John Stanesby sole surviving executor of Caesar Prince.
- John Bird administrator of Joseph Pierce.
- Thomas Jones executor of John Reycroft.
- Mary Stanesby (alias Mary Harmer) executrix of Johanna Spry.
- Arthur Taylor executor of John Taylor.
- Margaret Therrell widow & executrix of Richard Therrell.
- Elisabeth Uty widow & administratrix of Col. Nathaniell Uty.
- William Hollis & James Phillips administrators of Thomas Winfield.
- Rachell Towers widow & executrix of John Towers.
- Benjamin Bennet administrator of his brother Andrew Bennet.
- William Yorke administrator of Capt. John Collier, unadministrated by Lodowick Williams.

4C:13
- Florence Lee widow & executrix of John Lee.
- Thomas Jones administrator of Walter Marcanallie.
- Col. George Wells executor of James Ogdon.
- Edward Monfret executor of William Poultney.
- Henrietta Swanston widow & executrix of Edward Swanston.
- Katharine Shadwell widow & administratrix of John Shadwell.

Sheriff (KE) to summon the following to render accounts:

4C:14
- Christopher Andrews administrator of Robert Carpenter (CE).

Page 211

Court Session: <no date>

4C:15
- Elisabeth Head daughter & administratrix of Edward Coppedge.
- Lewis Blangey administrator of James File (AA).
- Patrick Sullivant executor of John Nevill (CV).
- Joseph Weekes & John Hinson executors of John Rodaway (TA).
- Henry Hosier (g), Cornelius Accomagies, & John Bowles executors of Walter Spencer.
- Mary Wright widow & administratrix of John Wright.
- Mary Wells widow & administratrix of Tobias Wells.
- Hannah Baxter widow & executrix of Thomas Baxter.
- Joane Workman relict & executrix of Robert Dun.
- Mary Eaton widow & executrix of Jeremiah Eaton.
- Alice Ginne widow & administratrix of Arthur Ginne.
- Thomas Warren executrix of Margaret Hill.
- John & Matthew Erickson administrators of Edward Jones.
- Isaac Winchester administrator of Richard Moore.
- Mary Plum widow & executrix of John Plum.

4C:16
- Anne Rye widow & administratrix of John Rye.
- Thomas Marsh sole surviving executor of Ralph Williams (AA).

Sheriff (TA) to summon the following to render accounts:

4C:17
- John Rowsby administrator of Francis Allen.
- Mary Bridges widow & executrix of Richard Bridges.
- Mary Clements widow & administratrix of John Clements.
- Elisabeth Foster widow & executrix of Seth Foster.
- Edward Man (merchant) administrator of Robert Harwood.
- Mary Roe widow & executrix of Edward

Court Session: <no date>

4C:18

- Roe, who was administrator of Robert Hale.
- Sarah Hancock widow & executrix of Benjamin Hancock.
- vidua Martin executrix of Robert Martin.
- Matthew Ward & William Bishop administrators of Robert Mackline.
- Mary Tilghman widow & executrix of Dr. Richard Tilghman.
- Thomas Hinson (g) administrator of John Vine.
- Ralph Dawson executor of Humphrey Archer.
- Mary Campher executrix of Thomas Campher.
- Joyce Hewton widow & administratrix of Matthew Hewton.
- Elisabeth Loggins relict & administratrix of John Hendricks.
- Mary Lorkie widow & executrix of Nicholas Lorkie.
- Mary Noake widow & administratrix of William Noake.
- Mary Price widow & executrix of William Price. Said Mary renounced administration & William Hemsley is administrator.
- Edward Man (merchant) administrator of Thomas Reede.
- Henry Wilcocks & Charles Hollingsworth administrators of John Singleton.

4C:19

- Executor of William Sturdenant.
- James Coursey administrator of John Scott.

Sheriff (AA) to summon the following to render accounts:

4C:20

- Capt. Richard Hill administrator of Edward Gardner, who was executor of Dorothy Bruton.
- William Russell administrator of Thomas Chandler.
- James Crouche executor of William Crouche.
- Capt. Richard Hill administrator of Philip Dawson.
- Elisabeth Edwards widow & executrix

Page 213

Court Session: <no date>

of John Edwards.
- John Welsh administrator of John Grose.
- Richard Guinne administrator of his brother Thomas Guinne.
- John Watkins executor of John Grose.
- Jane Hilliard widow & administratrix of Daniell Hilliard.
- William Russell administrator of Thomas Chandler, who was administrator of Symon Harrison.

4C:21

- Mary Hawkins widow & executrix of John Hawkins.
- John Gray executor of Hopkin Jones (BA).
- Alice Roper relict & administratrix of Jervase Morgan.
- Susanna Neale widow & executrix of William Neale.
- Edward Parish administrator of John Peck.
- Sarah Porter widow & administratrix of Peter Porter.
- Elisabeth Reade widow & executrix of William Reade.
- Henry Lewis (g) administrator of Thomazin Stinchcombe, unadministered by Thomas Turner.
- Henry Lewis (g) & John Ricks executors of William Slade.
- Henry Lewis (g) administrator of Thomazin Stinchcombe, unadministered by Thomas Turner. Said Thomazin was executrix of Nathaniell Stinchcombe.

4C:22

- Sarah Thomas widow & executrix of Philip Thomas.
- Magdalene Smith relict & executrix of Edmund Townehill.
- Henry Lewis (g) administrator of Thomas Turner.
- Mary Bucknall relict & administratrix of Edward Wheellock.
- Nehemiah Birckhead the son executor of Christopher Birckhead.
- Stephen Burle the son executor of Robert Burle.
- Margaret Cooper widow & administratrix of Thomas Cooper.
- Robert Francklin (g) executor of William Collier.

Court Session: <no date>

4C:23
- Rachell Clarke widow & executrix of Neale Clarke.
- Diana Fitting widow & administratrix of Robert Fitting.
- John Watkins administrator of Jonas Kinsey (TA).
- Mary Luffman widow & executrix of William Luffman.
- Robert Procter & John Gather executors of Joseph Morley.
- Peter Barnet & Richard Beard executors of Daniell Taylor.

4C:24
20 August 1677. Sheriff (CH) to summon the following to render accounts:
- Richard Beck administrator of his brother Lewis Beck.
- Henry Hawkins executor of Giles Cole.
- Thomas King administrator of Samuell Cooper.
- Margaret Downes widow & administratrix of Robert Downes.
- Thomas King executor of Jenkin Jones.
- Jane Matthews widow & executrix of Dr. Thomas Matthews.
- Maj. Benjamin Rozer administrator of Robert Prowse (VA, late inhabitant of this county).
- John Stone (g) executor of Verlinda Stone.

4C:25
- Elisabeth Corker widow & executrix of Thomas Corker who was administrator of Clement Theobald.
- Thomas Clipsham administrator of John Williams.
- James Tyer executor of John Bowls.
- Sarah Barnes executrix of Henry Barnes.
- Thomas Clipsham administratrix of Roger Bowder.
- Philip Lynes administrator of Robert Clarke.
- Thomas Casey executor of Patrick Farlum.
- Robert & Francis Goodrick sons & executors of George Goodrick.
- William Deane & William Stannard

Page 215

Court Session: <no date>

4C:26
- executors of John Greene.
- Penelope Helmes administratrix of John Helmes.
- Joanna Jones widow & administratrix of Owen Jones.
- Maj. Benjamin Rozer administrator of Edmund Lindsey.
- John Finning (g) administrator of Seabright Meacock.
- William Wells administrator of David Maddox.
- Mary Blackfan executrix of John Blackfan, who was administrator of Richard Owen.
- Mary Pope widow & administratrix of Thomas Pope.
- Thomas King administrator of Samuell Sherrill.
- Margery Stone widow & executrix of Matthew Stone.
- Mary Blackfan relict & executrix of Thomas Stone.
- Maj. Benjamin Rozer administrator of Joseph Pearse (Dartmough, old ENG).

4C:27
21 August 1677. Sheriff (CV) to summon the following to render accounts:

- Henry Exon executor of Thomas Arnold.
- Francis Hopewell administrator of John Booth (SM).

4C:28
- Robert Taylor administrator of Coniers Barber.
- Rebecca Brooke widow & administratrix of John Brooke.
- Anne Bigger widow & executrix of John Bigger.
- Sarah Clarke widow & executrix of Thomas Clarke.
- Joseph Edloe executor of William Cane (alias William Keene, SM).
- Henry Exon executor of Thomas Cosford.
- George Parker (Clifts) administrator of Lownes Eason.
- Capt. John Cobreath executor of Richard Evans.
- Anne Ewen widow & executrix of

Court Session: <no date>

- William Ewen.
- Robert Fisher administrator of his brother Henry Fisher.
- Margaret Gittings widow & executrix of John Gittings.
- Roger Brooke (g) sole surviving executor of Philip Harwood.

4C:29

- Jackelina Moore (alias Jackelina Harris) relict & executrix of James Moore.
- William Parker (Herring Creek) administrator of Thomas Preston.
- Isabella Swanston widow & executrix of Dr. Francis Swanston.
- Anne Tapticoe widow & administratrix Peter Tapticoe.
- Capt. Samuell Bourne administrator of Robert Taverner (merchant, London).
- Susanna Wadsworth widow & administratrix of Richard Wadsworth.
- William Kent administrator of Richard Williams.
- George Young administrator of his brother William Young.
- Mary Anderson widow & executrix of John Anderson.
- Joyce Brummale widow & executrix of Richard Brummale.
- Robert Blinckhorne executor of William Cussin.

4C:30

- Hester Ennis widow & executrix of William Ennis.
- Richard Fenwick administrator of his brother Cuthbert Fenwick.
- Phillis How widow & administratrix of Thomas How.
- Anne Jones (Clifts) widow & administratrix of Meridith Jones.
- Samuell Vines executor of Cornelius Jones.
- Capt. Samuell Bourne administrator of Levin Johnson.
- Tabitha Mill widow & executrix of William Mill.
- Mary Stockley widow & executrix of James Stockley.
- Mary Stacey widow & administratrix of William Stacey.
- Jane Thompson widow & administratrix

Court Session: <no date>

of James Thompson.
- Sarah Evans relict & executrix of Guy White.

4C:31
4C:32

22 August 1677.
Sheriff (SM) to summon the following to render accounts:

- Garret Vansweringen administrator of William Baker.
- Katharine Bartley widow & administratrix of George Bartley.
- Roger Diggins sole surviving executor of William Bourke.
- Rebecca Beale widow & administratrix of John Beale.
- Sarah Claw (alias Sarah Younger) administratrix of William Claw (St. Jerome's).
- Morgan Jones administrator of George Charlesworth, unadministered by Thomas Matthews (CH).
- Peter Watts sole remaining executor of Robert Cager.
- Col. William Calvert & Thomas Keiting administrators of Bryan O'Daly.
- Thomas Griffin administrator of Peter Eure.
- Joseph Edley administrator of his brother John Edley.
- Vincent Mansfield administrator of his father-in-law Richard Foster.

4C:33

- Joanna Farrar widow & executrix of Robert Farrar.
- Elinor Forrest & George Dundasse the widow & son-in-law executors of Patrick Forrest.
- Henry Elliot administrator of his mate William Gifford.
- Gilbert Turbervile administrator of Francis Graile.
- Frances Hyde widow & executrix of Henry Hyde.
- James Lewis executor of Benjamin Hunton.
- Richard Chilman administrator of John Hall.
- Thomas Griffin executor of Thomas Hunt.
- Mary Haile widow & administratrix of

Court Session: <no date>

John Haile.
- Randolph Hinson administrator of Thomas Hatton.
- William Hatton administrator of Richard Hatton, Sr., during executor's minority.
- Margaret Jolley widow & administratrix of Edward Jolley.
- Marmaduke Semme administrator of Abell James, unadministered by Diana widow & executrix.

4C:34
- William Rosewell (g) administrator of Francis Montefort.
- Robert Carvile (Gentleman) executor of Elisabeth Moy, widow & executrix of Richard Moy.
- Anne Mackall widow & executrix of George Mackall.
- Robert Carvile executor of Elisabeth Moy.
- Elisabeth Mackey widow & executrix of John Mackey.
- Elinor Newman widow & administratrix of Abraham Newman.
- Thomas Pinck administrator of Jane Paine.
- Lydia Pierce widow & administratrix of Thomas Pierce.
- Sarah Claw (alias Sarah Younger) administratrix of William Claw, who was sole surviving executor of John Reynold.
- Richard Edelen (g) executor of Samuell Cressey (CH), who was administrator of Daniell Russell (SM).

4C:35
- Elisabeth de la Roche widow & executrix of Charles de la Roche.
- William Rosewell (g) administrator of Nicholas Rithson.
- Thomas Gerard administrator of Marmaduke Snow.
- Richard Edelen (g) executor of Samuell Cressey (CH), who was administrator of Alexander Smith (CH).

Richard Edelen (g) executor of Samuell Cressey (CH), who was administrator of John Waas (CH).

Court Session: <no date>

4C:36

- Elisabeth Royall executrix of Francis Barnell.
- Thomas Cooke administrator of John Cooke.
- William Watts administrator of Thomas Cager.
- Mary Connery widow & administratrix of Edward Connery.
- Capt. John Coode administrator of Thomas Ceely. Executor is in ENG.
- Thomas Carlisle & John Watson only remaining executors of John Cunningham.
- Elisabeth Dundasse (alias Elisabeth Phippes) executrix of George Dundasse.
- Rebecca Addison relict & executrix of Thomas Dent.
- Marmaduke Semme administrator of Samuell Dickeson.
- Elisabeth Dundasse (alias Elisabeth Phippes) executrix of her mother Helena Forrest.
- Thomas Carvile executor of Robert Hunt.
- Morgan Jones executor of John Harrington.
- Mary Goffe relict & administratrix of Lt. Col. John Jarboe.
- Elisabeth Mackart widow & executrix of John Mackart.
- Anne Medley (alias Anne Cole) administratrix of John Medley, who was executor of his brother George Medley.

4C:37

- Anne Medley (alias Anne Cole) widow or relict & administratrix of John Medley.
- Elisabeth Mackey executrix of Elisabeth Rawlins.
- Kesia White widow & administratrix of Rowland White.
- Jane Gray administratrix of Alexander Gray.

18 October 1677. Joseph Chew (CE) vs. John Browning (CE) administrator of Capt. John Gilbert (CE). Caveat.

Court Session: <no date>

13 November 1677. Francis Swinfin vs. estate of John Bigger (CV). Caveat.

4C:38 Michael Miller (KE) vs. John Browning (CE) administrator of Capt. John Gilbert (CE).

27 November 1677. Sheriff (SM) to summon John Doxey to render accounts on estate of Richard Chapman.

12 April 1678. Anne Hood executrix of Robert Hood (KI or KE) vs. estate of Edward Chicken (KI or KE). Caveat.

13 April 1678. Johannah Goldsmith (BA) vs. John Browning (CE) administrator of John Gilbert (g). Caveat.

4C:39 3 May 1678. Henry Howard (AA) in right of Henry Howard (executor of said John) vs. estate of John Possum (AA & NY). Caveat.

General Index

(no surname)
  Andrew 147, 170
  Augustine 62
  Edith 107
  Edward 14
  Elisabeth 145
  Frankham 23
  Grace 145
  Harrie 17
  Hendrick 66
  Henrietta 18
  Jade 188
  James 23, 165
  John 110
  Joseph 137
  Mary 62, 145
  Mathias 62
  Maurice 112
  Richard 145
  Sarah 145
  Saunders 84
  Suffia 57
  Symonds 23
  Thomas 18, 145

Abbestone
  Will. 178
Abbington
  Mr. 23, 140
Abbott
  Samuell 157
Abercromby
  David 30
Abestone
  William 166
Abingdon
  John 18
Abington
  John 33
  Mr. 62
Abraham(s)
  Cornelius 11
  Elisabeth 44
  Isaac 165, 167, 179
  Isaack 19, 152, 179
  Isack 70, 167
Abrahamson
  Cornelius 53
  Cornely 162
  Frances 10
Accheson
  Vincent 37

Accomagies
  Cornelius 212
Acheson
  James 35
  Vincent 62, 154
Ackellis
  Peter 54
Ackillis
  (N) 107
Ackworth
  Anne 210
  Richard 104, 210
Acthezon
  Vincent 101
Acton
  Rich. 53
Ad(d)am(e)s
  Charity 39
  Elisabeth 127
  George 127
  Henry 19, 22, 26, 29,
    30, 38, 44, 50, 52,
    60, 63, 69, 72, 93,
    94, 124, 125, 129,
    130, 136, 153, 159,
    169, 172, 176, 179,
    186, 187, 191, 193,
    195
  Isabella 127
  James 11, 127, 133,
    144
  John 127
  Margarett 127
  Mr. 88
  Phebe 127
  Richard 110
  Thomas 55
  William 117, 129, 149
Addenbrooke
  Nicholas 129
  Roger 129
  Thomas 129, 141
Addison
  John 78
  Rebecca 220
Adwick
  Grace 93
  James 93
  John 93
  William 93, 101
Adwicke
  Grace 93
Adwicks

James 101
Ahalwen
  Lathline 74
Aixell
  Thomas 112
Alanson
  Thomas 8
Alberry
  Edward 145
Alcox
  Thomas 23
Alder
  Will. 164
Alderson
  Geo. 63
  George 33, 63, 70, 141, 148, 176
Aldeson
  Geo. 48
Aldridge
  George 78, 153, 185
Alexander
  Charles 117, 119
  Chas. 42
  Henry 11, 41, 47, 52, 53
Alexson
  John 182
Alkocke
  Thomas 124
Allanson
  Tho. 107
  Thomas 8, 93, 94, 99, 107, 124, 150, 151
Allcock
  Sam. 102
Allcocks
  Tho. 175
Allemby
  Philip 108
Allen
  Francis 212
  James 22, 26, 32, 36, 95, 97, 101
  Jasper 200
  Jesper 183, 184
  John 159, 179, 191, 193, 194, 203, 206, 209
  Mary 183, 184
  Patrick 142
  Richard 90
  Solomon 173
  Thomas 143
  William 1, 44, 120, 162, 175
Allenbie
  Joyce 100
Allenby
  Jane 100
  Phillip 100
Allenson
  John 40
  Mr. 162
Allexander
  Henry 26
Allibane
  Thomas 153
Allily
  Edw. 164
Allin
  Mary 79
Alline
  William 35
Allomby
  William 48
Allsta
  John 79
Alonson
  Thomas 70
Alvey
  Pope 150, 151
Alveys 96
Ambrose
  Richard 181
Anderson
  David 154
  George 159
  Gilbert 154
  Henry 185
  John 27, 40, 71, 110, 151, 154, 187, 217
  Mary 217
Anderton
  Andrew 163
  John 3, 33, 80, 145, 151, 153
  Roger 8
Andrew(e)s
  Christopher 211
  John 139
  Tho. 145
  Thomas 64, 138, 150
Anketile
  Francis 71
Anketill
  Francis 3, 71, 80, 148
  John 3
Antonio

Simon 2, 3, 11, 12
Appleford
  Tobias 182
Archer
  Humphrey 213
  John 152
  Peter 149
Archilles
  Peter 109
Argent
  Margarett 115
  William 106, 115, 154
Armestrong's Quarter 147
Armiger
  Thomas 190, 194
Arminger
  Thomas 207
Armstrong's White Marsh 162
Arm(e)strong(e)
  Edward 67, 148, 152
  Elisabeth 162
  Fran. 172
  Frances 166, 173, 175
  Francis 33, 53, 70, 80, 159, 162, 166, 173, 174, 175, 179
  Philemon 162
  Rich. 68, 69
  Richard 62
Arnold
  Rich. 164
  Thomas 216
Arrisbrooke
  Suzanna 106
Arthur
  Edward 23
Asbeston
  William 124
Asbestone
  William 175
Asbiston
  William 152
Ashbrooke
  John 19
  Thomas 154
Ashcomb(e)
  John 22, 24, 141, 176
Ashton
  Capt. 171
Asiter
  Will. 161
  William 56, 76, 77
Askom

  John 33
Asseter
  William 6, 7
Assiter
  William 35, 44, 46, 56, 78
Atcheson
  James 30, 68
  Susan 30
  Vincent 30, 105, 194, 197, 206
Atkeson
  Roger 40
Atkin(s)
  John 206
  Richard 176
  Robert 176
  Thomas 55
Attchison
  Vincent 12
Attkins
  Edward 13
  George 150
Attwicks
  Humphrey 42
  Humphry 42
Atwick
  James 40
  John 40
Aues
  John 122
Austin
  Annah 73
Austure
  Robert 54
Avery
  John 154, 177
Axell
  Thomas 91
Axton
  John 171
Ayliffe
  William 42
Ayres
  Edward 104, 153

Bacer
  Thomas 139
Bacheler
  Frances 36
  Francis 47
Backer
  Joseph 149
Backhouse

William 13
Bagby
  Dyna 185
  John 33, 68
Baggley
  William 146
Bagley
  Mr. 77
Baily
  Hen. 72
  Rich. 164
Baker
  Caleb 190, 192
  John 55, 200, 206
  Roger 187
  Tho. 70, 72, 179
  Thomas 34, 83, 92, 94, 125, 136, 179
  William 32, 56, 198, 208, 218
Baldwin
  George 14
Balf
  Oliver 107
Ball
  Richard 111, 208
  Thomas 130
  William 208
Ballard
  Charles 77, 121
Balley
  John 155
Balls
  Alphonsus 68
Balte
  Oliver 136
Balts
  Oliver 171
Balye
  Rich. 68
Baman
  John 61
Bamby
  Richard 59
Bamsday
  Will. 52
Bancke
  George 167
Banckes
  Adam 167
  Richard 29, 37, 144, 146, 151
Banister
  Henry 152
  Tho. 23

Bank(e)s
  Capt. 13
  Margarite 83
  Richard 7, 13, 32, 42, 88
Bann
  James 79
Banyster
  Henry 40
Barbary
  Thomas 20
Barber
  Coniers 216
  Dr. 6, 49
  Elisabeth 156
  John 52
  L. 3
  Luke 1, 4, 6, 15, 68, 156, 189
  Numan 148
Barbery
  Tho. 68
  Thomas 153
Barbier
  Elisabeth 166
  Luke 166
Barecroft
  Humphry 192
Barke
  John 28
Barker
  William 59
Barly
  Ann 137
Barnabe/Barnaby
  Elisabeth 115, 121
  James 115, 121
  Mary 115, 121
  Rebecca 115
  Rebeckah 121
Barnell
  Francis 220
Barnes
  Christopher 138, 174
  Dorathy. 139
  Francis 116, 139, 140, 146
  Henry 136, 215
  Isab. 140
  Isabell 139
  Issabella 146
  Izabella 150
  James 115
  John 153, 162, 190, 191

Mary 139
Sarah 215
Thomas 139, 204
William 51
Barnet
  Peter 215
Barnett
  William 149
Barns
  Christopher 78
Barnum
  Frances 64
Barren Island 173
Barrens
  Francis 89
Barret(t)
  John 114, 132, 206
Barrows
  John 7
Barthowse
  William 4
Bartle
  Gabriell 159
Bartley
  George 218
  Katharine 218
Barton
  Edmond 117
  Robert 173
  William 31, 54
Basey
  Michaell 151
  Miell 151
Basha
  Andrew 62
Bashachis
  Andr. 72
Bashaw
  Andrew 126, 151
Bashey
  Andrew 62
Baskett
  Thomas 55
Bassett
  Thomas 117, 119
Basy
  Michaell 68
  Miell 153
Batchelor
  Francis 62, 69
  Sarah 62
Bateman
  John 18, 19, 27, 33,
    37, 40, 51, 59, 65,
    66, 67, 71, 74, 89

  Mary 51, 65, 66, 67,
    69, 71, 89, 108,
    110, 111, 138, 140
  Mr. 22, 24, 62
  Mrs. 114, 152
  William 59
Bates
  Edward 15
  Mr. 41
  Thomas 30
Bath(e)
  Christopher 23
  Peter 4, 5, 8, 14,
    15, 17, 22, 23, 37
  Richard 23
Batterson
  Robert 19
Battin
  Margery 39, 40
  Will. 55
  William 39, 40, 46
Batty
  Fernando 73
Baxter
  Hannah 212
  John 58
  Rodger 28
  Roger 163, 179
  Thomas 179, 212
Bayes
  Bridgett 141
Bayley
  Godfrey 96, 97, 106,
    119, 188, 190
  John 206
  Richard 66, 75, 84,
    86, 91, 92, 113,
    118, 149, 152, 176,
    185
  Thomas 163
  Tobias 107, 109
  Tobyas 111
Baylie
  John 205
Bayly
  Godfrey 126, 127, 151
  Godfry 14, 53
  John 44
  Richard 68, 74, 76,
    80, 117, 119, 123,
    129, 131, 183
  Tobias 107
Baylye
  Rich. 76
Bayne

Gualteri 131
Lewis 111
Walter 111, 158
Bayward
  Peter 153
Beach
  Anne 42
  Elias 42
  Mary 42
  Rebecca 42
  Thomas 42
Beachamb
  Edmond 176
Beachamp
  Edmund 151
Beadle
  Thomas 55
Beage
  John 82, 85
Beale
  John 150, 218
  Neman 149
  Ninian 182
  Rebecca 218
Beane
  Ralph 26
  Walter 54, 76, 94, 101, 112, 121, 136, 153, 155, 158
Beard
  John 107
  Richard 215
Beath
  William 54
Beauchamp
  Edm. 115, 116
  Edmund 130
Beauchampe
  Edmond 154
Beaven
  Hugh 36
Beavin
  Charles 95
Beck
  Lewis 215
  Richard 215
Becker
  Edward 5
Beckwith
  Fran. 84
  Frances 83
  Geo. 123
  George 84, 107, 123, 150, 201
Becworth

Mrs. 85
Bedlam
  Elisabeth 65
  William 65
Bedlow
  Isaack 155
  Isaacke 150
Bedworth
  Rich. 164
Beech(e)
  Elias 151, 164, 204
  Humphry 17
  Sarah 164, 205
Beedle
  Thomas 151
Beeson
  Thomas 52
Beesson
  Tho. 91
Beeston
  William 67
Beetle
  Edward 159
Begerlye
  Will. 101
Belcher
  Mr. 27
  Sarah 184
  Thomas 184
Bell
  Harves 16
  Nineon 133
  Thomas 141
Bellamin
  Jane 114
Bellard
  Charles 115
Bellott
  Michaell 15
Bellows
  Francis 163
Bellus
  Francis 156
Ben
  Walter 35
Benbo
  John 91
  Mr. 13
Benbow
  John 37, 174
Bendall
  Robert 111, 140
Benett
  Henery 116
  Henry 118

Benjamin's Choice 119
Bennet(t), Bennitt
  Andrew 211
  Benjamin 211
  Desboro 28
  Disboro 166
  Disborough 21, 28,
    206
  Henerietta Maria 113
  John 55, 56, 85, 87,
    95, 101, 164, 166
  Peter 74
  Richard 16, 32, 56,
    64, 80, 113, 117,
    119, 145, 151, 153
  Robert 153
  Thomas 37, 53, 144,
    146, 151, 162
  William 162
Bennitt's Purchase 162
Benson
  Elisabeth 85
  John 38, 150
  Stephen 33, 85, 91,
    152
  William 85
Bentley
  Nicholas 154
  Richard 34
Bently
  Richard 20
Benton
  Edmond 150
Berkitt
  Richard 126
Berkley
  Edm. 3
Berredge
  John 67
Berrey
  William 150
Berrudge
  John 140
Berry
  James 48, 173
  William 48, 85, 92,
    113, 140, 141, 152,
    173, 174, 176, 187,
    188
Berrymore
  John 33
Besson
  Capt. 65
  Tho. 142
  Thomas 10, 14, 65,
    73, 82, 100, 135,
    141, 188
Bette's Cove 162
Beven
  Hugh 39
Bevett
  Thomas 53
Bevin
  Alice 179
  Hugh 48
Bevrm
  Charles 164
Bewling
  James 136
Bigby
  James 53
Biger
  John 187
Bigger
  Anne 216
  John 52, 82, 85, 121,
    126, 129, 133, 187,
    188, 216, 221
Biggs
  John 148
Billingsley
  Edmond 57
  Elisabeth 81
  Francis 142
  James 50, 57, 62
  John 22, 81
  Mrs. 22
  Susan 59
  Susannah 57
  Suzan 69
  Tho. 52
  Thomas 50, 57, 59, 74
  Zuzan 62
Billingsly
  Francis 149
Billinstia
  Major 36
Binckes
  Thomas 149
Birch
  Roger 142
Birckhead
  Christopher 214
  Nehemiah 214
Bird
  John 211
Birkles
  Garrett 122
Bisco(e)
  John 23, 135, 158

Biscooe
  Hannah 146
  James 146
  John 146
  Jonathon 146
  Joseph 146
  Mary 146
  Thomas 146
Bishop
  Abr. 53
  Henry 9, 10
  William 182, 213
Biss
  William 30, 36
Bisse
  Thomas 60
  William 48, 61
Bissie
  Will. 52
Bisson
  Tho. 100
Black Wallnutt 124
Black
  Ann 161
  George 161
  William 152
Blackfan
  John 216
  Mary 216
Blackhall
  Ralph 198
Blackhurst
  Roger 170, 171
Blackiston
  George 169
  John 169
  Nehemiah 158
Blackiter
  George 142
Blackston
  Nehemiah 155
Blackstone
  Georg 169
Blackwood
  Phine 86
Blake
  Edward 201
  Elias 54
Blakwell
  John 55
Blanch
  Francis 198
Bland
  Damaris 199
Blangey

Lewis 203, 212
Blaye
  Guenbtheon 27
  William 27
Blin(c,k)horne
  Robert 10, 11, 18,
    33, 61, 73, 78, 103,
    148, 160, 163, 217
Blomfeild
  John 152, 164, 165,
    178, 189
Blount
  Richard 168
Bloyce, Bloys(e,s)
  Thomas 77, 116, 151,
    181
Blunt
  Ann 166, 169
  April 166
  Josias 166
  Rebeccah 166
  Rich. 53
  Richard 16, 28, 98,
    102, 166, 169, 182,
    189, 209
  Robert 166, 175
  Samuell 166
  Thomas 166
  vidua 209
Boage
  John 26, 33, 126, 140
  Mary 126, 140
Boages
  Philip 85
Boague
  John 16, 108, 110,
    126, 133
  Mary 108, 126
Boareman
  William 1, 3, 5, 41
Boarman
  William 114
Bodell
  Jone 109
Bodlam
  widow 62
Bodwell
  Elisabeth 29
Boge
  John 34
Bogisse
  John 54
Bogue
  John 18, 68, 107
Boing

David 7
Bolanie
  John 60
Bolayn
  Elisabeth 60
  John 60, 72
Bold
  William 149
Bolds
  William 176
Bond
  Hatton 33, 171
  John 125
  Richard 40
  Sarah 171
Bone
  John 138
Bonner
  John 83
Booker
  Richard 153
  Tho. 175
  Thomas 166, 174
Booth
  John 73, 154, 155, 216
  Thomas 33, 152
Boreman
  Mrs. 5
  William 1, 4, 5, 15, 17, 23
Borgis
  William 127
Boroughs
  John 182
Bosman
  Ellinor 78
  George 77
  John 77
  William 77, 79
Boston Clifts 182
Boston
  Henry 210
  Mary 202, 210
  Samuell 202, 210
Boteler
  Charles 141, 148, 150, 152, 159, 176
  Mr. 139
Boud
  Ellnor 52
Boudell
  Tho. 157
  Thomas 90
Boudle

Thomas 90, 149
Bouge
  John 22, 138
Boughton
  Richard 124
  William 210
Bougue
  John 89
Bould
  William 140
Boule
  Cornelius 78
  John 137
Boules
  Edward 7
  John 42
  Sarah 42
  William 7, 42, 155
Bouls
  Sarah 42
Boulton
  (N) 195
  John 42, 193
Bourke
  William 208, 218
Bourne
  Samuell 217
Bowdell
  Tho. 90
  Thomas 90, 127, 136, 144
Bowder
  Roger 215
Bowdle
  Thomas 153
Bowles
  Edward 7
  John 39, 40, 46, 50, 155, 179, 193, 194, 204, 212
  Margery 194
  Sarah 76
  William 29, 50, 54
Bowles
  William 7, 76
Bowlin
  James 153
Bowling
  James 151, 158
  John 193
Dowlls
  Edward 7
Bowls
  John 215
  William 59

Boy
  John 62
Boyce
  John 72
Boyden
  William 136
Boyss
  Jane 114
  William 114, 115, 130
Bozman
  Anne 77
  Bridget 77
  Ellenor 77
  George 77
  John 77
  Katherine 77
  Mary 77
  William 77
Braban
  William 78
Brackenbury
  John 61
Brad
  George 56
Bradaway
  Nich. 61
Braddaway
  Nicholas 100
Bradle
  Thomas 199
Bradley
  Thomas 154, 155
  William 152
Bradmore
  Katherine 126
Bradnox
  Mary 30, 39, 53
  Thomas 28, 30, 31, 81, 106
Bradshaw
  George 41
  Mr. 72
Bradway
  Nicholas 28, 106
Bramble
  Thomas 139
Bramhaite
  Ant. 65
Bransh
  Edward 142
Brasheurs, Brashieur,
  Brassears, Brasseur,
  Brassier, Brassieur,
  Brassieurs
  Ann 49

Ben. 32
Benjamin 49, 60, 73, 88
Elisabeth 49
John 49
Martha 49
Mary 49, 60, 85
Rob. 95
Robert 49, 85, 86, 87, 88, 89, 95, 98, 101
Susanna 49
Brawne
  Richard 55
Brent
  Capt. 62
  Edmond 13
Brett
  John 81, 91, 112
Bretton
  Mr. 61
  William 13, 15, 21, 41, 75, 117, 150, 178, 181
Brewer
  (N) 188
  Elisabeth 135, 141, 142, 187, 188, 189
  John 10, 14, 46, 47, 52, 57, 135, 186, 187, 188, 189, 196
  Rachell 135
  William 135, 188
Brian
  Mathias 23
Bridges
  Accoliah 155
  Anthony 119, 136
  Mary 212
  Richard 212
Brien
  Lewis 122
Briges
  John 172
  Mary 207
  Richard 207
Brigge
  Humfry 175
  Tim. 175
Brigger
  John 33
Briggs
  John 173
Bright
  Thomas 181

Brimington
  Jacob 93, 174
Brimston
  John 66, 89
Brimstone
  John 75
Brinstone
  John 76
Brisco
  Arthur 164, 186
Briscoe
  Rich. 57
Bristo
  John 113
Britten
  William 140
Britting
  Stephen 26
Britton
  Temperance 195
  William 13
Broadnox
  Mary 189
  Mr. 189
Broadoake 178
Broadway
  Nicholas 109
Brockett
  Samuell 62
Brockson
  Thomas 173
Brodnox
  Mary 34
  Thomas 34, 39
Bromale
  Richard 201
Bromall
  William 23, 27, 45
Bromefield
  Christian 36
Bromfeild
  John 132
Bromfield
  Christian 46
  Marke 175
Brook(e)(s)
  Baker 125, 141, 177
  Charles 53, 64, 75, 78, 88, 136, 149, 157, 176
  Dr. 149
  Elisabeth 125, 141, 177
  Fran. 20
  Frances 31, 60

Francis 10, 11, 12, 14, 15, 16, 17, 89, 149
John 60, 64, 66, 67, 78, 79, 101, 117, 121, 149, 150, 153, 177, 191, 208, 216
Maj. 61
Major 148, 177
Mary 12, 14
Mathew 168
Michael(l) 34, 48, 60, 67, 68
Nicholas 54
Rebecca 208, 216
Rob. 176
Robert 16, 125, 130, 140, 141, 149, 176
Roger 141, 176, 198, 200, 202, 207, 217
Tho. 26, 65, 71, 140, 145
Thomas 20, 31, 34, 49, 65, 66, 67, 81, 86, 106, 113, 176, 181
William 23, 153
Broome
  Mr. 152
Brorkers
  Samuell 151
Brothers
  John 90
Brough
  Joseph 150, 152, 158, 184
Brougham
  William 164
Brought
  Joseph 146
Broughton
  Richard 153
Brown(e)
  David 43, 176
  Daniell 34
  David 141
  Elisabeth 93, 107
  Francis 154
  Gerrard 107, 114, 117
  Henry 102
  James 102, 131
  John 6, 39, 56, 58, 92, 93, 97, 99, 102, 107, 114, 117, 131, 140, 142, 147, 150,

 162, 165, 180, 183,
 195, 196
 Jonathon 153
 Margaret 6
 Margrett 165
 Mary 6, 140, 142
 Patrick 162
 Richard 38, 174, 182
 Thomas 142, 151
 Walter 23
 William 5, 6, 144
Brown(e)ing
 John 209, 220, 221
 Thomas 81, 91, 92,
 112
Brownrigge
 Christ. 1
Bruckfeld
 Mary 32
Bruer
 John 53
Brumale
 Charles 26
 Luke 26
 Richard 26
 William 26
Brumfeild
 Margarett 165, 169
 Marke 169
Brummale
 Joyce 217
 Richard 217
Brundally
 Mr. 154
Brunfeild
 Marke 165
Bruntwhite
 Mr. 65
Bruton
 Dorothy 213
Bryan(t)
 John 6, 57, 77
 Thomas 150
 William 103, 110,
 141, 149, 176
Buchwood 66
Bucknall
 Mary 214
Buckson
 Francis 198
Buckstone
 Francis 133
Budd
 Katherine 38
Buddens

 Elisabeth 50
Bugg
 John 73
Bull
 John 155
 Thomas 155, 158
Bullett
 Joseph 26
Bulleyne
 Mary 61
Bulline
 Henry 22
 Mary 22
Bulling
 Henry 29
Bullock(e)
 Francis 168
 Jean 168
Bulner
 John 33
Bumbery
 Thomas 55
Bundicke
 Rich. 111
Burdett
 Mr. 61, 62
 Tho. 1, 68
 Thomas 34, 44
Burditt
 Thomas 131, 141, 151
 Virlinda 124, 131
Burges(s)
 Capt. 57, 135, 188
 Captaine 149
 Thomas 91
 William 47, 48, 53,
 62, 73, 82, 96, 99,
 100, 102, 119, 131,
 135, 166, 188, 189,
 207
Burgh
 William 81
Burghill
 Row. 112
Burgis
 John 116
Burke
 Robert 94
 William 48, 111, 113,
 121
Burle
 Robert 10, 14, 16,
 92, 104, 113, 118,
 121, 124, 129, 131,
 141, 142, 144, 157,

159, 160, 170, 175, 180, 192, 214
  Stephen 214
Burlein
  John 17
Burley
  Robert 53, 150
Burlin
  John 15
Burly
  Robert 66, 120
  Stephen 66
Burnett
  Thomas 66, 69
  William 87
Burridg(e)
  John 111, 116, 118, 140, 153, 161, 164, 184
  Margarett 161
Burrisone
  Robert 81
Burrows
  John 182
Burton
  Edmon 165
  Edmond 122, 155, 158, 166
  Edward 137, 186
  Mary 186
  Rebecca 155, 166
  [torn] 182
Burtton
  Robert 168
Buschill
  Geo. 100
Bushell
  Thomas 35
  William 35, 64
Bussey
  Ann 137
  George 137, 140, 148, 152
  Paul 148
Bussy
  Geo. 27
Bustard's Island 7
Butler
  Henry 154
Butmore
  Mary 24
Buttin
  Margery 194
Butting
  William 193

Buttler
  Charles 79
Button
  Nathaniel 51
Bynam
  John 94
Bysse
  Thomas 61
  William 60

Cable
  John 166
Cadd
  Bartholomew 71, 74
Cadger
  Robert 7, 16, 93
Cage
  Ann 94
  John 74, 76, 94, 203, 206
  Robert 102
Cage(e)r
  Dorothy 17, 120
  John 101
  Rob. 2
  Robert 17, 53, 56, 62, 101, 105, 120, 127, 128, 139, 151, 218
  Robertt 198
  Thomas 151, 205, 220
  William 198
Call
  Robert 6
Callaway, Cal(l)oway
  Ant. 102
  Anthon 111
  Anthony 89, 102, 117, 122, 131, 133, 137, 145
Calvert
  Charles 75, 95, 103, 145
  Esq. 105
  Governor 29
  Jane 95
  Philip 7, 8, 9, 53, 83, 87, 89, 95, 100, 108, 145, 146, 151, 200
  Phillip 37, 51, 62
  Phip 140
  Will. 105
  William 39, 68, 75,

89, 101, 102, 112,
116, 131, 143, 145,
151, 172, 175, 177,
183, 184, 218
Cam
  Godfry 147
Camall
  Christopher 53
Cambes
  Enock 32
Came
  James 77
Cam(m)ell
  John 16, 32, 42, 50,
    63, 70, 88, 99, 152
  Patrick 30
Campher
  Mary 213
  Thomas 71, 213
Canady
  Cornelius 20
  Susan 73
Cane
  Henry 90
  John 9, 99, 124, 156
  Richard 137
  William 216
Canedy
  James 133
Cannaday
  John 51
  Suzan 51, 52
  William 16, 51
Cannady
  James 51
Cannons
  William 207
Cantwell
  Edmond 122
  Edmund 209
Caplin
  Henry 14
  Hester 14
Car
  Walt. 19
  Walter 32, 36
Caree
  Walter 57
Carew
  Evan 204
Carey
  John 176
Carleton
  Arthur 201
  Thomas 201
Carlile
  Henry 82, 86
Carline
  Henry 28, 170
Carlisle
  Thomas 204, 220
Carlton
  Arthur 209
  Thomas 209
Carmell
  Christopher 55
Carnell
  Christofer 34, 35
  Elisabeth 34
Carpender
  Sy. 172
Carpenter
  Edmund 21
  Fran. 20
  Francis 19, 20, 33,
    41, 61, 154
  John 155
  Robert 211
  Simon 128, 137, 138,
    139, 145
  Symon 137, 138
  Thomas 4, 5
Carr
  John 209
  Peter 54, 60
  Walter 57, 142, 148,
    186
  William 57, 61
Carraden
  Peter 76
Carraway
  John 193, 194
Carre
  John 199, 200
Carridine
  Peter 58
Carrington
  John 83, 154
Carter
  Michaell 54
Cartland
  William 29
Cartwright
  Demetrius 141, 145,
    149, 150, 152, 177,
    181
Carvile, Carvill(e)
  Rob. 177
  Robert 177, 181, 183,
    219

Thomas 220
Carwardin(e)
  Peter 39, 47, 73, 76, 152
Carwaren
  Peter 32
Caryduter
  Phillip 54
Carye
  John 140
Casey
  Thomas 215
Cather
  John 50
Catlen
  Henry 172
Catlin
  Henry 180
Catlyne
  William 166
Caton
  Peter 74
Cattland
  William 152
Cattlin
  Henry 56
  Robert 114, 115
Cattline
  Henry 142
Cattling
  Ann 114
  Robert 114, 130
Causeen
  Ignatius 120
Causeene
  Ignatius 124, 159
Causine
  Ignatius 99, 105
Caussin
  Ignatius 191
Cavett
  Elisabeth 145
Ceely
  Thomas 220
Chadborne
  William 202
Chafe
  Miles 150
Chaireman
  John 19
Chamberlaine
  Leonard 19
Chamberlayne
  Leonard 20
Chambers

John 129
Chamon
  George 59
Champ(e)
  Will. 53, 143
  William 83, 126, 132, 151
Champhey
  Richard 112
Chandborne
  William 193
Chandler
  An 9
  Edward 134
  Job 2, 3, 9
  Jobe 9
  Mr. 23
  Richard 9
  Thomas 213, 214
  William 9, 141
Chanels
  Tho. 145
Chanler
  Mr. 9
Chaplaine
  William 78
Chaplin(e)
  Elisabeth 177
  Mary 177, 181
  William 66, 78, 106, 108, 131, 132, 139, 144, 148, 152, 156, 177, 181
Chaplyn
  William 148
Chapman
  Richard 136, 221
Charlesworth
  George 151, 152, 218
  John 152
Charl(e)ton
  William 172, 173
Charman
  John 124
Chase
  Nathaniell 108
Chatterline
  (N) 159
Chease
  William 34
Cheaswick
  Robert 33
Cheeke
  Thomas 167, 171
Chercliffe

Page 236

John 31
Cherendine
 Thomas 27
Cheseldine
 Thomas 13
Cheseldyn
 Kenelm 191, 195, 200, 203
Chesholm
 James 184
Chestnut Point 181
Chew
 Joseph 55, 157, 161, 169, 172, 220
 Sam. 68, 172
 Samuel(1) 52, 98, 110, 116, 117, 119, 127, 135, 138, 146, 157, 161, 169, 181, 196, 197
Cheyney
 Richard 53, 189
Chicken
 Edward 139, 221
Chilcott
 James 73
Chilld
 Abraham 196
Chilman
 Richard 218
Chisecke
 Robert 149
Chisick
 Robert 129
Chittam
 John 82, 83
Chivers
 Peeternell 108
 Peternelle 82, 83, 84
Chope
 Joseph 131
Christison
 Wenlock 182
Churchyard
 Francis 162
Cizell
 Joseph 122
Clackson
 Edward 5
Claer
 Mark 95
Clagett
 Mrs. 197
Clamton
 Marke 94

Clandman
 George 182
Clarck
 Robert 33
Clare
 Mark 32, 36, 87
 Marke 87, 157
 Markes 37
 Mathew 180
Claris
 Markes 61
Clark(e)
 Abraham 122, 166
 Alice 142
 Edward 44, 49, 97, 140, 151
 John 63, 69, 136
 Mary 63, 69, 157, 160
 Mathew 52, 55, 59, 118, 121, 124, 157, 160
 Mr. 62
 Neale 65, 73, 215
 Rachell 215
 Robert 1, 3, 54, 63, 69, 70, 215
 Samuel(1) 40, 102
 Sarah 120, 210, 216
 Thomas 63, 69, 78, 79, 152, 154, 159, 216
Clarkson
 Elisabeth 92
 Mary 92
 Milcah 92
 Milkia 92
 Robert 56, 92, 98
Clarkston
 Edward 39
Claw
 Sarah 218, 219
 William 218, 219
Clawson
 Jacob 122
Clay
 Francis 55
 Henry 28, 53, 110, 154, 162
Clayfall 122
Clayland
 James 191
Clayton
 James 54
Cleamond
 William 55

Clear
  Mark 101
  Marke 85
Cleares
  Mark 32
Cleggatt
  Mrs. 197
Clemens, Clement(s)
  John 179, 207, 208, 212
  Mr. 154
  Mary 207, 208, 212
Clerk
  Jonathon 203
Clese
  Nathaniell 199
Clew
  William 192
Clifton
  Dr. 90
  Francis 65
  Jone 57, 67
  Mr. 23, 61
  Stephen 8, 33, 51, 58, 61, 63, 67, 78, 90, 109, 115
  Stephen Brooks 53
  William 57, 58, 67
Clipsham
  Thomas 215
Clocker
  Dan. 27
  Daniel 113, 145, 151, 168, 206
  Daniell 17, 24, 26, 123, 143, 149, 206
  Mary 4
  Mrs. 143
Cloufeild
  Richard 27
Coale
  Bartholomew 179
  Charles 164
  John 164
  Mary 164
  Richard 164
  Robert 13
  Sanders 52
  Sarah 164
  Will. 106
  William 164
Coat(e)s
  Bartho. 171
  Bartholomew 153, 176
  John 16, 23, 155

Coatestoole Close 64
Cobathwaite
  Robert 187
Cobertwait
  Robert 187
Cobham
  Tho. 20
  Thomas 147
Cobr(e)ath
  John 19, 36, 60, 69, 73, 87, 101, 161, 180, 216
Cobret(h)
  John 22, 26, 36, 63, 81, 85, 95, 97, 98, 101, 145, 161
Cobrith
  John 22
Cock
  Mr. 65
  Samuell 64
Codasck
  John 201
Coddington
  John 54
Coffer
  John 136
Coffin
  Abraham 52, 209
Colclouch
  Geo. 68
Colclough
  Mr. 54
Cole Parke 167
Cole
  Alexander 52
  Anne 220
  Edward 48, 49
  Elisabeth 48, 49
  Giles 215
  Hen. 126
  Henry 126, 206
  Jone 49
  Mary 48, 49
  Richard 16, 204, 205
  Rob. 48
  Robert 21, 25, 27, 31, 48, 49, 116
  Sarah 164
  William 14, 36, 43, 48, 49, 62, 101, 103, 105, 108, 150, 152, 164, 205
Coleburne
  William 154

Coleman
 John 32, 45, 77
Coler
 Henry 109
Coles
 William 35, 174
Colleck
 Joane 196
Collens
 George 158
 James 108
Coller
 Henry 109
Collerton
 Michaell 144
Collett
 Elisabeth 136
 John 25, 91, 96, 97,
  112, 134, 153, 159,
  190, 194
 Mr. 3, 13, 30, 61
 Rich. 70, 90
 Richard 40, 65, 70,
  71, 78, 80, 133,
  136, 145, 149, 150,
  153, 155
 Samuell 96
Collier
 Anne 189
 Henry 109
 John 44, 53, 66, 104,
  118, 119, 134, 156,
  189, 211
 William 214
Collinion
 Robert 171
Collins
 Daniell 54
 George 159
 Thomas 178
Collison
 George 182
Collough
 George 64
Collyer
 John 92
Comages
 Cornelius 69
Comb Hills 128
Comer
 Ancton 148
Comes
 Philip 27
Compt
 Enoch 145

Compton
 James 52
Conaway
 James 57
Congee
 Anthony 135
Congo
 Anthony 146
Congue
 Anthony 138
Conley
 Mr. 3
 Thomas 3
Connaway
 William 164
Conner
 Philip 102, 131
 Phillip 27
 Sarah 102, 131
Connery
 Edward 220
 Mary 220
Conneway
 James 173
Conngo
 Anthony 146
Connor
 Mary 47
 Philip 47
Connoway
 Mr. 127
Connyers
 John 64
Constable
 Jane 25
 Marmaduke 25
Coode
 John 220
Coodery
 Edward 68
Cooke
 Andrew 37, 67, 115,
  140, 149, 152
 Capt. 40, 49
 Edward 186, 187
 Elisabeth 140
 John 78, 220
 Miles 204, 205
 Thomas 220
Cookeman
 Rice 147
Cookey
 Elisabeth 108
Coomes
 Enoch 174

Enock 33
Phillip 33
Cooper
  Bridget 64
  John 118, 182
  Jonathon 64
  Josias 148
  Judith 183
  Margaret 214
  Mr. 147
  Sampson 24, 49, 64
  Samuell 49, 64, 215
  Sarah 196
  Thomas 119, 124, 147, 160, 162, 176, 214
Cootes
  John 109
Cootnall
  Christopher 9
Cooy
  Joseph 54
Copeland
  Samuel 110
Coperthwayte
  Robert 187
Copland
  Samuel 110
Coppedge
  Edward 212
Corbyn
  Henry 37
Cordea
  Hester 195
  Marck 191
  Mark 198
  Marke 128, 138, 143, 145, 146, 168, 185, 205, 206
Cording
  Roger 130
Corke
  Robert 150, 152
Corker
  Elisabeth 215
  Thomas 171, 215
Cornelius
  John 16, 52
Cornelos
  John 40
Corner
  Ellinor 181
  Gilbert 181
  Job 181
Cornwaleis, Cornwaleys
  Tho. 37

Thomas 2, 10
Corsey
  Henry 34
Cortney
  James 33
Cosford
  Thomas 216
Cotes
  Mr. 147
Cotterill
  Walter 26
Cottingham
  Thomas 130
Cottmer
  Richard 153
Cotton
  Edward 45, 58
Coudle
  Anne 52
Coughing
  Thomas 39
Coulton
  George 107
Coursey
  Henry 12, 28, 81, 89, 119, 128, 136, 139, 153, 163, 174, 206
  Henry. 91
  James 28, 213
  John 16, 53
  Katheren 8
  Katherine 28
  Mary 28
  Will. 53
  William 8, 28, 68, 100, 102, 131, 138, 139, 162, 164, 172, 180, 198, 203, 206
Courseyton 28
Court(e)(s)
  John 60, 136, 158
  William 54
Courtney
  James 149
  Thomas 62, 145, 150, 152
Courts
  John 34, 94, 101, 155
Cousins
  Ignatius 179
Covant
  Absolam 80
  Mary 185, 186
  Thomas 150, 185
Covell

John 157
Covent
  Thomas 140, 162
Coventon
  Nehemiah 68, 154
Coventrey
  Jonathon 159
Covey
  Absolom 55
  Thomas 166
Covinton
  Nehemiah 79
Cowch
  Mr. 62
Cowd(e)ry
  Edward 110, 148, 187
Cox(e)
  Anthony 157
  Edmund 199
  Edward 141
  Henry 139, 148
  Joseph 157
  Thomas 206
Crackborne
  Richard 21
Cragbone
  Richard 35
Crakson
  Thomas 53
Cranly
  Michaell 143
Craordley
  Michaell 33
Cray
  John 57, 141
Creacroft
  John 148
Cres(s)(e)y
  Samuel(l) 83, 88, 124, 136, 191, 208, 219
  Susannah 83
Crispen
  Jeane 159
Crissey
  Samuell 37
Croe
  Sam. 101
Crombe
  David 37
Cromwell
  Greshom 170
Cronheeck
  John 36
Croscombe

Cross
  Ezechiell 179
  Roger 189
  William 188
Crossman
  Robertt 195
Crostley
  Samuell 153
Crouch
  Ralph 8, 58
  Ralphe 1
  Raph 3, 45
  Will. 116
  William 60, 142, 168, 172, 180
Crouche
  James 213
  Jane 209
  John 209
  William 213
Crow
  Samuell 97, 101
Crowtch
  William 113
Crumell
  Grehan 53
Crumwell
  Gresian 189
Crymer
  William 60
Cullams
  James 183
Cullin(n)(e)s
  James 134, 149, 150
Cullough
  George 64
Cumber
  John 31, 52, 55, 57
Cummin(e,g)s
  John 59, 73, 79, 84
Cunday
  Joseph 102
Cunikin
  Jeremy 78
Cunningham
  John 204, 220
Cur(r)er
  John 195
Cursina
  Ignatius 99
Curtice, Curtis
  Daniel 130
  Daniell 114, 115
  Robert 79
Cusale

Mary 52
Cusseene
  Ignatius 179
Cussin
  William 217
Cutt
  Rich. 188

Dabney
  Henry 141
Dagger
  Peter 151
Dal
  Brian 27
Dale
  David 153
Daley
  Brian 105
  Bryan 89, 101, 105, 112, 150, 158, 178
Daly
  Brine 27
  Bryan 62
Damrell
  John 186
Dandy
  John 2
Dangly
  John 154
Daniell
  Constant 178
  Thomas 189, 210
Darcy
  Thomas 114
Dare
  William 188, 201, 202, 203
Darling
  Thomas 66, 82, 83, 84, 85
Darnell
  Hen. 164
  Henry 148, 151
  Thomas 91
Dasen
  Abraham 172
Dauner
  Robert 43
Daves
  James 161
  John 56, 57
Davies
  Anne 78
  Hopkin 109
  James 78, 79, 147
  John 76, 112
  Mary 112
  Thomas 27
  William 89, 97
Davis
  Alexander 150, 155
  David 103
  Edward 163, 171
  Elisabeth 181
  Evan 164
  Hopkin 151, 179, 181, 182
  James 161
  John 27, 113, 123, 149, 150, 151, 152
  Katheryne 56
  Rebecca 163
  Richard 114
  Thomas 32, 130
  Walter 168
  Will. 52
  William 31, 92, 114, 130, 189
Dawkins
  Joseph 141, 176
Dawnes
  Henry 179
Dawse
  John 79
Dawsey
  Ralph 173
Dawson
  Anthony 157, 179
  Jane 157
  Joyce 157
  Philip 213
  Ralph 213
  William 157
Day
  Dorothy 22
  George 54, 145
  John 22, 27
  Robert 75
  Thom. 64
Dayley
  Bryan 178
de la Roche
  Charles 193, 198, 219
  Elisabeth 198, 219
de Ringh
  Hans 134
Deane
  William 215
Deaver, Deavo(u)r

Grace 16
Richard 53, 122, 145, 155, 199
Decosta, Decoster
  Mathias 150, 152
Deeme
  Daniel 158
Delahay(e)
  Arthur 6
  Charles 6
  John 22, 37, 43, 54
Delamus
  Jane 130
Demery
  John 154
  Thomas 150
Demondidier
  Anthonie 15
  Anthony 15, 141
Denahoe
  Daniel 114
Denby
  William 162
Dench
  Walter 173
Denly
  William 154
Denning
  Christopher 163
Dennis
  Richard 54
Denny
  Christopher 182
Denrell
  James 52
Dent
  John 70
  Mr. 49, 62
  Rebecca 50
  Rebecka 50, 70
  Tho. 26, 27, 50
  Thomas 26, 45, 50, 70, 93, 102, 103, 120, 126, 144, 151, 160, 220
  William 50, 70
Denton
  James 210
Deparkes
  Thomas 130
Deulin(e)
  George 174
Devine
  Daniel 150, 152
Devom
  Rich. 164
Devour
  Richard 16
Dew
  Patrick 20
Deynly
  John 54
Dick(e)
  James 22, 26, 36
Dickason
  Andrew 177
Dickenson
  Jeremie 18
  Jeremy 15
  Roger 124
Dickerson
  Jeremiah 23
Dickes
  Thomas 31
Dickeson
  Andrew 20, 33, 141
  Arther 15
  Edward 130
  Roger 93, 107, 117
  Samuell 160, 203, 220
Dickinson
  Mary 172
  Sam. 160
Dickison
  Jerimiah 175
Digbey
  John 130
Dig(g)ins
  Roger 208, 218
Dike
  Daniel 65
  Daniell 73
Dikes
  Thomas 20
Diniard(de)
  Thomas 6
Diveare
  William 194
Dixon
  John 111
Dobbs
  Annah 98
  John 97, 98
Dobe
  John 174
Dobson
  Lucy 114
  Samuell 34, 114, 127, 139, 156
Dod(d)

Rich. 43
Richard 54, 70
Dodman
  Mr. 16
Dol(l)by
  John 167, 179
Doppen
  John 150
Dorazell
  Joseph 44
Dor(r)ington
  Ann 40
  Francis 149
  William 40, 58, 67,
    71, 73, 74, 75, 78,
    80, 90, 132, 149,
    153, 163
Dormand
  Francis 122
Dorsey
  Edward 15, 196, 197
  James 173
  John 173
  William 210
Dossey
  James 173
  John 173
  Ralph 173
Doud(e)
  James 167
Doughty
  Francis 7
Douglace, Douglas(s)
  Jo. 111
  John 7, 30, 35, 71,
    74, 136
Dougles
  John 29
Dowd
  James 179
Dowglas
  John 102, 121, 129,
    153
Dowkins
  John 45
  Joseph 26
Dowling
  John 194
Downes
  Henery 174
  Henry 182
  Margaret 215
  Richard 40
  Robert 151, 179, 215
Dowsey

  Ralph 172
Doxey
  John 221
  Mary 146
  Thomas 135, 146, 150,
    178
Doyne
  John 55
Draver
  Richard 182
Dreure
  William 190
Driver
  David 167
Drue
  Elisabeth 170
  Emanuel 175
  Martha 170
  Samuell 170
  Thomas 170
Drury
  Richard 141, 177
Duall
  John 164
Duarte
  Emanuell 5
Dudley
  Richard 75
Due
  Patrick 148
Duglas
  John 54
Duhatto
  Jacob 47
Dun
  Robert 212
Duncan
  David 50, 63, 70
Dunch
  Barnaby 127
  John 57, 129
  Mr. 93
Duncun
  David 43
  David. 43
Dundasse
  Elisabeth 220
  George 207, 218, 220
Dunkin
  Patrick 52
Dunn
  Pasco 97
  Robert 168, 169, 175
Dunoons
  Patrick 59

Dunston
  John 130
Dunstone
  John 131
Durand
  Alice 16
  Elisabeth 16
  Mrs. 16
Durin
  Richard 149
Dustan
  John 150
Dutton
  Abr. 112
  William 34
Duvall
  Maren 73
  Murrian 65
Dyke
  Mr. 59
Dylate
  John 133

Eale
  William 9
Earle
  Thomas 205, 208
Early
  Thomas 55
Eas(s)on
  John 53, 110, 126, 151, 189
  Lownes 216
Eaton
  Jeremiah 212
  Jonathon 204
  Mary 212
  Nathan. 123
  Nathaniel(l) 116, 131
  Samuell 123, 136
Ebben
  Bernard 64
Eclinor
  Andrew 53
Edelen
  Richard 208, 219
Edinborough 167
Edley
  John 218
  Joseph 62, 218
Edloe
  John 103
  Joseph 103, 108, 206, 216

Edly
  Barnaby 154
  Joseph 129
Edmonds
  James 84, 105, 152
  John 87
Edmondson
  John 33, 70, 144, 146, 153, 162, 173, 176, 181, 190
Edmunds
  James 84
  John 80
Edmundson
  John 125, 138, 172, 198, 199, 201, 205
Edmuns
  James 94
Edwards
  Debera 133
  Elisabeth 213
  Emanuell 23
  James 167, 179
  John 52, 214
  Thomas 56, 141, 145, 148, 163, 176
Edwin, Edwyn
  Michael 56
  William 17, 43, 45, 46, 53, 56, 62
Eirne
  James 20
Eldridge
  William 116, 118
Elery
  Henry 61
Elie
  John 74
Elis
  Elisabeth 168
  John 168
  Mary 168
Ellees
  Thomas 129
Ellens
  Ann 97
Ellery
  Elisabeth 136
  Henery 41
  Henry 15, 44, 45, 46, 53, 56, 83, 90, 126, 132, 136, 137, 144
Elleyeatt
  William 165
Ellickson

John 181
Ellingsworth
　Richard 157, 160
　William 80
Ellins
　Sara 97
Elliot(t)
　Edw. 28
　Henry 218
　Jane 108
　John 108, 122
　Mary 168, 169, 171, 183
　Will. 52
　William 165, 168, 169, 171, 183
Ellis
　Francis 147
　John 28, 174, 181, 182
　Philip 130
　Thomas 176
　William 130
Ellstone
　Thomas 31
Ellwis
　Thomas 188
Elly(e)
　John 74, 152
Elston(e)
　Thomas 21, 35
Elstonhead
　Thomas 27
Elton
　James 33, 142, 149
　John 48
Eltonhead
　Edward 8
　Jane 2, 8
　William 3
Elwes
　Ann 132
　Thomas 132, 133, 142
Elwood
　William 111
Elzey
　John 40, 68, 77, 79
Emanson
　Nich. 150
　Nicholas 107, 124, 150
Emerson
　Anthony 134
　John 75
　Nicholas 100

Thomas 15, 182
Empson
　William 22, 30, 34, 42, 55
England
　John 145
Englis
　Edward 202
English
　George 124, 136
　Henry 71
Engrum
　John 159
Enis
　William 149
Ennes
　Thomas 68
Ennis
　Hester 217
　Mr. 62
　Tho. 23
　William 89, 217
Erickson
　John 20, 31, 212
　Mathew 20, 31
　Matthew 212
Esford
　John 131
Eure
　John 54
　Peter 198, 218
Eures
　Thomas 8, 17
Evans
　Capt. 9
　Col. 27, 55, 77, 162
　Elisabeth 161
　Richard 216
　Sarah 218
　William 6, 7, 16, 21, 28, 33, 44, 49, 107, 109, 125, 132, 140, 152, 161, 176
Evens
　Col. 31
　John 164
　Mary 197
Evers
　Peter 167
Evett(s), Evitt(s)
　Nathaniel 117, 125, 137, 146
Ewen(s)
　Ann 57
　Anne 216

John 57, 62, 100, 108, 122, 153, 166
Rich. 52, 108
Richard 52, 57, 100, 135, 141, 153, 184
Sarah 166
Will. 159
William 217
Exon
  Henry 216
Eylett
  William 168

Fantleroy
  M. 1
Fardel
  William 129
Farguson
  William 199
Farloe
  James 82
Farlum
  Patrick 215
Farmer
  Michael(1) 117, 121, 122
Farrar
  Joanna 218
  Robert 218
Fearnley
  Francis 34
Felton
  John 34
Fendall
  Capt. 22, 31, 69, 131
  Josias 3, 7, 38, 40, 62, 136, 153, 171
  Tobias 167
Fenly
  Robert 79
Fensons
  Peter 86
Fenwick(e) 18
  Cutbeard 81
  Cutbord 81
  Cuth. 18
  Cuthbert 2, 18, 29, 59, 79, 110, 217
  Elisbath 169
  Ignatius 18, 33
  Jane 2, 18, 29, 61
  Jeane 38
  John 18
  Mr. 34

Richard 3, 18, 217
Robert 3
Teresa 18
Ferman
  Nicholas 55
Ferson
  John 159
Figett
  Daniell 74
File
  James 203, 212
Fillpott
  Edward 136
Finning
  John 216
Fishborne
  Ralph 182
Fisher
  Anne 207
  Daniel 111
  Daniell 114
  Dr. 91, 112
  Henry 217
  Robert 217
  Thomas 176
Fitting
  Diana 215
  Robert 215
FittzAlley
  Rich. 102
FittzAlleyne
  Richard 131
FittzAllin
  Rich. 108
FitzAllen
  Richard 88, 93, 98
FitzHarbert
  Mrs. 6
Fitzherbert
  Edward 190, 192
  Fran. 132
  Francis 24, 25, 41, 44, 48, 82
  Mr. 25, 28, 29
Flambert
  Jasper 199
Flanagan
  Darby 58
Fleming
  John 77
  Patrick 115
Fletcher
  Curtis 151, 160, 161
Flin(e)
  Nicholas 99

Flint
  Richard 55
Foard
  John 165
Fooke(s)
  Francis 153
  Garr. 25
  Gerrard 153
  Richard 161
Fookitt
  Peter 106
Foote
  James 118, 186
  Robert 80
Foott
  Robert 71
Forbes
  Elisabeth 103
  James 33, 103, 106
  Margaret 103
  Margarett 103
Ford
  John 165
  Tho. 164
Forest
  Patrick 132
Forke
  James 67
Forrest
  Elinor 218
  Helena 220
  Patrick 11, 13, 14,
    15, 41, 51, 62, 120,
    126, 136, 137, 160,
    161, 171, 218
  Patricke 2
  Pattrick 51
Forster
  Armpow 23
Fortly
  Ralph 207
Foster
  An 21
  Elisabeth 212
  John 97, 141, 156,
    188, 189, 190
  Michael 177
  Mr. 154, 189
  Richard 61, 151, 153,
    169, 200, 218
  Seth 53, 92, 109,
    143, 153, 170, 189,
    212
Fouke
  Anne 172

Gerrard 172
Foukes
  Col. 136
Fountaine
  John 154
Fountlin
  Hanna 65
Fowke
  Col. 55
  Richard 169, 180, 181
Fowkes
  Ann 169
  Gerrard 169
  Richard 182
Fowler
  Edward 58
Fox(e) 162
  Henry 1, 2, 4, 9, 10
  Mary 4, 13
Foxall, Foxell
  John 68, 154
Foxcroft
  Isack 68
Foxen
  Richard 138, 146
Foxes
  Henry 81
Foxhall
  John 94, 105
  Mr. 116, 140
Foxon
  Richard 128, 193
Foxun
  Richard 128
Foyle
  John 109
Frame
  Christofer 34
Frances
  Elisabeth 134
  Thomas 95, 96
Francis
  Jacob 159
  Sarah 200, 207
  Thomas 207
Franckain
  Henry 160
  Mary 160
Franckam
  Henry 197
Franckcum
  Henry 43, 62
Francklin
  Robert 56, 65, 135,
    214

Franckling
  Hanna 65
Francum
  Henry 69
Franklin(g)
  Robert 55, 73, 142
Frankrume
  Henery 162
Franlyn
  Mr. 59
Freak
  William 55
Freeman
  John 12
  Richard 149
  Thomas 147, 160, 161, 176
Freland
  William 142
Fremen
  Randall 124
Fresell
  Tho. 27
Fresh Pond Neck 177
Frisby
  James 127, 141
Fris(s)ell
  Alexander 17, 102
  Allexander 32
  Denish 32
  Dennis 6
  Forker 32
  Rebecca 17, 32, 102
  Sarah 17, 102
Frizall, Frizell
  Alexander 40, 43, 105
  Ellick 37
  Forker 32, 39, 43
  James 141
  Robert 64
  Sarah 93
  Tho. 23
  Walter 45
Frost
  Tho. 85
  Thomas 85, 87, 95, 98, 150, 155
Fryzall
  Alexander 41
Fuller
  Humphry 53
Furbee
  Benjamin 134
  Elisabeth 134
Furbus
  James 61
Furby
  Benjamin 156
Furms
  Nicholas 148

Galley
  Thomas 171
Gallion
  Joseph 59, 118
Galloway
  Rich. 47
  William 11
Gallyan
  Joseph 66
Games
  Mary 153
  Richard 33, 62
Gammack
  William 182
Gammer
  John 124
Gane
  Thomas 67
Gannt
  Thomas 123
Gant
  Thomas 176
Gard
  Mr. 155
Gardner, Gardnor
  Capt. 76
  Edward 213
  Elisabeth 25
  John 24, 25, 54
  Joseph 155
  Luke 21, 24, 25, 27, 41, 49, 51, 63, 70, 76, 93, 94, 105, 116, 117, 147, 152, 169, 190
  Mr. 6
  Richard 82, 83
Garey
  Stephen 34
Garinier
  John 121
Garland
  Sam. 164
Garms
  John 150
Garner
  James 140, 176
  John 154

Garret
  James 185
  Nath. 185
Garrett
  Richard 24, 27
  Rutten 122
Gary
  Stephen 11
Gassaway
  Nicholas 73
Gater
  William 166
Gates
  Robert 127
  Thomas 15, 52
Gather
  John 215
Gatherill
  Bartholomew 54
Gaunt
  Thomas 125
Gaylard
  Mr. 62
Gaymes
  William 56
Gearing
  Stephen 153
Gees
  Walter 16
Gell
  Francis 149
George
  Griffen 148
  John 86
Gerard
  Mr. 62
  Thomas 219
Gerd
  John 6
Gerrall
  Richard 61
Gerrard
  Justinian 154
  my father 34
  Thomas 33, 55, 56,
    107, 156
Gerrardy
  Mathias 204
Gerrat
  Thomas 28
Gerry
  Stephen 68
Gib(b)s
  Richard 71, 133
  Thomas 82, 83, 85

Gibson
  Miles 210, 211
  Thomas 42, 158
Gie
  John 41
Gifford
  William 178, 218
Gilbert
  John 209, 220, 221
Giles
  Tho. 79
Gill
  Ann 14
  Beniamin 13
  Benjamin 2, 14
Gillam
  Zachariah 71
Gillem
  Zachariah 74
Gillett
  German 61
  Jerman 62
Gilley
  Thomas 111
Gillinge
  Michell 26
Gillum
  Zachariah 72
Gilly
  Hannah 104
Ginn(e)
  Alice 212
  Arthur 182, 212
Girdling
  Richard 143, 156
Gitting(s)
  John 51, 67, 89, 97,
    107, 108, 140, 141,
    149, 153, 177, 217
  Margaret 217
  Margarett 115
  Mr. 62
Glanvile
  William 115
Gleven, Glevin
  Bartholomew 59, 73,
    88, 93, 131, 132
  Mary 88, 93, 131, 132
Glewin
  Bartholomew 102
Glover
  Daniell 209
  Giles 117
  Gyles 124
  Mr. 127

Tho. 177
Thomas 90, 141
Gnerin
  Jasper 151
Goad
  Edward 145
Goat
  Henry 89
Goate
  Richard 30
Goddard
  Anthony 47, 52
Godgon
  Robert 172
Godscrosse
  James 180
Godserosse
  James 115
Godsgrace
  James 33, 106
Goff
  Mary 200
Goffe
  Mary 207, 220
Gold
  Richard 143
  Thomas 55
Goldhacke
  George 155
Goldhauke
  George 102
Goldsmith
  George 202, 210
  Johannah 221
  John 55
  Mary 202
  Mathew 154
  Samue 145
  Samuel(l) 127, 134, 190, 191, 194, 202
Gongo
  Anthony 146
Good
  Edward 11
Gooddeker
  Christo. 16
Gooddricke
  Geo. 64
Goodeker
  Dorothy 58
  Richard 58
Gooding
  George 152
  John 151
Goodman
  Edward 55
Goodrick(e)
  Francis 215
  George 12, 63, 69, 215
  Henry 112, 150, 151
  John 15
  Mr. 153
  Robert 124, 215
Goodridg(e)
  Henry 80
  Katherine 111
  Mr. 23
  Timothy 125, 132, 149, 151, 153, 159, 163
  Tym. 159
  Tymothy 26, 146
Goodwin
  Robertt 197
Goosey
  Samuell 149, 180
Gordion
  Daniell 72
  Mary 72
Gordon
  Patrick 204
Gore
  Richard 209
Gorge
  John 113
Gorsuch
  Charles 120
  Richard 185
Gosson
  Anthony 68, 69
Gott
  Henry 138, 179
  Richard 42, 52
  Susan 42
Gotts
  Henry 86
Gough
  Henry 139
Goulden
  Gabriel 73
  Gabriell 78
  Mary 73
Gouldhake
  George 93
Gouldhawk
  George 158
Gouldin
  Gabriell 11
Goulding

Gabriell 78
Gabrill 73
  Mary 73
Gouldsmith
  Elisabeth 96
  George 96, 97, 106, 118
  John 34, 35
  Maj. 122
  Mary 96, 97
  Mathew 96, 134, 156
  Matt. 97
  Petronella Penelope 134
  Sam. 96, 156
  Samuell 96, 134
Goulson
  Daniell 68
Gowdree
  Edw. 186
Graile
  Francis 218
Grainger
  Will. 31
Grammer
  John 149, 150, 152, 194
Granger
  Benjamin 123
Graunte
  Pat. 1
Graves
  Sam. 79
  Samuel(l) 20, 45, 64, 67, 69, 71, 80, 127, 133, 144, 194
  William 20, 34, 51, 52, 141, 176
Graw
  Henry 54
Gray
  Alexander 220
  Francis 54, 55
  Jane 220
  John 47, 59, 73, 150, 188, 214
  William 146, 149, 152
Great Thicketts 21
Greeer
  John 33
Green(e)
  Elisabeth 78
  John 216
  Leo. 99
  Leonard 44, 99, 152,
205
  Luke 36, 206
  Mary 142
  Robert 25
  Walter 78, 153
  William 54, 62, 104, 111, 142, 161
Greenewood
  Armigell 31
Greengoe
  William 23, 56
Greenhill
  John 2
Greere
  William 37
Gregory
  Charles 203, 206
  Thomas 10
Grey
  John 188
Griffen
  Anthony 28
Griffin
  Anthony 53, 55, 128, 138
  Jane 128
  Jean 128
  Lucie 128
  Lucretia 128
  Rice 166
  Suzanna 52
  Tho. 62, 108, 164, 174
  Thomas 103, 152, 164, 198, 204, 218
Griffith
  Auth. 29
  Lucey 96
  Samuell 98
  Tho. 96
  Thomas 101
Griggs
  Mary 208
Grimes
  Daniel 150
  Richard 45, 46, 62
  Robert 151
Grimsted
  William 68
Grimston
  John 163
Gringer
  William 128
Gringoe
  William 168

Grinoway
  James 58
Groce
  Anne 198, 200
  Elisabeth 198, 199, 200
  Francis 198, 199, 200
  John 198, 199, 200
  Roger 197, 198, 199, 200
  William 198, 199, 200
Groom(e)
  Moses 135, 138
  William 66, 67, 71, 74, 75, 78, 83, 85, 86, 90, 106, 109, 110, 125, 127, 131, 132, 152, 160, 180, 181
Grose, Gross(e)
  Anne 91, 100, 131
  John 135, 214 John 135
  Rog. 53
  Roger 42, 48, 63, 65, 69, 91, 100, 131, 135
Groves
  Samuel(l) 45, 63, 67
Gudgion
  Robertt 196
Guibert
  Joshua 166, 189
Guinn
  William 122
Guinne
  Richard 214
  Thomas 214
Guither
  Capt. 16
  Nicholas 11, 14, 15, 17
Guleman
  Jeremiah 157
Gum
  Arthur 147
Gunby
  Francis 150
Gundry
  Joh. 135
  Joseph 158
Gungo
  Anthony 150
Gunn
  John 164

Gunnell
  Edward 201
  James 47
  Will. 164
Gunnery
  Joseph 155
Gunnion
  Elisabeth 22
  James 22
Gunter
  Timothy 149
Gurling
  Richard 111
Guthrey
  James 208
Gutteridge
  Henry 91
Guy
  Ann 38
  Anne 26, 30
  John 26, 30, 38
Guyanagh
  Morgan 114
Guyther
  Nich. 30
  Nicholas 5, 29
Gwanh
  Jean 6
  John 6
Gwither
  Nicholas 105, 155
Gwy
  John 35
Gwyther
  Capt. 62, 68
  Nicholas 61, 77, 79, 81, 87, 89, 95, 100

Hacke
  Dr. 154
Hacker
  Thomas 209
Hacket
  Humphry 37
Hackett
  Mr. 68
  Thomas 54
Hackney
  Joseph 105, 150
Hackworth
  Richard 104
Hactcoot
  Thomas 61
Haddaway

George 143
James 12
Margarett 143
Peter 143
Rowland 143, 156
Ursula 143
Hagel
  Edward 101
Haggatt
  Humphrey 43
Haggett
  Anne 47
  Humphrey 47
Haggott
  Humph. 43
Haile
  John 219
  Mary 218
Haird
  William 59
Hale
  Robert 213
Hales
  Spencer 173
Half(e)head
  John 29, 65, 146, 148, 152, 155, 156, 205
  Mr. 62
Haling
  Thomas 25
Hall
  Charles 115
  Christofer 128
  Christopher 125, 145, 163
  Ellen 196
  Emanuel 111
  John 31, 47, 54, 201, 218
  Mary 56
  Mr. 62, 156
  Patrick 181
  Walt. 13
  Walter 3, 4, 10, 58, 152, 166, 167
  William 9, 94, 101, 136
Halles
  James 32
  Mary 32
Halloway
  Olliver 170
Haly
  Clement 201

Hambleton
  John 56, 139, 145, 149, 150
  Will. 168
  William 172, 174
Hamblton
  John 152
Hammett
  Stephen 57, 59
Hammond
  Alice 87, 89
  Anne 1, 44
  John 1, 44, 46
  Mordecai 48
  Nic. 89
  Nicholas 93
  Nicolas 87, 88
  Thomas 12
Hamon
  Beniamen 6
  John 6
Hamond
  Mr. 62
  Percivall 54
  Stephen 59
  Thomas 56
Hamper
  Thomas 54
Hampstead
  Mr. 62
  William 150
Hance
  John 148
Hanck
  Thomas 154
Hanckes
  Henry 49
Hancock
  Benjamin 213
  Sarah 213
Handley
  Robert 38
Handson
  Randall 50
  Randolph 79, 99
Hanman
  William 204
Hanson
  Barbara 144
  Katherine 97
  Padrick 97
  Rand. 58
  Randall 15, 18, 29, 73, 82, 84, 110, 144, 152

Randell 32
Randolph 91, 144
Harbott
  John 54
Harcase
  Thomas 108
Harcott
  Joseph 154
Hardesty
  George 148
Hardey
  Henry 109
Hardginson
  William 78
Hardy
  Joseph 115
Hare
  Henry 145, 154
  William 120, 124
Harenton
  John 112
Hares
  Henry 80
Hargust
  William 130
Harinton
  Ann 49
Harison
  Elisabeth 99
  Joseph 99
Harman
  Augustin 178
Harmer
  Godfrey 68, 69
  Mary 211
Harper
  Elisabeth 32
  Thomas 33, 68, 114, 150
  William 32, 62, 129, 173
Harrington
  Jeremiah 123
  Jeremy 77
  Jerome 77
  John 76, 112, 151, 191, 220
  Mary 76
Harrinton
  John 112
Harris(e)
  George 105, 124, 150, 153
  Henry 208
  Jackelina 217
  John 12, 37, 66, 136, 139, 157
  Joseph 23, 37, 58
  Mary 2
  Richard 2, 136
  Samuel(1) 23, 34, 120, 124
  William 136, 164
Harrison
  Elisabeth 193
  Joseph 19, 25, 31, 36, 43, 47, 48, 54, 99, 105, 107, 116, 119, 120, 131, 193
  Mary 99
  Mr. 179
  Peter 204
  Symon 214
Harriss
  William 188
Harrisson
  Joseph 36, 130
Harrod
  Robertt 197
Har(r)wood
  Alce 47
  Alice 29, 45, 46
  Allice 7
  Capt. 115, 122
  John 7, 13, 16, 23, 46, 73
  Philip 217
  Phillip 141, 177, 186
  Robert 172, 173, 212
  Robertt 198
Hasbazdier
  Maharshalal 145
Haseling
  Marie 15
  Phebia 15
Haselridge
  Tho. 65
  Thomas 65
Haslewood
  Henry 159, 190, 194
Hassard
  Mary 24
  William 24
Hatch
  John 41, 54, 123, 153, 168
  Joseph 78
Hatfield
  James 8
  Joseph 19

Hattly
  William 79
Hattoft
  William 190, 192, 195
Hatton
  Elisabeth 50
  Elizabeth 70
  John 39, 46, 48, 52,
    186, 187, 188, 189,
    196
  Margaret 15
  Margarett 2
  Mrs. 18
  Richard 88, 219
  Robert 151, 152
  Samuell 186, 188,
    189, 196
  Thomas 2, 3, 11, 16,
    51, 114, 120, 137,
    152, 155, 186, 219
  William 16, 26, 27,
    50, 70, 219
Haukings
  Elisabeth 170
  Thomas 170
Hawes
  George 173
Hawkings
  John 73
Hawkins
  Henry 156, 192, 215
  John 16, 45, 164,
    186, 197, 214
  Joseph 170
  Margarett 104
  Margrett 170
  Mary 214
  Ralf 170
  Ralph 104, 118, 142,
    170, 175
  Robert 186
  Thomas 170
  William 170
Hawley
  Edward 54
Hawlings
  John 78
Hawly
  James 154
Haybeard
  Richard 54
Hayes
  Hercules 23
Haylens
  Thomas 154

Haynes
  Thomas 154
Hayward
  Ralph 56
  Thomas 11
Haywood
  Raphael 63, 76, 84
  Raphaell 149, 152
  Raphel 70
Hazel(l)wood
  Henry 96
Head
  Adam 93, 102
  Elisabeth 195, 197,
    212
  William 82, 88, 147,
    193, 195, 197
Heard
  Bridget 74, 76
  Bridgett 71
  William 29, 42, 50,
    54, 71, 74, 76, 93
Heathco(a)t(e),
  Heathcott
  Nath. 47, 196
  Nathaniel(l) 100,
    135, 141, 145, 153,
    186, 188, 189
Heeds
  Williams 174
Heigh(e)
  Robert 49, 63, 69,
    74, 80, 85, 95, 97,
    101, 133, 134, 142,
    155, 172
Height
  Robert 136, 164
Helding
  Richard 154
Helle
  Edward 96
Helmes
  John 216
  Penelope 216
Helyard
  John 45
Hemsley
  Will. 53
  William 20, 21, 31,
    53, 88, 117, 125,
    128, 138, 139, 162,
    166, 172, 173, 182,
    189, 191, 213
Hemstead
  William 46

Henderson
  Alexander 5
  Andrew 34
  William 10, 12
Hendricks
  John 213
Hendson
  Randall 32
Henfield
  Capt. 68, 69
Henings
  Susanna 108
Henl(e)y
  Edward 55
  Rob. 40
  Robert 35, 54, 62,
    102, 129, 134, 168,
    191
  Sarah 62
Henshall
  Thomas 130
Henson
  Andrew 110
  Randall 88, 110
  Richard 110
Herbert
  William 141, 149, 176
Herd
  William 163
Herman's Mount 53
Herman
  Augustine 25, 81, 91,
    112, 151
  Casparus 25
  Ephraim Georgius 25
  Godfrid 52, 53
  John 56
Herring
  Bartholomew 106, 115,
    186
  Margarett 115
Hewes
  Jonathon 54
  Robert 55
  William 49
Hewett
  William 209
Hewse
  Thomas 183
Hewton
  Joyce 213
  Matthew 213
Heylens
  Thomas 154
Heynes

William 5
Hichinson
  John 175
Hickes
  Robert 55
Hide
  Henry 120, 128, 144
Higgen
  Mich. 190
Higgins
  Michaell 71
  Patricke 23
Higgnen
  Michael 194
Higgs
  Andrew 201
Hill
  Ann 21
  Assidia 21
  Azadiah 16
  Clement 110, 111
  Daniell 54
  Elisabeth 94
  Francis 11, 12, 32,
    37, 39, 151
  Grace 166
  John 45
  Margaret 212
  Michaell 54
  Rich. 68
  Richard 56, 92, 97,
    150, 205, 213
  Roger 211
  Thomas 39, 93
  William 94, 124, 179
Hillan
  Fra. 53
Hillary
  Thomas 140
Hillen
  John 164
Hilliard
  Daniell 214
  Jane 214
  John 33, 45
Hillingsworth
  William 151
Hillis
  William 120
Hills
  Richard 118
  William 60, 118, 120
Hillyard
  John 151
Hilton

Page 257

John 160
Hinchman
  Edmund 140
Hinderson
  Alexander 132
  Patricke 152
Hinsey
  William 54
Hinshman
  Edmund 27
Hinson
  John 128, 137, 138,
    212
  Randall 144
  Randolph 219
  Tho. 172
  Thomas 89, 102, 131,
    137, 138, 141, 142,
    147, 151, 179, 213
Hinton
  Thomas 93, 150, 151
Hitchcoke
  Richard 54
Hitchenson
  John 179
Hitchinson
  John 159
Hix
  Mary 19
  Richard 19, 20
Hob(b)s
  Richard 8, 14
  Robert 45
Hocker
  John 6
Hockings
  John 146
Hodgkeys
  Rich. 69
Hodgson
  John 167, 171
Hoford
  George 111
Hogge Necke 3
Holdcraft, Holdcroft
  George 87, 94, 105,
    130
  Susanna 84, 130
Holdman
  Abraham 118
Holland
  Dennis 161
  Elisabeth 118
  Francis 46, 119, 188,
    189

  James 197
  John 145
  Math. 10
  Sarah 51
Hollaway
  Oliver 159
Hollegar
  Philip 151
Hollen
  Langhnel 75
Hollingsworth
  Charles 213
  William 72, 74, 150
Hollins
  Johannes 106
  John 78, 95, 103,
    106, 148, 150
  William 44
Hollis
  William 44, 118, 134,
    147, 156, 161, 211
Holliway
  John 177
Holloway
  John 177
Hollowdays
  John 15
Hollyday
  Robert 121
Holmes
  George 158
Holmwood 66
Holshott
  John 113
Holt(e)
  Abraham 174
  Christian 38
  David 36, 38
  Dorothy 38
  Elisabeth 38
  Robert 37, 41
Holton
  Robert 39
Homan
  Harbert 17
  Herbert 40
Homes
  George 73
Homper
  Tho. 153
Hood
  Anne 221
  Robert 221
Hooke
  Thomas 31

Hooker
  Thomas 101, 197
Hooper
  Ann 114
  Hen. 30
  Henry 42, 68, 74, 85,
    108, 109, 149, 176,
    181, 210
  Mary 193
  Richard 109, 147,
    148, 181, 193
  Robert 36, 61, 114
Hopewell
  Francis 146, 216
  John 154
  William 186
Hopkins
  Alice 185
  Gerrard 164
  John 97, 102, 155
  Jonathon 59, 93, 131,
    138, 139
  Joseph 179
  Mr. 154
  Robert 56
  Thomas 56, 185
  Will. 162
  William 56, 94, 102,
    118, 131, 142, 147,
    172, 176, 193, 196
Hopkinson
  John 100
  Jona. 172
  Jonathon 73, 162, 173
Hopper
  Dorothy 160
  John 160, 163
  Richard 177
Horne 173
  Thomas 101
Hunting North 66
Horne Point 92
Horner
  Nicholas 26
  Volentine 172
Horsey
  Stephen 77, 78, 79,
    104
  Steven 104
Horsle(y)
  (N). 187
  Jo. 109
  Jos. 94, 159, 163
  Joseph 74, 94, 109,
    125, 145, 149, 150,
    153, 160, 183
  Mr. 62
Horssi
  Stephen 130
Horsy
  Joseph 142
Hortley
  John 75, 86
Horton
  Joseph 155
  Mr. 54
Hosier
  Henry 147, 161, 176,
    185, 204, 212
Hoskeys
  Richard 17
Hoskins
  Edward 155
  Mr. 62, 68
Hosley
  Joseph 91
Hotchkey(e)s
  Richard 1, 18
Hough
  Dr. 143
  Henry 152
Houkins
  Elisabeth 13
  Nicholas 13
Houldcroft
  Michaell 84
  Susanah 84
  Valentine 84
Houldman
  Abraham 66, 104
  Isabell 104
  Izabell 66
Hoult
  Christian 36
  Robert 36
Houlton
  Robert 20, 31
House
  William 148
Houton
  Thomas 141
How
  Phillis 217
  Thomas 131, 139, 148,
    149, 150, 153, 217
Howard
  Cor. 59, 102
  Cornelius 56, 57, 59,
    92, 97, 98, 131,
    153, 196, 197

Edward 180
Elisabeth 185
Henry 120, 124, 182, 221
John 57, 59, 94, 113, 116
Mathew 92, 97, 98, 159, 180
Richard 179
Thomas 16
William 209
Howbacke
  James 154
Howell
  Capt. 159, 179
  Humphry 23
  Johanna 5
  John 209
  Thom 14
  Thomas 14, 16, 44, 55, 56, 81, 96, 97, 106, 119, 122, 126, 127, 190, 209
  William 160
Howes
  William 20, 34, 70
Howeton
  Thomas 177
Howker
  Thomas 62
Howman
  Harbert 161
  Herbert 26, 29
Howton
  Thomas 139
Hubbar
  Simon 52
Hubdon
  Mary 145
Hudgins
  Francis 87
Hudlestone
  Valentine 152
Hudson
  Henry 168
  John 16
  Valentine 148
Hues
  Joseph 130
Huff
  Henry 145
Huffe
  Dr. 149
Hufte
  Mr. 94

Huggins
  Richard 55, 56, 59, 141
Hughes
  Thomas 62, 112, 124, 150, 152, 165, 166
  William 16
Hughs
  Tho. 175
Hulinworth
  Charles 168
Hull
  Edward 122, 165, 166, 168, 169, 170, 175, 182
  Margrett 170
Hulls Neck 50
Humber
  James 193
Hume(s)
  Grace 185
  James 49, 60, 73, 87, 95, 97, 101, 133, 140, 141, 181
  Sarah 95, 101
  Thomas 97
Humfery
  Robert 106
Humphreyes
  Christopher 152
Humphreys
  Mary 120
  Robert 100
  Thomas 54
Humphry
  Alexander 164
Humphryes
  Robert 179
Humphrys
  Robert 109
Hundley
  Robert 62
Hunt
  Elisabeth 95
  Isaac 173
  John 65, 151
  Robert 127, 220
  Thomas 95, 218
  Will. 31, 53
  William 94, 98, 110, 189
Huntchens
  Francis 33
Huntington
  William 33

Hunton
　Benjamin 218
Hunts Mount 98
Hurd(e)
　William 29, 34
Hussey
　Mewell 155
　Thomas 34, 105, 108, 153
Hustey
　Thomas 136
Hutch
　John 55
Hutchings
　Francis 142, 152
Hutchinson
　Fra. 164
　Francis 145
Hutt
　Daniell 55
Hutton
　Tho. 144
Hyde
　Frances 218
　Henry 45, 46, 64, 120, 139, 151, 218
Hynson
　Thomas 128
Hyott
　John 110

Illin(gs)worth
　Richard 121
　William 121, 149
Inglesbey
　Joseph 153
Inglish
　Edward 207, 208, 209
Inglsbey
　Joseph 151
Ingram
　John 195, 205
　Major 145, 173, 179
　Thomas 150
Ingrum
　John 157
Innes
　Tho. 24, 42
　Thomas 145
Innis
　Thomas 4, 5, 105, 123, 143
　William 19, 97
Iperer

William 61
Ireland
　John 203
　William 93, 150
Ireton
　Thomas 154
Irland
　William 31
Isaack
　Edward 152
Isham
　Roger 9, 33

Jackman
　Elisabeth 68
Jackson
　Barnabie 17
　Barnaby 49, 58, 64, 138, 151
　Francis 38, 69, 83
　Mary 26
　Mr. 62
　Tho. 26
　Thomas 16, 21, 27
　William 191
Jacob
　Paul 154
　Sebyna Frances 170
Jacobe
　John 196
Jagger
　James 164
James Hill 95
James
　Abell 200, 204, 205
　Ann 95
　Charles 55, 96, 154
　Diana 219
　Dianna 200
　Edward 114
　Elisabeth 95
　John 99
　Mathew 200
　Mr. 12
　Owen 11, 13, 17
　Thomas 146, 151
　Will. 164
　William 70
Jane
　James 151
Jarbo
　John 2, 3, 4, 11, 21, 44, 46, 200
Jarboe

John 146, 207, 220
  Lt. Col. 152
Jarnings
  Mr. 64
Jarues
  Thomas 7
Jarvis
  Robert 88
Jeffers
  William 43
Jefferson
  Mrs. 64
Jefferys
  Ann 109
Jenifer
  Brian 143
  Daniel 88, 123, 124, 125, 127, 129, 143, 145, 183
  Daniell 137, 145, 185
  Mary 155, 185
  Mr. 140, 175
Jenkin(s)
  Capt. 23
  Griffith 109
  John 52, 100, 106, 109, 110, 139
  Obadiah 179
  Walter 65, 89, 106
  William 206
Jenkinson
  John 125
  Robert 179
Jenkson
  William 193
Jennyngs
  William 154
Jenus
  Arthur 86
Jerves
  Robt. 85
Jervis
  Robert 85
Jinifer
  Daniel 72
Jinkinson
  Robert 179
Joanes
  Isabella 49
  Robert 16
Johns
  John 144
Johnson
  Cornelius 11, 34
  Daniel 83
  Daniell 54, 55, 62, 69, 80, 92, 124, 136, 184
  Elisabeth 25, 41, 184
  Emma 24, 25
  Francis 188
  George 104, 115, 116, 130, 176, 178
  Henry 139
  Hugh 152
  James 13, 34, 37, 41, 150, 158
  Levin 217
  Peter 89
  Richard 185
  Rowland 59
  Sibel 48
  Thomas 55
  William 24, 25, 28, 31, 109, 126, 187
Joll(e)y
  Edward 219
  James 20, 33, 149, 154
  Margaret 219
Jones
  Anne 217
  Cadwallader 204
  Cornelius 217
  David 124, 151, 155, 171
  Edward 82, 86, 212
  Frances 127
  Francis 127
  Hopkin 214
  James 115, 176, 178
  Jenkin 215
  Joanna 216
  John 52, 68, 102, 154, 158, 189
  Leonard 139
  Meridith 217
  Mor. 112
  Morgan 112, 150, 200, 218, 220
  Owen 124, 216
  Peter 158, 159
  Rice 127, 139, 156
  Richard 128, 132, 138, 143, 162
  Robert 54, 58, 106, 122, 151, 154
  Tho. 164
  Thomas 93, 140, 148, 184, 211

William 116, 139,
    148, 174, 191, 199
Jordaine
  John 167, 182
Jordan
  Daniel 51
  Jonas 78
  Sarah 77, 79
  Tho. 77
  Thomas 66, 67
Jowles
  Henry 201
Joy
  Edmond 110
  Edmund 98
  Peter 34
  Robert 109
Joyne
  Abraham 54
Joyner
  Robert 6, 7, 62, 107,
    111, 151, 162
Justice
  William 174

Kades
  Thomas 148
Kannaday
  Susan 11
Keate
  William 29
Kedger
  Robert 45
Kedmore
  Edward 55
Keene
  Edw. 85
  Edward 33, 141, 176,
    180, 190, 202, 207
  Henery 61
  Henry 61, 90, 154
  Richard 85, 123, 149,
    208
  Susanna 202
  William 216
Keerke
  Edward 39
Keetting
  Nicholas 4
Keiting
  Ellenor 29
  Thomas 29, 218
Keitting
  Audery 5

Nicholas 4, 5
Kellaway
  Anthony 122
Kelley
  Tho. 23
  William 35
Kelly
  Thomas 56
Kemon
  Richard 59
Kemp(e)
  Peter 132
  Thomas 83, 89, 148
Kenckby
  William 78
Kendall
  William 69, 130
  [torn] 68
Kenington
  Robert 66
Kennaday
  Suzan 52
Kennady
  William 151
Kennemont
  John 113
Kent
  Ann 133, 185
  Dyana 133
  Henry 31, 87, 133,
    134, 140
  John 54
  Mary 133, 185
  Robert 138, 165
  William 31, 133, 134,
    139, 145, 152, 185,
    217
Kerke
  Martin 158
Kernall
  Christopher 41
Kerney
  Thomas 154
Kettell
  Robert 8
Key
  Peter 138
Keyes
  John 179
Keyton
  Thomas 178
Kidmore
  Nicholas 94
Killam
  Zachariah 151

Killy
 Thomas 41, 58
King
 Hugh 68
 John 126
 Marg. 183, 184
 Margarett 183
 Robert 151, 158, 181
 Tho. 175
 Thomas 58, 215, 216
 Walter 116, 175
 William 86, 92, 113, 123, 125, 149, 150, 183, 184
Kingbury
 Rob. 65
 Robert 65
Kingsberry
 Robert 101
Kingsboro
 Robert 39
Kingsborough
 Robert 20
Kingsbury
 Robert 24, 27
Kingston 128
Kinsborro
 Robert 61
Kinsbury
 Mr. 62
Kinsey 124
Kinsey
 Elisabeth 120
 Hugh 120, 124
 Jonas 215
 Katherine 111
 Margarett 120
 Paul 61, 111
 Paule 61, 120, 122, 124
Kinsman
 Edmond 61
Kirerne
 Richard 114
Kirke
 Martin 23, 152
Kitchin
 Nicholas 65
Knap
 Elisabeth 140
 Mr. 108
Knapp
 John 154
Knight
 Edward 158
 Jane 104, 108
 John 104, 108
 Peter 20
Knighton
 Thomas 181, 183, 199
Knott
 Francis 48, 49
Knowles
 Guy 68, 69
Kydd
 William 81
Kyll
 James 160

Lacie, Lacy
 Francis 20, 63, 65, 70
 William 147
Ladd
 Richard 187, 201
Lafel
 John 38
Lam
 Henry 179
Lamare
 Peter 133
Lamb
 Henry 195
Lamberd, Lambert
 Edmond 124
 Ellen 72
 Hubbert 150
 Jeffery 42
 John 29, 30, 36, 38, 72, 124
 Josias 53, 79, 141
 Sam. 38
 Samuell 29, 36, 38, 43, 54
Lamer
 Peter 141
Lames
 Peter 177
Lamman
 William 55
Lampen
 Thomas 152
Lamphigh
 Nathaniell 191
Land
 Ann 9
 Anna 23
 Mrs. 62
 Philip 2, 4, 5, 9

Phillip 10, 178
Thomas 9, 178
William 9, 178
Landon
  Robert 38
Lands
  Samuell 85
Lane
  Ann 107
  Francis 39, 58
  John 54
  Margaret 184
  Mary 4
  Sam. 164
  Samuel(l) 116, 135, 184
  Thomas 201
  Walter 172, 180
  William 170, 180
Langford's Neck 118
Langford
  John 118
Langley
  John 113
  Thomas 70
Langworth
  Agatha 24, 25
  Elisabeth 25
  James 24
  John 25
  Mary 24, 25
  William 24, 25
Large
  Robert 145
  Thomas 148
Larkin(s)
  John 146, 164, 188, 201
Larrance
  John 89
Laurence
  John 174
Lawleme
  John 21
Lawrence
  John 182, 186
  Mary 183
  Will. 152
  William 61, 139, 143, 145, 183
Lawson(e)
  Darcus 144
  Dorcas 45
  Jean 144
  John 1, 7, 13, 16, 17, 19, 32, 37, 42, 43, 45, 50, 58, 63, 70, 73, 76, 103, 120, 144, 146
  William 72
Le Count
  Anthony 91
Leach
  John 148
Leacthworth
  Thomas 33
Leadbeather
  Samuell 204
Leads
  William 174
Leagwort
  Mr. 51
Leake
  Edward 168
  Richard 158, 209
Leaven
  John 190
LeCompte
  Anthony 192, 195
  Hester 192
LeCount
  Anthony 112
Lee
  Edward 146, 151
  Florence 211
  Hannah 30, 40
  Hugh 22, 23, 30, 40, 46, 61, 62, 63
  James 23, 37, 43, 54, 124
  John 211
Leeds
  Robert 93
  Will. 52
  William 20, 31, 55, 89, 146, 151
Lees
  James 25
Legate
  Mrs. 167
Legg
  Mr. 45
Leigh
  Francis 137, 149
Leitchworde
  Thomas 51
Leitchworth
  Elisabeth 135, 159
  Thomas 135, 159
Lemactre

Abraham 84
Lemaistre
  Abraham 84
Lemall
  Peter 148
Lendsy
  James 105
Lenthall
  Joseph 26
Lerry
  Lettice 113, 114, 121
  Peter 113, 114, 121
Letchworth
  Mr. 157
  Thomas 79, 157
Leucas
  William 31
Lewan
  Robert 115
Lewes
  Capt. 9
  John 68
  Richard 153
  William 12
Lewgar
  Martha 171
Lewger
  Elisabeth 171
  John 3, 43, 124, 153, 171, 182
  Thomas 171
Lewis 182
Lewis
  Evan 120, 150
  Henry 214
  James 146, 150, 152, 218
  Mary 182
  Sarah 182
  Theophilus 49, 73, 82
  Thomas 142, 151, 153
  William 42
Lewling
  John 151
Lille
  William 133
Lilly
  Edward 142
  Henry 26
Linckhorne
  William 119
Lindsey, Lindsie
  David 64
  Edmond 93
  Edmund 23, 125, 136, 139, 153, 195, 216
  Elisabeth 99
  James 2, 3, 4, 19, 54, 94, 99, 100, 105, 107, 120, 124, 158
  Mary 99
  Mr. 23
Lingen
  George 206
Linhecom
  Thomas 144
Linsey
  Edmond 54
  Edmund 193
Linstead
  Thomas 163
Linton
  Anthony 54, 154
  Widd 30
Lisle
  William 12
Lister
  Edmond 152
Littell
  John 34
Little Wells 118
Little
  John 33, 102, 103
  Lawrence 124
  Mary 103
Livinstone
  Tho. 23
Lizman
  William 149
Lloyd
  Edward 10, 14, 16, 56, 91, 110
  John 10
  Margarett 10
  Mr. 62, 97
  Philemon 192
  Richard 17, 152, 160
  Robert 135, 150, 153, 188
Loboty
  Deliverance 82
Lodge
  George 171
Loes
  Rich. 96
Loggins
  Elisabeth 213
  Jonathon 204
Loker

Thomas 152
Lomax
  Mr. 62
  Tho. 38
  Thomas 38, 47, 136, 152, 155, 158
London
  John 66, 78
Long(e)
  Jemima 109, 111, 112, 121
  John 61
  Mathew 17
  Mrs. 153
  Robert 109, 131, 136
  Samuell 154
  William 22, 31
Longlines
  Elisabeth 110
Longworth
  John 59
Lord
  John 54
Lorkie
  Mary 213
  Nicholas 213
Losy
  Tho. 146
Loudell
  George 56
Love
  John 45
  Judith 132
  Robert 141
  Thomas 132
  William 39, 54, 136
Lovely
  Deliverance 86
Lovilye
  Mr. 93
Lowder
  Richard 168
Lowry
  William 121
Loyd
  Ed. 102
  Edward 104, 109, 131, 145
  Moris 95
  Mr. 39, 110
  Philemon 128
  Richard 17, 110
Lucar
  John 180
  Martha 180
Lucas
  Francis 206
  Samuel 155
  William 35, 36, 101, 103, 105, 198, 206
Lucus
  William 62, 150
Ludford
  Arthur 51, 52, 59, 68, 69, 73, 79, 106, 111, 114, 115, 121, 136, 148, 157, 186
Luen
  Philip 151
Luffman
  Mary 215
  William 215
Lugar
  Martha 181
Luger
  John 4, 10
Lumbard
  Rebecca 28
Lumbert
  John 99
Lumbro
  Jacob 55
Lumbrozo Distewy 93
Lumbrozo
  Dr. 72
  Elisabeth 93
  Jo. 72
  John 72, 93, 100, 154
  Rebecca 93
Lunbrey
  Humphry 187
Luombroz
  John 46
Lupton
  Thomas 79
Lyle
  James 160
Lyles
  William 122
Lylly
  Henry 99
Lyndsey
  Edmond 11, 55, 124
  Edmund 12
  James 11
Lynes
  Philip 215
Lyngham
  George 23
Lynton

Ursly 21
Lyster
  Edmund 99

Macall
  George 39, 160
Macannark
  Dennis 73
Macay
  James 99
Macc(k)all
  Geo. 27
  George 26, 43
Macckenny
  John 24
Maccounough
  Dennis 142
Macdowall
  William 74
Macenna
  Annah 98
  Macam 98
Macenne
  John 97
  Macam 97
Machell's Necke 3
Macheny
  Martin 139
Machie
  John 37
Mackahill
  George 32
Mackall
  Anne 219
  George 163, 219
Mackart
  Elisabeth 220
  John 220
Mackary
  Daniell 209
Mackdoc
  William 22
Mackdodalt
  William 26
Mackeaneday
  Phillip 36
Mackennie
  Martin 125
Mackenny
  John 22, 48
Mackey
  Elisabeth 219, 220
  James 117
  John 161, 219

Mackine
  John 31
Mackinnie
  John 31
Mackline
  Robert 213
Macklyn
  Robert 68, 152
Macky
  James 107
  John 143, 160
Macou
  James 124
Maddock
  Robert 211
Maddox
  David 216
  Edward 197
  Laserus 77
Magrouder
  Dennis 132
Magrowder
  Alexander 133, 149
Magruder
  Alexander 20, 92
  Sanders 33
Mailam
  John 1
Makey
  John 32
Makgreger
  James 54
Male
  Anthony 181
Mallett
  William 27
Malom
  John 120
Man
  Edward 203, 204, 205,
    212, 213
Manchfeild
  Vincent 139
Mane
  Samuell 20
Manfeild
  Ranson 94
Maning
  Mr. 61
Manlove
  Christopher 104
  Elisabeth 104
  Marke 104, 111
  Mary 104
  Persy 104

Thomas 111, 130
Mannder
  Mr. 55
Manne
  Edward 204
Manning
  Capt. 33, 68
  Mr. 33
  Thomas 31, 42, 45,
    67, 103, 104
  Mannor of Bohemia 25
  Mannor of Nangemy 7
Mannyng
  Tho. 87, 90, 95
  Thomas 60, 67, 78,
    82, 84, 87, 88, 89,
    91, 94, 101, 148,
    153
Manrow
  Tho. 135
Mansell
  John 43
  Mary 161
  Vincent 6
Mansfeild
  Mr. 37
  Vincent 105
Mansfield
  Benjamin 200
  John 23
  Vincent 218
Manwaring
  Georg 186
  George 180, 187, 191,
    193, 195
Many(i)ng(e)
  Tho. 71, 86
  Thomas 86
Marakin
  John 37
Marcanallie
  Walter 211
Marcekin
  John 61
Marchall
  George 35
Marear
  Andrew 148
Mareday
  John 113
Maris
  Thomas 9
Marke
  Couden 125
  John 34

Markhes
  George 55
Markin
  Thomas 33, 144, 153
Markline
  Robertt 198
Markum
  Ann 116
  John 116
  Thomas 154
Marland
  Robert 23
Marler
  Jonathon 94, 153, 192
Marlow(e)
  William 76, 77, 151
Marsh Point 165
Marsh
  John 155
  Paull 153
  Sarah 56
  Thomas 122, 131, 153,
    192, 193, 212
Marshall
  George 152, 178, 207
  Isaack 148
  Thomas 150
  Will. 63
  William 16, 54, 60,
    111, 112, 136, 153,
    158, 193
  William. 123
Marsham
  Richard 141, 176
Martin
  Abdaloe 178
  Abdelo 117, 118, 153
  Abdeloe 178
  Abdlo 119
  Abdloe 113
  Abedlow 86
  Abelor 117
  Ablomar 92
  Ann 167
  Anne 167
  Elisabeth 178
  James 11, 76, 77, 78,
    84, 161, 167, 181
  John 83, 84, 85, 168,
    179, 200
  Lodowick 149
  Lodwick 108
  Mary 157, 178
  Robert 52, 168, 174,
    213

Sarah 157, 178
Thomas 98, 157, 161
vidua 213
Martine
  Patience 29
  Thomas 29
  William 24, 29, 31
Martyn
  Thomas 154
Martyne
  Abdelo 139
  Mary 97
Mas
  John 23
Mascall
  Richard 122
Maskhum
  John 79
Masley
  Ralph 158, 159
Mason
  Edward 157
  John 149
Masses
  John 16
Massey
  Robert 167
  Winifred 168
Masson
  Mathew 174
Masters
  Charles 192
Maston
  Robert 23, 62
Mastrix
  John 62
Mathewes
  John 54, 152
  Mr. 9
  Tho. 37
  Thomas 1, 3, 4, 5, 8, 21, 45, 58, 69, 159
Mat(t)hews
  Henry 152, 204
  Jane 215
  John 178, 184
  Love 184
  Mr. 8, 23, 24, 39
  Tho. 4, 36, 72, 83, 92, 151
  Thomas 8, 15, 17, 18, 22, 28, 52, 58, 60, 63, 69, 72, 83, 124, 136, 153, 187, 191, 193, 195, 215, 218

Mattingl(e)y
  Elisabeth 63
  Tho. 76
  Thomas 63, 70
Mattix
  Dr. 55
Mattrick
  John 4
Maxall
  James 53
Maxell
  James 164
Maxfeild
  Alexander 174
  James 55, 56
Maxwell
  Alexander 153, 168, 181
  James 181
Mayhan
  Samuell 54
Maylam
  John 124
Mayle
  Anthony 151, 153
Maynard
  Agnes 132, 167
  Ann 132
  Charles 6, 167
  Elisabeth 132, 167
Meacock
  Seabright 216
Meadly
  John 11, 12
Meale
  Anthony 143
Meare(s)
  John 174
  Thomas 12
  William 110, 152
Meayl
  Anthony 143
Mecammey
  Macam 53
Mecard
  John 132
Mecconnak
  Dennis 199
Mechie
  James 179
Meckenny
  Martin 125
Mecoakin
  John 182
Meconnah

Dennis 98
Medford
  Fortune 126
Medley
  Anne 220
  George 28, 220
  John 2, 28, 77, 220
  Thomas 28
  William 28
Mee
  George 35, 43, 61
Meech
  Tho. 178
  Thomas 161, 164
Meekin(g)s
  Richard 139, 145, 152
Meere
  Thomas 154
  William 150
Mees(e)
  George 36
  Henry 37, 61, 91
  Mr. 13, 154
Meggison
  John 169
Mekenne
  Markeham 102
Mekenny
  Martin 125
Mekeny
  Mecom 20
Meles
  William 16
Melton
  Thomas 151, 152
  William 190
Mentiall
  Jeffery 104
Meredith
  John 91, 183, 184
Merest
  Henry 167
Meriday
  John 183
Meridith
  John 112
Meriken
  William 160
Meriton
  Joshua 192
Merryweather
  John 154, 155
Metcalfe
  John 5, 23, 29, 77
  Mr. 62

Metford
  Bulmer 83
  Fortune 83, 126
Mettcope
  George 55
Michaelson
  Jacob 154
Micheelson
  Jacob 68
Michell
  Hen. 86
  Henry 31, 94, 95
  Tobya 189
Middlefield
  Thomas 209
Mid(d)leton
  Thomas 14, 154
  William 110
Midwinter
  Mary 165
Miles
  John 111
  Margarett 169
  Mr. 16
  Tho. 78, 91, 172
  Thomas 169
  Tobias 87, 88, 89, 137
  Tobyea 93
  William 188
Mill
  Tabitha 217
  William 18, 19, 217
Miller
  John 145, 153
  Mich. 195
  Michael 195, 204, 221
  Phill. 61
  Richard 147, 148, 156, 184
Milles
  Tobias 149
  William 166, 182
Millner
  Thomas 25, 35
Mills
  Bartholomew 159
  George 17
  Jacob 17
  James 210, 211
  John 10, 11, 179
  Mary 51
  Peter 10, 11, 44, 140, 144, 152, 167
  Thomas 141

Tobias 34, 148
Will. 126
William 2, 18, 26,
  33, 51, 59, 68, 148
Milner
  Thomas 31, 47
Minshall
  Jeffery 111
Minton
  Richard 131
Mirth
  John 34
Mitchell
  George 151
  Henry 59, 91, 142,
   146, 149, 150
  John 181
  Thomas 146, 152
Mit(t)ford
  Bulmer 83, 90, 103,
   110
  Fortune 83, 90, 103,
   110
  Thomas 83
Mitton
  Mary 133
Mockey
  John 161
Moffett
  William 137, 146,
   150, 152, 163
Moffitt
  William 90
Mogg
  Francis 79
Moll
  John 200, 206
Monfret
  Edward 211
Montague
  Stephen 104
Monteague
  Cornelius 182
Montefort
  Francis 219
Montfort
  Tho. 90
Monyan
  Imben 77
Moore
  Francis 151, 154
  Henry 72, 136
  Jackelina 217
  James 71, 217
  Richard 139, 148, 212

Robert 136
Mooreley
  Joseph 148
More
  James 133
  Mary 98
  Richard 149
  Tho. 40
  William 179
Morecraft, Morecroft
  John 83, 89, 103,
   129, 150, 151, 159,
   170, 183, 184, 194
Morely
  Joseph 164
Moreram
  John 149
Mores
  Samuel 110
Morga(i)n
  Abraham 91
  Aler 112
  Barbara 203
  Bennet 209
  Elisabeth 44, 138,
   209
  Frances 203
  Henry 28, 39, 55,
   124, 203
  Jarvis 203
  Jervase 214
  John 21, 39, 53, 138,
   139, 153, 162, 209
  Robert 112, 209
  William 154, 210
Morgen
  Robert 91
Moricroft
  John 83
Moring
  Edward 36
Moris
  John 31
  Samuel 111
Morkin
  Thomas 33
Morley
  Joseph 215
Morlin
  Francis 158
Morne
  Elisabeth 125
Morrice
  Hannah 122
  Richard 94

Morris
  Capt. 66
  Elisabeth 24
  John 19, 36, 54, 158
  Richard 54, 158, 182
  Rob. 175
  Robert 66, 101
  Tho. 164
Mortine
  Thomas 36
Morton
  Hammon 107
Mosely
  Robert 54
Mosley
  Joseph 166
Moss(e)
  Richard 59, 86, 157, 160, 170
Mott
  Ann 150
  Elisabeth 70
  John 70
Mounroe
  George 120, 124
Mount Arakat 96
Mountagne
  William 174
Mountague
  Henry 210
  Katharine 210
  Mr. 54
  Stephen 8, 99, 105, 107, 119, 120, 124, 153
Mounteyne
  Alexander 122
Mountford
  Thomas 140
Mountfort
  Tho. 90
  William 90
Mounthope 182
Mountigue
  Mr. 23
Mountique
  William 168
Moy
  Elisabeth 219
  Rich. 165
  Richard 105, 128, 146, 150, 158, 180, 185, 219
Mudge
  Gregory 169

Muffett
  William 61, 90, 186
Mugg
  Francis 76, 81
  Mary 76, 77
Mulattoes
  Jeffery 135
  Richard 135
Mulleken
  Patrick 152
Mullekin
  James 123
Mullican
  Patrick 106
Mulliken
  James 123
Mullikin
  James 33
  Mary 123
  Patrick 18
  Pratriack 104
Mumford
  Tho. 90
Munn
  John 120, 124
Munni
  Thomas 8
Munroe
  George 133, 166
Munrow
  George 136
Murrah
  William 123
Murraine
  John 180
Murray
  William 123
Murrell
  Gregory 28
Murty
  Stephen 205, 206
Mustian
  Edmond 178
Muttershed
  Mr. 55
Mutterslued
  Samuell 54
Mychell
  Henry 93
Myles
  John 140
  Margreat 172

Nanfann

Edmund 29
Nanton
  Edmond 54
Nash
  Alexander 182
  Anne 209
  Hugh 154
  Richard 182
Neale
  Capt. 68, 193, 195
  James 13, 14, 30, 40, 113, 150
  Jonathon 56, 92
  Susanna 214
  Will. 52
  William 56, 118, 170, 175, 189, 214
Neall
  Samuell 191
Nedham
  Mathew 24
Needham
  Dorothy 24
  Margarett 24
Neglect 173
Negroes
  Alckaman 9
  Ann 9
  Dorothy 18
  Dugo 137
  Emmanuel 96
  Flora 108, 111, 140
  Francisco 9
  Inde 135
  Marea 111
  Margarett 23
  Mary 145
  Moccaton 9
  Peter 135, 145
  Philip 23
  Robert 145
  Suzanna 135
  William 145
Nell
  Peter 85
Nesfolde
  William 199
Nettlefeild
  George 14
Nettles
  Mr. 163
Neugwett
  John 109
Nevell
  John 30, 54, 150, 163
  Richard 12
  William 154
'Nevett
  Richard 16
  Serjeant 23
Nevill
  Johannah 72
  John 60, 72, 74, 75, 160, 212
  Mr. 80
  William 72, 136
Nevitt
  Richard 16
Newell
  Rich. 164
Newman
  Abraham 219
  Elinor 219
  George 39, 40, 54, 62, 153
  Margerite 39
  Thomas 145
  William 39
Newport
  William 150, 152
Newton
  John 211
Niccolls
  John 83
Nicholas
  John 137
Nicholls
  John 45, 177
Nichols
  Thomas 132
Nickall
  John 144
Nicolas
  Mordecay 52
Nicolls
  John 90
Noake
  Mary 213
  William 213
Nobes
  Margarett 115
  Thomas 115
Norman
  Edward 139, 173
  John 34, 35
North
  Charles 200
Norton(n)
  Mr. 51
  Tobias 51, 106, 110,

130, 148, 176
Tobyas 117, 121, 125
Norwood
  Ben. 59
  Capt. 122
  John 11, 12, 37, 61,
    94, 118, 148, 158,
    159
  Judith 37
Not(t)l(e)y
  Mr. 58, 76
  Tho. 67, 94, 188
  Thomas 105, 127, 129,
    167, 171, 187, 200
Noubes
  Margarite 106
  Thomas 106
Nowell
  John 60
Nugent
  William 4, 10
Nut(t)(h)all
  Arthur 113
  Ellinor 143
  James 13, 143
  John 46, 63, 103,
    123, 127, 143, 145,
    151, 152
Nutthell
  John 43
Nutwell
  John 40

O'Bryan
  Anne 208
  Denis 208
O'Daly
  Bryan 218
Oackly
  John 101
Oakel(e)y
  Thomas 107
Oazey, Oazie
  James 88, 99
Obder
  John 133
OBowen
  Davy 148
OBryan
  Mathias 124
Odber
  John 24, 116, 117,
    125
Odenhanway

Elisabeth 57
Odonell
  Thomas 189
Odovell
  Thomas 53
Ogdon
  James 211
Ohoggan
  Paul 95, 101
Okeham
  John 130
Okeley
  John 95
  Thomas 150
Oldfeild
  Christopher 153
Oldfield
  Peternella 209
Oliver
  Thomas 144
Omaile
  Bryan 180
Omale
  Brett 91
  Bryan 112
Oneale
  Hugh 131, 150, 153
Oonell
  Mary 40
Oonelle
  Mary 52
Orchard
  William 134, 147
ORelly
  Edward 136
Orris
  James 10, 12, 13, 14
Orson
  Richard 52
Osbaston
  William 112
Osbisson
  William 105
Osborn(e)
  Henry 34
  Thomas 98, 169, 175,
    178
  William 156
Osbourn
  Henry 75
Osbourne
  Katherine 75
  Thomas 175
  William 161
Osburne

Thomas 98
Ososton
  William 150
Osterlin
  Henry 154
Oston
  Robert 38
Ostrine
  Robert 30
Ouldfeild
  Christopher 110
Ourmstronge
  Edw. 78
Ouzen
  James 91
Oversee
  Symon 9
Overseyes
  brother 9
Overson
  Francis 109
Overton
  Francis 81, 92, 109, 111
  Mary 92, 109
  Thomas 45, 134, 147, 202
Overzee
  Elisabeth 19
  Mr. 9
  Simon 11, 12, 13
  Symon 19
Owen
  Christopher 150
  John 41, 170
  Richard 68, 127, 216
  Thomas 65, 151
Owsey
  James 99

Paca
  Robert 47, 98, 116
Pacey
  Thomas 109
Packer
  Edward 1, 15
Packyt
  Walter 76
Paddison
  James 166
Padifitt
  Nathaniell 160
Padock
  Henry 105

Page
  Robert 102, 151
Pag(g)ett
  Tho. 90
  Thomas 33, 90, 143, 149, 150, 152
Paine
  Jane 219
  Tho. 106, 178
  Thomas 105, 164, 178
Pake(s)
  Francis 21
  George 37, 149
  Walter 1, 9, 10, 11, 12, 14, 21, 23, 48, 55, 61, 117, 130, 150, 151
Palmer
  George 123, 125
  Samuell 25
  William 11, 17, 29, 40, 41, 42, 43, 49, 54, 62, 134
Panther
  George 150
  John 148
Paratt
  William 165
Parish
  Edward 42, 214
Parkall
  Geo. 164
Parke
  Robert 1
Parker's Land 177
Parker
  Edward 177, 180
  Elisabeth 177
  George 207, 216
  Henry 151, 153
  Joane 29
  John 35, 186, 187, 188, 201, 202, 203
  Mr. 108
  Phillip 132, 177
  Rober 53
  Robert 189
  Samuell 29, 177
  Thomas 138
  William 31, 80, 148, 217
Parkes
  George 201
  Robert 59
Parnaphee

Robert 175
Parnell
  Henry 1, 3
Parr
  John 164, 166, 172
Parramore
  John 68
Parrat(t)
  Ann 165
  Beniamin 165
  Benjamin 165
  George 165
  Henry 165
  Will. 165
  William 165, 167
Parrett
  Robert 124
  William 26, 33, 61, 165
Parrey
  Robert 33, 67
Parrimore
  Arnold 210
  John 210
Parrish
  Edw. 164
  Edward 57
Parrot
  Anne 179
  Benjamin 179
  William 179
Parry
  Tho. 20
Parsons
  Margarett 25
  Thomas 12, 128, 131, 142
Pary
  Thomas 20
Pascall
  George 63, 69, 73, 98, 108, 116, 117, 118, 141, 150
Pasey
  Thomas 109
Pateson
  James 57
Patricke
  Forrest 4
Pattin
  John 153
Paulgrave
  Gregory 64
Pawly
  Lionell 164
Pawmer
  William 37
Payne
  Tho. 106
  Thomas 72, 152
  William 18
Paynter
  John 34
Peak(e)
  Geo. 129, 133
  George 8, 27, 60, 63, 74, 82, 84, 85, 86, 87, 88, 89, 90, 95, 97, 101, 103, 129, 133, 134, 137, 140, 155, 164, 166, 176, 180
  Johanna 166
  Katherine 166
  Martha 166
  Mary 166
  Thomas 174
  Walter 1, 27, 35, 41, 83, 146
Pearce
  John 145, 153
  Thomas 181
Peare
  Henery 54
Pearse
  Joseph 216
Peart
  John 138, 146
Peary
  Daby 8
Peca
  Robert 110, 150, 153
Peck
  John 214
Peek
  Robert 137
Peeke
  Robert 31
Peerce
  John 178
  William 209
Peeterson
  Jacob 179
Peirce
  Dr. 140
Peirpoint
  Anias 135
  Henry 135
  Jabez 135
Pekes

Walter 58
Pell
  William 16
Pellinger
  Sam. 164
Pen(n)ington
  Henery 174
  Henry 152, 158, 164
Penrin
  William 37
Penroy
  Margret 203
Pensax
  Samuell 189
Perce
  Robert 171
Percefor
  John 154
Perc(e)y
  Thomas 111, 112, 121
Pereman
  Ann 95
Perepoint
  Henry 188
Perey
  Constant 182
  Richard 138
  Tho. 90, 144
  Thomas 69, 70, 79, 80, 133
Perie
  John 150
  Richard 55
  Thomas 152
Perkins
  Ann 176
  Anne 171
  John 68
  Robert 171, 176
Perkone
  Henry 101
Perpoint
  Henry 153
Perren
  Edward 152
Perrepoint
  Amos 188
Perrey
  Margarett 51
  Thomas 144, 155
Porrie
  Thomas 194
Perrpoint
  Henry 188
Perry
  Margaret 51, 71
  Margarite 84
  Marguarite 67
  Micaiah 201
  Richard 140
  Robert 82, 84
  Tho. 63
  Thomas 15, 33, 63, 64, 67, 71, 127, 132, 149
  William 63
Perryneck 194
Pert
  John 135, 146
Pery
  Robert 33
Peryne
  Thomas 54
Peteate
  Anne 26
  Thomas 26
Petekin
  James 154
Peterson
  Jacob 184
  Mathias 179
Pether
  Richard 138, 163, 182
Petit
  Francis 193, 194
Petoson
  Jacob 136
Petro
  John 3
Pett's Gift 139
Pettipoole
  William 150, 152
Pettitt
  Francis 124
Phare
  Richard 52
Phebo
  Marke 151
Phelps
  Cuthbert 143
  Thomas 199
  Wa. 70
  Walter 70
Phenix
  Cuthbert 149
Phepo's Fort 178
Phepo
  Mark 77
  Marke 178
  Marks 32

Pheybo
  Marks 36
Pheypo
  Marcks 27
  Mareke 23
  Marke 4, 5, 23
  Markes 4
  Marks 17, 29, 35, 47
  Mr. 62
Philipps
  Thomas 126
Philips
  Alice 78, 79, 81
  Bartholomew 7, 84, 132
  Cuthbert 156
  Elisabeth 84
  Margaret 82
  Margarite 84
  Robert 157
  Thomas 16, 45, 92
  William 79, 81
Phillipps
  James 66
Phillips
  Barth. 6
  Batt. 6
  Ellen 6
  James 211
  Richard 122
  Thomas 6, 39, 110, 126, 179
  William 78, 81
Philpott
  Edward 158
Phippes
  Elisabeth 207, 220
Phrizell
  Suncomb 45
Pick
  Leonard 64
Pickard
  Ellinor 137
  Nicholas 137, 147
Pickenson
  Mary 173
Pickett, Pickitt
  Nicholas 82, 102, 131
Pickord
  Nicholas 88
  Nicolas 88
Pier
  Henry 35
Pierce
  Joseph 211

Lydia 219
Thomas 219
Will. 164
Pierse
  William 202
Piggott
  John 146
Pile
  John 58
Pilkinton
  Walter 171
Pille
  John 3
Pinck
  Thomas 191, 219
Pinke
  John 119
Pinkedacy
  Henry 6
Pinner
  Anne 105
  Richard 105, 107, 130
  William 130
Pinson
  edm. 61
  Maximilan 154
Pinsonn
  Edmund 40
Pinter
  Elisabeth 114
Piper
  Will. 55
  William 31
Pirke
  Edward 157
Pither
  William 15
Pitt(e)(s)
  John 92, 102, 109, 115, 145, 151, 153, 172, 173, 182, 205
Planter Delight 118
Platts
  John 34
Plaucleg
  William 189
Plead
  William 179
Pleasants
  John 171
Pledg
  William 174
Pleypo
  Markes 4
Plum

John 212
Mary 212
Plumer
  Tho. 188
Plumland
  Thomas 64
Poesey
  Francis 9
Pollard
  John 59, 152
  Mr. 61
Pollett
  William 23
Ponning
  William 192
Poole
  John 23, 209
  Sarah 209
Poor
  James 97
Poore
  Thomas 185
Pope
  Anne 79
  Fran. 72, 179
  Frances 41
  Francis 22, 26, 29,
    30, 34, 35, 38, 41,
    42, 46, 50, 54, 59,
    60, 74, 76, 80, 83,
    92, 94, 121, 123,
    129, 136, 153, 158
  Henry 79, 150
  Mary 216
  Michaell 135
  Thomas 181, 216
Poplar Knowle 47
Poppins Gaye 165
Porkeson
  Luke 145
Porter
  Dr. 188
  John 135
  Peter 214
  Sarah 214
Possum
  John 221
Pot(t)(s)
  Elisabeth 114
  John 33, 34, 114,
    140, 141, 152, 157,
    177, 186
  Mr. 113
Potter
  Adory 36

  Audry 27
  Henry 35, 47
  Thomas 207
Poultney
  William 211
Powell
  Edward 105
  John 209
  Tho. 125, 172
  Thomas 92, 109, 110,
    126, 147, 159, 161,
    165, 167, 181
  William 164, 201
Powick
  John 154
Prater
  Jonathon 65
  Samuell 69
Presley
  Peter 55
  William 64, 68
Prestoe
  Richard 27
Preston
  James 173
  Margaret 173, 174
  Mr. 62, 67, 140
  Rebeckah 173
  Ri. 174
  Richard 78, 85, 106,
    113, 142, 173, 174
  Samuell 173
  Sarah 173
  Thomas 148, 152, 173,
    207, 217
Prestone
  Robert 73
Prether
  Jonathon 33
Price
  Ann 26
  Col. 27
  Elisabeth 24
  Henry 47
  James 141, 154, 176
  Jenken 151
  Jenkin 154, 176, 180
  John 8, 11, 17, 26,
    29, 32, 40, 54, 55,
    72
  Mary 213
  William 56, 62, 72,
    83, 92, 99, 107,
    154, 155, 158, 213
Prichard

Daby 8
David 9, 10
  Nicholas 53
  Palador 84
Prichett
  Thomas 111
Pricklow
  Samuell 155
Pricthitt
  Thomas 140
Prince
  Caesar 211
  Cesar 24
Pritchard
  David 54
  Pallidere 82
  Thomas 150
Pritcher
  John 1
Pritchett
  William 33, 34, 148
Pritt
  John 65
Procter, Proctor
  Robert 141, 215
Proctor's Hall 96
Prooter
  Robert 59
Prouse
  George 58
Prowse
  John 150, 152
  Robert 151, 215
Pudd
  Bartho. 72
Puddington
  George 14, 65, 73, 82, 91
Pugsley
  James 49
Purnell
  Tho. 75
  Thomas 64
  William 173
Purnill
  Thomas 101
Purqua
  Nicholas 54
Purse(s)
  Anthony 137, 146, 147
  Antony 116
Pyle
  John 58
Pyne
  Francis 186

Pyper
  John 34, 53, 94, 105

Quigley
  Capt. 201
  John 195, 196, 198

Raile
  Thomas 204
Rainer
  Rd. 177
Ralley 167
Rallings
  John 34
  William 37
Rallus
  William 61
Ramsey
  John 164, 166
  Tho. 164
  William 58
Randall
  Ann 119
  Richard 80, 92, 117, 119, 124, 153
Raper
  John 8, 77
  Thomas 17
Rapier
  John 145
  Thomas 17
Ratcliffe
  Robert 154
Raton
  Samuell 116
Raven
  Jane 210
  John 154, 210
Rawbone
  James 205
Rawlings
  John 149, 150
  Nicholas 61, 143
Rawlins
  Elisabeth 220
Raynoldes
  John 62
Read(e)
  Alce 24
  David 110
  Eleis 61
  Elisabeth 214
  Geo. 66

George 16, 18, 19,
  24, 27, 33, 38, 61,
  85, 89, 101, 107,
  152, 191
John 18, 27, 38, 61,
  65, 68, 69, 115, 152
Jone 89, 101
Margaret 75
Margarete 65
Mary 110
Mathew 137, 155, 166,
  175, 181, 182
Maty 158
Percivall 145, 151
Simon 177
Thomas 19
William 102, 131, 214
Reader
  Simon 141
  Symon 141
Reave
  William 148
Redd Clift 25
Rede
  George 76
Reed
  George 39, 75, 76
  John 30, 39, 61
Reede
  Thomas 213
Reeves
  William 144
Refue
  Henry 190
Renolds
  Dorothy 162
Repland
  Michell 166
Reserve 165
Resurrection Mannor 51
Revell
  Mr. 161
  Randall 115, 116,
    130, 147, 154
  Rendell 176
Reycroft
  John 211
Reynold
  John 219
Reynolds
  Geo. 162
  George 10, 13, 14,
    35, 77
  John 24, 46, 63, 77,
    81, 123, 152, 192

Richard 22, 24
Reynols
  John 79
Rho(a)d(e)s
  Abraham 78, 188, 198
  John 114, 115, 130,
    151
Rhoden
  Mathew 62
Rice
  John 138
  Richard 54
Rich
  Richard 55
Richarbie
  Richard 173
Richard(s)
  John 158, 178
  Will. 53
  William 31, 65, 81,
    86, 89
Richardson
  Edward 93, 152
  Elisabeth 112
  Francis 88, 150, 153
  George 108, 121, 125,
    132, 145, 159, 163
  John 112, 125, 147,
    157, 159, 161, 163,
    165, 176, 179
  Lawrence 112, 113,
    116
  Mary 112
  Robert 210
  Sarah 112
  Simon 125, 159, 165,
    167
  Simond 165
  Symon 54
  Thomas 112
  William 172, 173
Richarson
  John 165
Richason
  John 157
Richeson
  Simon 179
Richisson
  Simond 163
Richmond
  Edward 94
Ricks
  John 214
Rico
  Benjamin 59

Rider
 Henry 206
 Richard 110, 144
Ridgell
 Richard 178
Ridgely
 Robert 200
 Robertt 192, 195
Rig(g)b(e)y
 James 158, 165, 170, 189
Rigg(e)s
 Francis 25, 70, 71, 80, 154
Right
 Ismaell 86
 William 39
Rigll
 Richard 132
Ring(e)
 Ellen 17
 John 73
 Richard 45
 Tho. 76
 Thomas 16, 17, 45, 72, 73
Ringgold
 James 126
Ringgould
 Thomas 82
Ringh
 Hans de 134
Ringold
 Francis 145
 James 145, 151, 153, 179
 Mr. 179
 Thomas 86, 147
Ringould
 Ja. 172
 James 119
 Thomas 21, 86
Rithson
 Nicholas 219
Rively
 John 179
Roach
 Henry 54
Roades
 Abraham 187
Robarts
 Edward 107
 Samuell 166
Robbinson
 Tho. 23

Robenson
 Henry 149
Roberson
 Andrew 33
Roberts
 Edward 107
 Fabby 77
 Fobber 158
 John 116
 Peter 97, 158
 Roger 158
 Stannop 7, 105
 Stannup 82
 Stanop 45, 46, 47, 102
 Stanup 151
Robertson
 Patrick 114
Robeson
 Charles 80, 92
 George 80, 92
 Susanna 80
 Zuzanna 92
Robesson
 William 94
Robin(e)s
 Robert 41, 42, 55
Robinson
 Andrew 68, 89, 97, 107, 144
 Hen. 68
 Henry 34, 142
 John 68, 119, 124
 Patrick 114, 130
 Richard 54
 Susannah 83
 Tho. 36
 Thomas 25, 31, 34, 47, 124, 142
 William 54, 83, 88, 148
Robison
 Andrew 19
Robson
 William 147
Robyne
 Robert 55
Roch
 Henry 154
Roche
 Charles de la 193
Rockhould
 Thomas 37, 61
Rockwell
 John 118

Rodaway
  John 212
Rodgers
  Anne 28
Rodwell
  William 182
Roe
  Anne 130
  Edward 153, 157, 165, 172, 173, 179, 201, 213
  Mary 212
  Richard 130
Rogers
  Cornelius 193
  David 68
  Edward 54, 137, 146
  John 64, 70
Roise
  John 128
Roper
  Alice 203, 214
  John 55
  Thomas 192
Rosewell
  Will. 182
  William 42, 63, 70, 76, 78, 84, 167, 219
Rosewill
  William 109
Roulands
  Okey 192
Roules
  Walter 137
Rousby
  Christopher 156, 169
Rouse
  Abraham 145
  Gregory 166
Rowdell
  Thomas 201
Rowe(s)
  Richard 34, 130, 179
Rowland
  Okey 201
  Robert 168
Rowles
  Christopher 180
Rowsb(e)y
  Barbara 203
  Christopher 148, 152, 174
  John 203, 212
  Mr. 148
Rowse

Abraham 136, 150, 155
  John 94, 102
Rowser
  Abraham 132
Roy
  Antony 50
Royall
  Elisabeth 220
Roz(i)er
  Ben. 134
  Benj. 171
  Benjamin 119, 129, 131, 146, 150, 153, 158, 215, 216
Rubel
  Joyce 78
Ruckeston
  Nicholas 124
Rushell
  Christopher 54
  Nicholas 54
Ruske
  William 55
Russell
  Christopher 19, 38, 40
  Daniel 47
  Daniell 219
  Elisabeth 38
  John 21, 139, 149
  Juliana 21, 28
  Richard 4, 32, 62, 178, 187, 192
  Sara 192
  Walter 38
  William 38, 213, 214
Russendall 21
Rustell
  Richard 151
Rutten
  Garratt 122, 159
  Garrett 122
Rye
  Anne 212
  John 212
Rynolds
  Tho. 188

Sacker
  Ewen 98
Sadches
  Thomas 92
Sadleir
  Gilles 20, 33

Gyles 27
Mr. 27
Sadler
  Giles 51
  Gills 61
  Gyles 33, 41
  Jules 20
  Mr. 61
Saffin
  William 112
Saffnie
  William 158
Sallaway
  Anthony 93
Sallmon
  T. 190
Salloway
  Anthony 119
Sallway
  Anthony 118
Salmon
  Ralph 59, 118
  Stephen 6
  Thomas 6, 202
Salsbury
  John 144
Salsby
  Nicholas 152
Salter
  Jane 28, 29
  John 28, 29
Sampell
  William 20
Samphell
  William 20
Sampson
  Robert 149
  Thomas 23, 44, 45, 127
Sanders
  William 64
Sandford
  John 59
Sandum
  William 76, 77, 78
Sanghier
  George 150
Saphines
  William 159
Sarah's Neck 182
Sarkey
  Lawrence 24
Satton
  John 33
Saunder(s)
  John 149, 206
Savage
  Edw. 78
  Edward 67, 75, 189
Savege
  Elisabeth 171
Savon
  Will. 92
Saward
  Mary 96
Sawyer
  Francis 130
Sayer
  Frances 203
Scale
  Peter 174, 179, 183
Scape(s)
  James 30, 33, 40
  William 144
Scarburgh
  Charles 68
  Henry 66, 67
Scarlett
  John 53
Scimmon Point 53
Scorey
  William 173
Scotcher
  John 14, 15
  Rose 14
Scott
  Edmund 18, 22, 30
  James 104, 108, 113
  John 153, 156, 163, 213
  Marmaduke 104, 118
  Roger 68
Scounn
  Edward 153
Scutt
  Henry 29
Seales
  Clement 179
Sealsbey
  Edward 172
Seamans
  Thomas 150, 158
Seamore
  Lettis 23
Seares
  Ann 16
  Joseph 16
Sech
  Robert 70
Sedgewick

James 204
Sedgwick
  Thomas 133
Seeling
  George 109
Seitclere
  William 2
Selby
  Edward 135, 180
Selleck
  Mr. 154
Semm(e)(s)
  Marmaduke 137, 150,
    152, 203, 205, 219,
    220
Sench
  Mary 70
  Robert 70
Sennott
  Garrett 124
Senott
  John 33
Sens
  John 25
Sensarfe, Senserf(e)
  Walter 30, 34, 40
Senserse
  Walter 67
Serchwell
  Thomas 20
Setton
  John 39
Seuell
  Johanna 196
Sewall
  Anne 75
  Elisabeth 75
  Henery 106
  Henry 30, 33, 34, 40,
    61, 68, 75, 78, 95,
    132, 143, 150, 152,
    163
  Jane 75
  John 68, 81
  Madam 78
  Mary 75, 78
  Nicholas 75
  Samuell 75, 153
  Secretary 68
Sewell
  Ellinor 184
  Henry 56, 59, 108
  John 81, 184
Sewwll
  John 35

Shacerly
  William 154
Shacklady
  James 148, 179
Shacocke
  Roger 151
Shaddock
  Henry 94
Shadwell
  John 211
  Katharine 211
Shaller
  Joshua 197
Shank(e)s
  Emma 24
  John 24, 167
Sharman
  John 153
Sharp(e)
  Peter 34, 68, 70, 85,
    140, 148, 174, 176
Shaw
  George 97
  James 141
  John 200, 207
  Joyce 209
  Martha 209
  Nicholas 209
  Thomas 54
  William 209
Sheale
  Bridget 44
  Robert 44, 46
Sheares
  Thomas 54
  William 142, 167
Sheeles
  Robert 61
Shehee
  Roger 187
Sheiredin
  Thomas 33
Shell
  Robert 28
Shelton
  Thomas 54
Sheppeard
  Nicholas 197
Shercliff
  John 51
Sherctcliff
  wid. 97
Sheridan
  Thomas 20
Sheries

William 179
Sherley
　Margrett 129
Sherm
　John 72
Sherreden
　Thomas 141
Sherredin
　Thomas 155
Sherriden
　Thomas 149, 153, 177
Sherridine
　Thomas 11
Sherrill
　Samuell 216
Sherrin
　Richard 154
Sherrwood
　Hugh 145
Shertcliff(e)
　Ann 6
　John 5, 6, 27
　William 6
Sherwood
　Alexander 54
　Hugh 181
Shills
　Thomas 210
　vidua 210
Shinkeler
　John 141
Shinkle
　John 177
Shipway
　John 181
Shirtcliffe Runne 43
Shirtcliffe
　Ann 44
　Anne 43, 44
　John 6, 11, 12, 13,
　　43, 46
　Mary 44
　William 43
Shourtie
　George 38
Shuall
　Warner 122
Shudall
　Wardner 195
　Warnar 122
　Warner 196
Sibery
　Jona. 172
Sibrey
　John 102

　Jonathon 131
Sicely
　John 201
　Mary 201
Sifick
　William 116
Sike
　John 65
Silvaine
　Daniel 113
Simes
　William 107
Simmonds
　Geo. 164
Simmons
　Lawrence 154
　Thomas 146
Simms
　Richard 211
Simon
　Richardson 179
Simons
　Lawrence 113
Simpson
　Alexander 158
　Paul 12, 13
　Paull 11, 12
　Tho. 26
　Thomas 102, 136, 139,
　　151
　William 129
Simpsor
　Hannah 134
　William 134
Sims
　William 201
Simson
　William 34, 141, 155
Sinckbury 64
Sinclare
　John 69
Singleton
　John 128, 132, 138,
　　162, 213
　William 66, 74, 75,
　　80, 86, 198, 200
Sinkle(a)r
　Jane 20
　John 19, 20. 80
Sison
　Benjamin 56
　Elisabeth 56
　Frances 56
　Jeane 56
　John 8, 56

Sissell
　John 58
Sisson
　Francis 56
　John 60
Six
　John 61, 108, 131, 133, 139
　Sibil 131, 133
　Sibill 150
Sixbe, Sixby
　Richard 167, 179
Sizon
　John 59
Skey
　Rich. 164
Skidmo(a)re
　Alice 208
　Edward 56, 208
　Nicholas 105
Skillington
　Thomas 167
Skinkler
　John 149
Skin(n)er
　Andrew 31, 104, 108, 153
　Edward 121
　Elisabeth 210
　Robert 154
　Thomas 210
Skippe
　Mary 6
Skippye
　Abraham 6
Skipwith
　Samuell 52
Slade
　William 158, 214
Slatter
　John 126
Slayd
　William 102, 160
Sleppey
　Richard 150
Sloper
　Samuell 155
Sly(e)
　Mr. 56, 76
　Robert 9, 22, 29, 30, 33, 34, 42, 58, 84, 94, 105, 127, 139, 143, 152, 167, 169, 175, 184
Smallpeece

　John 192
Smart
　John 179
　Thomas 192
Smith
　Alexander 60, 158, 219
　Ann 13
　Daniel 151
　Edmond 44
　Emperour 16, 178
　George 151
　Henry 152
　James 172, 180
　John 13, 28, 37, 61, 83, 87, 90, 94, 102, 105, 130, 145, 147, 150, 154, 155, 156
　Joseph 129
　Josias 36
　Magdalene 214
　Martha 54
　Mary 128, 143, 155, 185
　Mathew 33, 41, 152
　Mr. 62
　Nathan 157
　Ri. 74, 90, 114
　Rich. 50
　Richard 41, 46, 50, 52, 58, 59, 80, 111, 123, 152, 181
　Rob. 164
　Robert 33, 180
　Samuell 33
　San. 50
　Sander 179
　Susanna 130
　Tho. 85
　Thomas 85, 171
　William 38, 62, 90, 108, 114, 123, 125, 129, 143, 145, 148, 149, 154, 185, 199
Smithe
　Robert 28
Smiton
　William 150
Smoot(e)(s), Smote
　Joane 129, 134
　Richard 129
　Thomas 42, 50, 54, 59, 102, 129, 134
　William 31, 37, 54, 129

Smoth
  Richard 41
Smute
  Jone 40
  Thomas 40
  William 40
Smyth
  (N) 142
  Daniell 40
  John 82, 83, 84
  Mary 68, 142
  Miles 64
  Rich. 71
  Richard 53, 66, 67, 71, 110
  Robert 4
  Tho. 98
  Thomas 87, 95, 98
  William 67, 103, 117, 118, 121
Smyton
  William 79
Snaggs
  William 108, 156, 163
Snow
  Marmaduke 105, 219
  Thomas 53, 116, 194, 197
Snowden
  Elisabeth 198, 199, 200
  Richard 198, 199
Solby
  Nicholas 178
Sollers
  John 157
Solman
  Edward 54
Solsby
  Nicholas 191, 194
Somerford
  Sibil 133
Sondford
  Jeferry 149
Sone
  Joseph 172, 173
Sorell
  Robert 56
Souchorne
  Tho. 61
South Coatoid 92
South Petherton 178
South
  Mr. 116
  Tho. 164, 172
  Thomas 119, 126, 128, 132, 137, 171, 195, 196
Southcote
  Jane 28
Southeby
  William 182
Southersby
  William 202
Southrins
  Edward 178
Southward
  James 118
Soward
  William 54
Sowth
  Thomas 116
Sowthward
  James 53, 56
Spalding
  Thomas 43, 44
Spark(e)s
  Edward 34, 165
Sparrow
  Elisabeth 201
  Salomon 201
  Thomas 201
Spence
  Francis 148
Spencer
  Mr. 55
  Nicholas 68
  Thomas 141
  Walter 204, 212
Spinke
  Henry 27, 31, 44, 46, 57, 64
Spkinke
  Henry 54
Sprig
  Thomas 176
Sprigg(e)
  Brother 23
  Mr. 61, 101
  Tho. 67, 71, 90, 114, 118, 143
  Thom. 110
  Thomas 33, 39, 67, 81, 111, 113, 115, 123, 126, 133, 136, 143, 149, 153, 184
Sprouce
  George 58
Spry's Hill 53
Spry

Johanna 202, 211
Sprye
  Mr. 53
  Oliver 53
Spurdance
  John 53, 163
Squire
  Jonathon 194
St. Barbarys Manner
  171
St. Wynefride's 24
Stacey
  Mary 217
  William 217
Stacie
  Richard 133
Stagett
  Moses 98
Staggall
  Mary 165
  Thomas 165
Stagott
  Mary 98
  Ruth 98
  Tho. 98
Stagwell
  Moses 28, 153
  Thomas 39
Standish
  Alexander 153
Standl(e)y
  Hugh 41, 51, 52, 63,
    79, 103, 106, 110
  Hugo. 103
  Mr. 46
  William 89
Staneley
  Adam 85
Stanesby
  John 42, 85, 211
  Mary 211
Stanford
  William 32
Stanl(e)y
  Dorithy 170
  Dorothy 117, 180
  Edward 170
  Hugh 63, 68, 69, 70,
    73, 80, 90, 117,
    121, 149, 152, 169,
    170, 180
  John 127, 170
  Will. 53
  William 146, 178
Stannard

William 215
Stansb(e)y
  Dr. 140, 150
  John 53, 59, 67, 85,
    119, 136, 148, 150,
    152, 206
  Mary 202
Stansley
  John 108
Stanson
  John 80
Stantley
  John 129
Stapleford, Stapleford
  Mr. 149
  Raymond 148, 153, 184
  Raymund 75
  Reymond 74, 66, 177
  Robert 103
Starkey
  Lawrence 1, 3
  Mr. 25, 58
Starling(e)
  Thomas 49
Starr
  Robert 154
Startup
  John 133, 150
Staunton
  Francis 180
Stavel(e)y
  Adam 94
  Addam 91
Staymes
  John 176
Stead(e)
  Thomas 47
  William 170, 175
Stearman
  John 16
Steele
  Thomas 29
Steevens
  Richard 39
  William 22, 24, 181,
    210
Steevenson
  Phi. 172
Stenborgh
  Dedmoras 134
Stephens
  David 19
  John 105, 158
  Katherine 106
  Margaret 75

Robert 106
William 115, 154
Stephenson
  Elisabeth 10
  Fran. 64
  Nicholas 128
  William 10, 41
Sterling
  Mary 60
  Tho. 95
  Thomas 60, 101
Steuard
  Charles 174
Stevens
  Ailes 139
  Ann 105
  Francis 139
  John 105, 182
  Katherine 153, 155
  Robert 108, 155
  widow 108
  Will. 104
  William 104, 115, 151
Stevenson
  Richard 154
Steward
  Charles 89, 98, 182
Stile
  Mr. 189
Stiles
  Mary 3, 48
  Nath. 101
  Nathaniell 96, 102, 134
  Samuell 202
  William 9
Stinchcombe
  Nathaniell 192, 214
  Thomasin 192
  Thomazin 214
Stincklow
  John 63
Stinett
  William 149
Stockdale
  William 115
Stockden
  William 86, 113, 117
Stocket
  Fra. 164
Stockett
  Capt. 159
  Franc. 53
  Francis 14, 119, 122, 170
  Henry 150, 158, 161, 164
  Lewis 122, 150
  Thomas 53, 119, 122, 135, 146, 153
Stockitt
  Lewis 96
Stockley
  America 48
  Ann 48
  Elisabeth 48
  James 48, 217
  Mary 217
  Oliver 48
  William 137
Stocks
  John 178
Stokter
  William 86
Stone
  Capt. 16
  Catheryn 7
  Elisabeth 7
  John 7, 116, 124, 131, 136, 141, 175, 215
  John S. 142
  Margery 216
  Mary 7
  Mathew 7, 39, 79, 146, 148, 152, 175
  Matthew 216
  Nath. 78
  Richard 7, 116, 123, 124, 136, 153, 175
  Robert 7
  Tho. 68, 131
  Thomas 7, 19, 34, 124, 136, 185, 216
  Verlinda 54, 215
  Virlinda 7, 124, 136
  William 3, 7, 9, 19, 23, 50
Storey
  William 153
Storrip
  John 145
Story
  Avis 55
  Elisabeth 129
  Ralph 55, 72
  Walter 71, 75, 129, 136
Stran
  Abraham 202

Streete
  Will. 55
Stringer
  James 189
Strong(e)
  Elisabeth 170
  George 37, 61
  James 127
Stroude
  James 91
Strowd
  James 82, 83, 87
  Rebecca 82, 83, 87
Stuard
  Charles 102
Studd
  Tho. 74
  Thomas 152
Sturdenant
  William 213
Styles
  Mary 48
  Nathaniel(1) 8, 39, 53
  William 26, 48
Such
  Robert 54
Suchole
  William 168
Sudborough
  Peter 14
Sudena
  Jeremy 98
Sudward
  James 15
Sullivant
  Patrick 212
Surveyor's Point 96
Suseman
  Patrick 98
Susquehanna Point 136
Suthrine
  Vallentine 179
Sutton
  Barbary 32
  John 14, 27, 32, 61
Swan(n)
  Edward 136, 158
Swanson
  Dr. 76
  Fran. 148
Swanston(e)
  Dr. 152
  Edward 211
  Fran. 178

Francis 148, 178, 217
  Henrietta 211
  Isabella 217
Sweetsad
  Thomas 26
Swenfen
  Francis 149
Swillivant
  Jeremiah 181
Swinfen, Swinfin
  Francis 150, 221
Swinson
  Francis 181
Swyer
  Even 124
Symons
  Francis 55
Syndewood
  Peter 201

Tail(l)er
  Mathew 111
  Tho. 47, 135
  Thomas 100
Tailor
  Thomas 188
Talbot
  William 184, 185
Talbott's Ridge 47
Talbott
  Edward 47
  Elisabeth 47, 57
  John 47
  Richard 47
Tallent
  Robert 183
Tallie
  Thomas 16
Tany
  John 51
Tapticoe
  Anne 217
  Peter 217
Tarlin
  Richard 55
Tassell
  John 147, 168, 183
Taverner
  Robert 217
Tawn(e)y
  John 125, 130, 137, 148, 176
  Michaell 149
Tayler

George 38
Johan 129
Tho. 62
William 39
Tayller
  Mr. 135
Taylor's Folly 147
Taylor
  Anth. 68
  Arthur 211
  Daniell 215
  Elisabeth 147, 148
  Francis 154
  Henry 24, 166
  John 144, 147, 156, 211
  Mary 24
  Mr. 109
  Robert 10, 20, 24, 26, 27, 61, 94, 150, 216
  Samuell 24, 149
  Sarah 8
  Tho. 80, 96, 119, 146
  Thomas 8, 10, 14, 31, 33, 52, 71, 80, 91, 99, 100, 145, 148, 153, 156, 165
  Will. 53, 164
  William 119, 199
Taylour
  Michaell 179
  Thomas 174, 182
Tayton 116
Teage
  John 210
Teighe
  Robert 59
Temple
  Nicholas 55
Tenahill(s)
  William 50, 58, 76
Tench
  John 61, 122
Tennis
  John 11
Tenry
  Margarett 190
Terre
  John 134
Terry
  John 156
Tetershall
  William 44, 46
Tetherly
  William 173
Tettershall
  William 48, 57, 140, 144, 151
Teuge
  John 197
The Addition 119
The Folly 113
The Island 3
The Rich Necke 3
The Wallnutt 120
Thellwell
  William 168
Thelwall
  William 151
Theobald(s)
  Clem. 43
  Clement 9, 100, 125, 139, 171, 176, 215
  Elisabeth 99
Therrell
  Margaret 211
  Richard 211
Thickpenny
  Henry 68
Thimbellby
  John 6
Thimbleby
  John 14
  Rob. 1
  Robert 1
Thomas
  Ann 8, 105
  David 58
  Edward 95
  Elisabeth 23
  Henry 6
  Macon 210
  Macona 210
  Mecom 111
  Philip 68, 214
  Robert 6, 7
  Sarah 214
  Symon 54
  Thomas 6, 12
  Walter 111, 140
  William 150
Thomkinson
  John 54
Thompson
  Arthur 107, 149
  George 3, 7, 51, 54, 72, 124, 153
  James 49, 79, 82, 84, 86, 113, 121, 141,

    157, 176, 177, 218
  Jane 217
  John 25
  Mary 21
  Mr. 62
  Samuell 129
  Sarah 25
  William 21, 25, 35,
    78, 156, 161
Thompsonus
  Georgius 38
Thomson
  James 33, 93
Thornbury
  Sam. 164
  William 154
Thorne
  William 68, 77, 115,
    147, 151, 161, 178,
    181
  Winifred 178
Thorntine
  Francis 162, 181, 182
Thornton
  Francis 163, 180
  Nathaniell 137
  Richard 202
Thorowgood
  Mrs. 167
  THomas 121, 131, 167,
    169
Thorpe Freehould 51
Thorpe
  Richard 171
  Roger 207
Thortine
  Francis 161
Throughgood
  Thomas 158
Thurall
  Richard 122
Thurmar, Thurmer
  John 132, 133, 142
Thurston
  Gilbert 116
Thurstone
  Thomas 153
Tick
  William 173
Tideings
  Richard 188
Tilghman
  Capt. 62
  Dr. 146
  Mary 213
  R. 162
  Rich. 173, 196
  Richard 102, 131,
    132, 138, 153, 164,
    172, 213
  Samuell 2
Tille
  Joseph 149
Tillny
  Ann 33
Tilly
  Joseph 103
Tilman
  Richard 171
Tilney
  Ann 18
  John 79
Timber
  Hen. 164
Timberley
  Henry 135, 138
Timmes
  William 120, 124
Tinton
  Paul 80
Tipping
  Elisabeth 160
Titmash
  John 33
Todd(e)
  Thomas 10, 12, 14
Toll(e)y
  Tho. 52, 189
  Thomas 54
Tomkins
  Gyles 38
Tomkinson
  John 3
Tompkins
  Gyles 30
Tompkinson
  Jane 22
Tompson
  James 59, 149
  Tomson 162
Tomson
  James 86
Tonge
  John 84
Tonkinson
  John 124
Tootle
  Henry 53
Toster
  John 164

Toulson
  William 93, 95, 96, 135
Tourner
  Thomas 192
Tove
  Thomas 149
Tovey
  Nicholas 202
  Tho. 95
  Thomas 85, 87, 88, 98, 152
Tow(e)
  Elisabeth 95
  Robert 95, 142, 149
  Thomas 148
Towell
  Roger 78
Towers
  John 211
  Rachell 211
Towerson
  Alexander 52
Towlson
  Will. 142
Townehill
  Edmund 214
Towneley
  Francis 154
Townell
  Edmond 14
Townhill
  Edmond 52
Townson
  Alexander 182
Tra(c)tman
  Francis 58, 63, 69
  Will. Bind. 63
Trayman
  Thomas 140
Treckson
  John 179
Trent
  Thomas 38
Trew
  Richard 72
Tripp
  Hen. 75
  Henry 153
Trippe
  Franc. 53
  Francis 190, 194
Trippen
  Mr. 154
Troop's Supply 99

Troop(e)
  Richard 4
  Robert 11, 12, 23, 58, 72, 80, 94, 99, 104, 107, 150
Troster
  John 59, 85, 95, 101, 133, 134, 140, 142, 155, 172, 189
Trostes
  John 74, 80
Trottin
  Francis 128
True
  Richard 93
Tru(e)man
  Tho. 67, 71, 74, 82, 83, 89, 129, 140, 171
  Thomas 33, 39, 51, 66, 82, 85, 90, 108, 110, 114, 126, 152, 170, 180
Trupp
  Robert 56
Trussell
  John 64, 65
Tubman
  Richard 177
Tuck
  Mr. 154
Tucker
  Frances 8
  John 11, 139, 144, 149, 150
  Thomas 8
Tull
  Thomas 130
Tulley
  Meverell 60
Tully
  Capt. 141
  John 39
  Stephen 139, 155, 162
  Tho. 164
Tunehill
  William 99
Tunnehill
  John 144
  William 73, 88
Tunnell
  Moses 134
Tunnhill
  William 76
Turbervile

Gilbert 218
Turbervill
  William 112
Turlen
  Paull 74
Turner
  Arthur 41, 54, 121, 130, 153, 158
  Bonham 119
  Edward 41, 57, 200
  Emma 25, 41
  John 18, 68
  Mary 25, 41, 170
  Mr. 23, 41, 154
  Nicholas 95
  Richard 57, 58
  Tho. 61
  Thomas 25, 28, 31, 41, 59, 132, 214
  W. 109
  William 20, 23, 26, 39, 45, 52, 53, 57, 61, 63, 67, 127, 149
Turnor
  Bonham 119
Turpen
  William 150
Turpin(ne)
  John 201, 202, 209
Turvile
  John 90
  William 78
Tydder
  Mr. 154
Tydings
  Richard 135
Tyer
  James 215
Tyler
  Frances 172
  Joan 191
  Robard 172
  Robert 53, 115, 189
Tylor
  Robert 150, 152
Tyre
  James 42
Tyrner
  Arthur 123

Ubbin
  Baerman 67
  Bernard 67
Umvin

  Nathaniell 129
Underwood
  Thomas 56
Upgate
  Richard 34
Upper Tayton 112
Utie, Uty(e)
  Bernard 202
  Elisabeth 211
  George 15, 52, 134
  Nath. 14, 16, 153
  Nathaniel(l) 16, 37, 56, 134, 174, 211

Vandervorte
  Michaell 68
Vanhack(e)
  John 22, 24, 35, 36, 39, 48, 154
  Mr. 77
Vanheck(e)
  John 79, 127, 141, 209
Vanhee(c)k
  John 62, 77
Vanswaden
  Mr. 163
Vanswearing
  Garret 180
Vansweringe(e)n
  Garret 168, 190, 205, 208, 218
Varlo
  James 86
Vaughan
  Capt. 65
  Mary 160
  Mr. 154
  Robert 53, 65, 98, 117, 122, 160, 163, 170
  Tho. 102
  Thomas 111, 131, 150, 151, 152, 190
Vaughen
  John 82
Vaune
  Thomas 181
Veake
  George 69
Veatch
  James 148
Veich
  James 12, 26

Veitch
  James 45, 68, 80, 85,
    141, 144, 152
Vendall
  Joseph 171
Venson
  Stephen 149
Verd
  John 59
Verlo
  James 86
Verroff
  Cornelius 154
Verroof
  Cornelius 155
Vicar
  John 102
Vicaris
  John 131, 140, 146,
    155, 165, 175
  Mary 175
Vicars
  John 131, 147, 169
Viccaridge
  Mary 106
Viccaris
  John 68, 178, 182
Viccoredge
  John 81
Vickeres
  John 168
Vickiricus
  John 174
Vickorice
  John 86
Vigris
  Thomas 145, 151, 153
Vincent
  Henry 11
Vine
  John 213
Vines
  Samuell 217
Viney
  Henry 166
Vinson
  Mr. 55
Vitch
  James 176, 177
Vizard
  Henery 41

Waas
  John 219
Wackfield
  Thomas 192
Waddis
  John 54
Waddy
  Eli. 103
  Thomas 141
Waddys
  Sarah 144
Wade
  Edward 13
  George 13
  John 13, 15
  Mary 13
  William 13
  Zachariah 13, 16, 180
  Zacharias 13, 62
  Zachary 26, 35, 37,
    43, 47, 54, 62, 162,
    181
Wadsworth
  Richard 141, 177,
    208, 217
  Susanna 217
Waghob
  Archbald 171
  Jane 171
  John 93
Waghop
  John 120
Wahob
  John 35, 127
Wale
  Edward 111
  George 154
Wales 103
Waley
  Tho. 151
Walker
  Daniel 15, 166, 174,
    175
  Daniell 15, 163
  George 103, 150, 152
  James 9, 22, 34, 39,
    46, 111, 121, 131,
    136, 153, 158
  John 93, 101
  Rich. 86
  Richard 74
  Thomas 210
Wallcops
  Elisabeth 45
Waller
  Mary 74
Walley

Tho. 79, 116
Thomas 78
Wallton
Tho. 40
Thomas 40
Walsh
  John 172
Walter
  Alexander 174
  Christopher 154, 180
  James 158
Walterlin
  Walter 190
Walters
  John 189
  Richard 204
Walton
  Ellinor 40
  Francis 29
  John 54, 136
  Tho. 62
Ward(e)
  Alice 16
  And. 136
  Andrew 71, 75
  Elisabeth 96
  Francis 29
  Henry 96, 101, 151, 209
  John 35, 54, 94, 100, 105, 108, 120, 124, 161, 162, 163, 171, 202
  Matthew 213
  Ralph 89
  Richard 30
  Tho. 108
  Thomas 36, 39, 103, 108, 129, 150, 152
  Zachary 161
Warding
  Mr. 154
Wardner
  George 35
  Izabel 34
  Mary 34
Ware
  Richard 60
Waren
  Sampson 152
Warfeild
  Richard 56
Warfield
  Richard 196
Waring

Basill 82
Bazill 87
  Capt. 142
  Edward 142
  Humphrey 74
  Mr. 88
  Sampson 12, 48, 50, 60, 85, 86, 87, 88, 89, 93, 95, 98, 129, 147
  Samson 30, 82, 141
Warner
  Andrew 35
  Elisabeth 196
  James 53, 59, 196
  Thomas 151
Warren
  Bassell 132
  H. 177
  Henry 81, 128, 151, 195
  Humfry 74
  Humphery 136
  Humphrey 134
  Humphry 26, 129, 134, 136, 155, 158, 167, 168
  Humprey 102, 127
  Ignatius 58
  John 58, 97, 140
  Sampson 176
  Samson 33, 132
  Thomas 212
  William 22, 31
Warrine
  Robert 27
Warring
  John 77
  Sampson 129, 176
Wast
  Francis 54
Wastson
  Andrew 53
Waterline
  Miles 159
Waterlyn
  Walter 5
Waters
  Alexand. 97
  Alexander 182
  Peter 43
Waterton
  J. 122
  John 122, 127
Watkins

John 148, 164, 214, 215
Tho. 164
Waton
  Edward 7
Wats
  Sand. 75
Watson
  Abraham 33
  Andrew 43
  John 204, 220
  Richard 54
  William 16, 177
Wattkins
  John 139, 153
  Thomas 152
Wattline
  John 139
Watt(s)
  Alexander 68
  Allexander 19, 33
  George 151, 159
  John 68
  Jone 74
  Peter 150, 160, 163, 218
  Petter 206
  Sander 80
  Saunders 74
  William 64, 82, 102, 120, 127, 150, 151, 203, 205, 220
Wattson
  Abraham 67
  Richard 136
  William 141, 145
Wayhopp
  John 152
Webb
  John 19, 23, 113, 177
  Richard 149
  Robert 139
Webley
  Richard 55
Webster
  John 153, 178, 182, 185, 197
Weeden
  James 104
Week(e)s
  Joseph 53, 212
  Margarett 170
Welch
  John 131, 149, 169
Wellen

Robert 153
Wells 118
Wells Hill 118
Wells Neck 118
Wells
  Ann 119
  Benjamin 118, 119
  Geo. 122
  George 97, 106, 118, 119, 122, 127, 191, 194, 202, 211
  John 118, 119
  Martha 119
  Mary 81, 119, 212
  Mr. 154
  Ralph 178
  Richard 118, 119, 126, 181
  Robert 118, 119
  Roby 153
  Tobey 34
  Tobias 102, 131, 163, 169, 174, 179, 212
  Toby 28, 34, 93, 150, 160, 165
  Tobye 28, 39
  William 216
Welsh
  Anne 198, 199
  John 188, 198, 199, 200, 214
  Mary 196
Wenham
  Alice 185
  William 185
Wentworth
  Tho. 23, 29
  Thomas 8, 47
West Wells 118
West
  Edward 46, 62, 63
  John 68
Whaakop
  Archibald 4
Whaley
  Edward 104
Wharton 165
Wharton
  Jane 133
  Thomas 124, 154
Whealey
  George 112
Wheately
  John 58
Wheatley

George 91
Wheatlie
  John 17, 18
Wheeler
  Cesar 143
  John 47, 49, 107
  Thomas 62
Wheel(l)ock
  Edward 197, 214
Whelock
  Mary 197
Wherell
  Robert 132
Whindell
  Richard 136
Whiston
  John 48
White Clift 53
White
  Alexander 54
  Casiya 201
  Daniell 54
  Ellynor 4, 5
  Guy 59, 66, 86, 91, 113, 183, 218
  Gwy 84, 89, 123, 148, 150
  James 57, 63, 69, 144, 190, 194
  Jerome 146, 151
  Kesia 220
  Mary 4, 5
  Nicholas 4, 5, 29
  Rachel 47
  Richard 172, 173, 179
  Rowland 201, 220
  Susanna 190, 194
  William 54, 55
Whitehed
  John 115
Whiteman
  Stephen 158
Whitewell
  Francis 179
Whitle
  Susanna 58
Whitt
  Robert 106
Whittell
  George 31
Whittington
  Capt. 9, 23
Whittle
  Geo. 68
  George 149

Robert 149
Susannah 72
WIlliam 23, 73, 76, 83, 84
Whitton
  Richard 209
Whitup
  Thomas 176
Wick(e)s
  Joseph 65, 89, 141, 188
  Josheph 89
Wiett
  Nicholas 55
Wigfield
  John 210
Wikes
  Margret 170, 171
Wilcocks
  Henry 182, 213
Wilcox
  Andrew 12, 18
Wild
  Joseph 59
Wilkenson
  Mr. 62
Wilkinson
  John 45
  Liddy 119
  Mr. 17
  Thomas 106
  William 17, 26, 50
Willan
  Elisabeth 51
  Grace 51
  Phillip 51
  Richard 3, 15, 17, 22, 23, 28, 44, 51, 58
Willchurch
  Henry 168
Willen
  Grace 204
  John 26
  Robert 151
  Thomas 125, 155
Willett
  William 145
  William Eriste & Co. 188
William
  Abijah 104
  Ann 104
  Christopher 104
  Elisabeth 104

George 104, 209
Hannah 104
John 48, 104
Luke 104
Richard 5
Thomas 104
William 104
Williams
  Elisabeth 113
  Francis 188
  James 47, 123
  John 16, 21, 29, 36, 38, 44, 151, 215
  Joseph 103
  Lodowick 156, 211
  Morgaine 169
  Morgan 20, 21, 28, 31, 53, 65, 81, 82, 86, 88, 89, 98, 140, 141, 160, 174, 175, 182
  Ralph 55, 131, 192, 193, 212
  Raph 102
  Richard 217
  Robert 154
  Robertt 201
  Sarah 20, 28, 31
  Susan 11
  Thomas 36, 54, 113
  William 41, 148, 151
Williamson
  William 142
Willin
  Thomas 128
Willkinson
  Mr. 32
  William 114, 130
Wills
  Richard 27
Willson
  Anthony 86, 92
  George 31, 39, 43, 154
Wilmer
  Luther 197
Wilson
  Anthony 86
  George 36, 151, 202
  James 33
  John 31, 79
  Robert 54, 188
  William 56, 59, 60
Wilton
  Anthony 86

Winale
  John 40
Winall
  John 48, 148
Winchester
  (N) 179
  Isaac 169, 212
  Isaack 174
  Isacck 147
  John 53, 86, 169, 174, 182, 199
  Mary 21
Wincles
  Edward 179
Winder
  John 115, 121
Wine
  Francis 61
Winfield
  Thomas 211
Winscomb
  John 171
Wins(s)low
  Isaack 151
  Joseph 141
  Sam. 172
  Samuel(1) 79, 151, 173, 182
Wise
  [torn] 68
Wis(e)man
  John 40, 145, 150
Witham
  Mr. 182
Withams
  Stephen 159
Witherall
  Mr. 154
Withers
  John 171
  Mr. 12, 188
  Samuel(1) 10, 14, 16, 48, 53, 55, 60, 91, 92, 94, 95, 96, 97, 98, 99, 100, 102, 104, 113, 131
Withnall
  Thurston 173
Woaker
  Richard 113
Wockare
  Elisabeth 137
Wolcott
  John 52
Woleman

Ri. 172
Wolford
  Roger 79, 161
Wollman
  Ri. 106, 175
  Richard 108, 192
Wood
  Edward 33, 54
  James 191
  John 59
  William 44, 48
Woodberry
  Andrew 52, 151
  Isaac 72
  Mr. 116
Woodbury
  Andra 59
  Andrew 59
  Mr. 154
Wooddall
  Mr. 13
Woodmorson
  Gaberell 56, 57
Woodriffe
  William 16
Woods
  William 48
Woodward
  Elisabeth 78
  John 107
  Joseph 7
Wool(l)ford
  Roger 77, 78, 147, 161, 176, 178
Wool(l)man
  Mr. 153
  Ri. 179
  Rich. 53
  Richard 100, 104, 113, 156, 165, 166, 189
Worell
  Robert 132
Worgan, Worgin(g)
  William 133, 149, 204
Workman
  Joane 212
Worland
  John 51, 109, 112, 191
Worrill
  Edward 173
Wright(e)
  Arter 168
  Arthur 100, 109, 110, 160, 163, 165, 166, 168, 169, 175, 192, 204
  Francis 96, 122, 127, 141, 190
  George 45, 145
  Ishmael 113, 183
  Ishmaell 86, 92, 119
  Ismaell 118
  Jane 103, 191
  John 18, 30, 56, 57, 64, 102, 112, 126, 129, 131, 132, 133, 140, 147, 150, 153, 174, 175, 178, 179, 181, 186, 192, 195, 212
  Margarett 113, 183
  Margerite 118
  Mary 32, 113, 132, 212
  Mr. 54
  Nicholas 64
  Raphael 127, 190
  Raphaell 122
  Rich. 69
  Richard 96
  Robert 113
  Sary 113
  Thomas 86, 103, 113, 122, 150, 191
  William 13, 16, 32, 42, 47
Wyatt, Wyett
  Damaris 196
  Damorus 194
  Mrs. 197
  Nicholas 56, 194, 196, 197, 199
  Samuel(l) 196, 197
Wylde
  Thomas 80, 85
Wyn(n)(e)
  Francis 193
  John 70, 152
  Tho. 163
  Thomas 125, 128, 145, 149, 151, 193, 195
Wyott
  William 175
Wytherell
  Jeremyah 154

Yardley

Sarah 9
Yardly
  Capt. 9
Yate(s)
  George 147, 150
  Mr. 59
  Robert 158
  Thomas 12
Yeo
  Hugh 115
  Stephen 121
Yeog
  Hugh 115
Yoe
  Ann 117
  Stephen 117
Yorke
  Anne 189
  William 189, 211
Young(e)
  Elisabeth 82, 177, 180
  George 217
  James 83, 103
  Nich. 18, 166
  Nicholas 17, 72, 84, 89, 125, 132, 143, 146, 150, 151, 164, 177, 178
  Richard 82, 84, 86, 93, 116
  Sara 88
  William 172, 173, 217
Younger
  Alexander 205
  Sarah 205, 218, 219
  William 204
Yow
  Ann 117
  Stephen 117
Yowkins
  Katherine 74
  Mary 74

Index to Equity Cases

Allen vs. est. Fox 1
Allen vs. est. Gregory 206
Allen vs. King 183, 184
Atkins vs. est. Jenkins 206

Baker vs. est. Atcheson 206
Baker vs. est. James 200
Baker vs. Ladd 187
Bayley vs. est. Aldridge 185
Blake, et. al. vs. est. Turpinne 201
Boareman vs. Stone 3
Boudle vs. Montfort 90
Brookes vs. Brookes 60
Browne vs. Lawrence 183

Cage vs. est. Gregory 203
Cager vs. est. Cager 198
Carr & Brisco vs. est. Foote 186
Chesholm vs. Jones 184
Chivers vs. est. Darling 82
Clemens vs. est. Earle 208
Clements vs. est. Cannons 207
Codasck vs. est. Roe 201
Cordea vs. Covant 185
Cordea vs. est. de la Roche 198
Cornwaleys vs. Dandy 2
Cornwaleys vs. est. Fox 2
Coursey vs. est. Bennet 206
Crossman vs. est. Manwaring 195
Crouch vs. est. Pritcher 1

de la Roche vs. est. Baker 198
de la Roche vs. est. Head 193
de la Roche vs. est. Lucas 198

Edloe vs. est. Lucas 206
Edmondson vs. Vaughan 190
Edmundson vs. est. Carre 199
Edmundson vs. est. Earle 205
Edmundson vs. est. Harwood 198
Edmundson vs. est. Syndewood 201
Eltonhead vs. est. Harris 2
Englis vs. est. Turpinne 202
Evans vs. est. Sadler 33
Ewen vs. Lane 184

Fenwicke vs. est. Fox 2

FittzAllin vs. est. Elliott 108

Garret vs. est. Johnson 185
Glover vs. est. Clifton 90
Grammer vs. Graves 194
Griffin vs. est. Eure 198
Guither vs. est. Brookes 11
Guthrey vs. est. Wadsworth 208

Hall vs. est. Nugent 4
Hanman vs. est. Worgan 204
Hatton vs. est. Fox 2
Hatton vs. est. Hatton 186
Hatton vs. Heathcoate 196
Hatton vs. Heathcote 188
His Lordship vs. est. Armstrong 172
Holland & Wilmer vs. est. Harrod 197
Holt vs. Bromefield 36
Hooper vs. est. Goate 30
Hosier vs. est. Webster 185

Ingram & Miller vs. Wright 195

James vs. est. Simpson 13
Jarbo vs. est. Fox 2
Jones vs. est. North 200
Jowles vs. est. Higgs 201

Keene vs. Bowdell 90
Keitting vs. est. Land 5
King vs. Allen 183
King vs. est. Stone 116

Land vs. est. Fox 2
Lindsie vs. est. Nugent 4
Lloyd vs. est. Orris 10

Man vs. est. Earle 205
Man vs. est. Penroy 203
Man vs. est. Wright 204
Man vs. Ingram 205
Man vs. Loggins 204
Manne vs. est. Eaton 204
Mansfield vs. est. Foster 200
Medley vs. Dandy 2
Melton vs. est. Foster 190
Miller vs. est. Barnes 204
Miller vs. est. Head 195

Moffett vs. Dorrington 163
Moll vs. est. Atcheson 206
Moll vs. est. Carre 200
Morecroft vs. est. Lane 170
Moy vs. Hopkins 185

Neale vs. est. Lee 40
Notley vs. Goff 200
Notley vs. Parker 187
Nutwell vs Sewall & Sensarfe 40

Overzee vs. est. Brookes 11

Pakes vs. est. Simpson 12
Parker vs. est. Pyne 186
Parkes vs. est. Higgs 201
Perry vs. executrix of Bateman 67
Pitt vs. est. Earle 205
Ponning & Smart vs. Fitzherbert & Baker 192

Quigley vs. est. de la Roche 198
Quigley vs. est. South 195, 196
Quigley vs. Williams 201

Rhoades vs. est. Buckson 198
Rider vs. est. Lucas 206
Ridgely vs. Groce, et. al. 200
Roades vs. est. Parker 187
Rousby vs. est. Stanley 169
Rowdell vs. est. Bromale 201
Rowland vs. est. Sicely 201

Saunders vs. est. Greene 206
Seitclere vs. est. Fox 2
Sims vs. Dare 201
Smyth vs. est. Richardson 121
Stansby vs. est. Barret 206

Tilghman vs. Cager 2
Troster vs. est. Foster 189
Turner vs est. Bromall 45

Vansworingen vs. est. Cooke 205

Younger vs. est. Cole 204